Hunger for Freedom

First published by Jacana Media (Pty) Ltd, in association with the
Nelson Mandela Foundation, 2008

10 Orange Street
Sunnyside
Auckland Park 2092
South Africa
+2711 628 3200
www.jacana.co.za

Soft cover ISBN 978-1-77009-565-6
Hard cover ISBN 978-1-77009-578-6

Cover and text design banana republic
Back cover: Madiba and author Anna Trapido
            Photographed by Alet van Huyssteen
Set in Stempel Garamond 10/12.5pt
Printed and bound in Malaysia by Imago
Job No. 000639

See a complete list of Jacana titles at www.jacana.co.za

Hunger for Freedom

The Story of Food in the Life of
Nelson Mandela

Anna Trapido

Picture Editor and Photographer Richard Goode

Acknowledgements

It has been said that too many cooks spoil the broth but, in this case, the many people involved have made for a delicious cultural and culinary soup.

At the Nelson Mandela Foundation, Achmat Dangor (Chief Executive), Shaun Johnson (Acting Chief Executive) and Verne Harris (Project Manager) provided invaluable support and assistance at all stages of the project. Sahm Venter worked with extraordinary skill, dedication and kindness throughout. Molly Loate offered extremely helpful insights into the cuisine of the Eastern Cape. Ruth Muller and Razia Saleh generously shared their remarkable knowledge of Madiba-related archives. Thoko Mavuso, Vimla Naidoo and Titise Make helped me to gain access to the Mandela and Machel households. Ahmed Kathrada was very effective in persuading people to talk to me when they weren't returning my calls.

The Mandela family and household staff were hugely generous not only with their time and insights but also with their kitchens. Nkosi Zwelivelile went above and beyond the call of duty when he organised the Qunu feast. Zindzi Mandela and Winnie Madikizela-Mandela could not have been kinder or more tolerant with my endless questions about dumplings. Xoliswa Ndoyiya helped me perfect my *amasi*, answered many *umphokoqo* queries and put to rest the great Fruit Loops-for-breakfast myth.

Zelda la Grange kindly facilitated time with Madiba and reassured his bodyguards that the cake I brought with me was not a threat to security. Maretha Slabbert arranged for Madiba, the cake and me to have our photograph taken. Graça Machel graciously allowed me access to Esmenia Rafael Gemo and, through her, to the glories of the Afro-Lusitanian food genre. Denise Vedor provided Portuguese-English culinary translations with the Mandela-Machel Maputo kitchen staff.

Richard Whiteing of the Robben Island Museum and Lailah Hisham of the Mayibuye Centre were invaluable sources of information on Cape-based Madiba-related archival material. Gwynne Conlyn published my first book, believed in the second, and introduced me to Jacana Media.

Stanley and Barbara Trapido inspired my interest in South African history. Richard and Josiah Goode made sure that there was always love in the sauce.

Most of all, thanks go to Madiba himself and to all those who cooked for and ate with him. The recipes and memories that they brought to this book deserve acknowledgement not only for their culinary contribution but also for their role in building a democratic and non-racial South Africa.

most of all, thanks go to Madiba himself and to all those who cooked for and ate with him

For Josiah Goode who was almost born in
Mvezo and whom Madiba offered to deliver.
Even if he did think you were twins ...

Contents

Introduction xi

Chapter One 1
THE TASTE OF NAMES

Chapter Two 17
FIGHTING WITH FOOD

Chapter Three 29
THE FOOD OF LOVE

Chapter Four 49
THE FOOD OF FRIENDSHIP

Chapter Five 63
MANDELA AND TAMBO AT LUNCH AND AT LAW

Chapter Six 83
MAZAWATTEE TEA ON THE RUN

Chapter Seven 95
ROBBEN ISLAND SOLDIERS MARCH ON THEIR STOMACHS

Chapter Eight 115
NO MAN IS AN ISLAND

Chapter Nine 137
POLLSMOOR AND THE BUZZING BEES

Chapter Ten 155
VICTOR VERSTER AND RIP VAN WINKLE IN THE KITCHEN

Chapter Eleven 165
FIRST MEAL OF FREEDOM

Chapter Twelve 175
ALL SIDES TO THE TABLE

Chapter Thirteen 185
PRESIDENTIAL POWER LUNCH

Chapter Fourteen 201
HAPPY ENDINGS AND JUST DESSERTS

Sources and interviews 208

Culinary and political glossary 210

Endnotes 212

Index 214

MATTERS OF HOUSEKEEPING

*Before there can be food, it is necessary to dispense with the
basic housekeeping of nomenclature and measurement.*

*Former President Nelson Mandela
has been referred to by many names and the significance
of each will be discussed in Chapter 1. For the sake
of clarity and consistency, the name used throughout this
book will be the clan name Madiba, which is the term of
address that he himself favours because it conveys both
affection and respect in the Xhosa language.*

*The majority of the recipes set out in this book have
been generously shared by home cooks. While professional
chefs work in exact measurements, home cooks tend to
move between grams, teaspoons, pinches and sloshes
with cheerful abandon. In the name of retaining the
authenticity of the recipes the ingredients are given
in a range of units depending on those used
by the individuals concerned.*

Introduction

In His Autobiography *Long Walk To Freedom* Madiba Declared: 'I was not born with a hunger to be free. I was born free. Free in every way that I could know. Free to run in the fields near my mother's hut, free to swim in the clear stream that ran through my village, free to roast mealies under the stars …

It was only when I learnt that my boyhood freedom was an illusion … that I began to hunger for it.'[1] This book explores Madiba's life and his hunger for freedom in a literal and metaphorical manner. What follows is not so much a cookbook as a gastro-political history with recipes. Food has provided the backdrop and occasionally the primary cause for momentous personal and political events in Madiba's life. *Umphokoqo* (mealie porridge and sour milk), crab curry and wedding cakes have borne silent witness to moments of joy, sadness, pain and glory. Life can be measured out in mouthfuls, both bitter and sweet. In the pages that follow the reader will taste the journey from the corn-grinding stone of Madiba's boyhood to prison hunger strikes, presidential banquets and beyond. Tales told in sandwiches, sugar and *samoosas* will speak eloquently of

intellectual awakenings, emotional longings and, always, the struggle for racial equality.

TASTE OF THE TIMES

Although such a project might initially seem trivial, to examine a life through food allows for unique insights into a man who has in recent years been as erroneously deified as he was once vilified. Such deification is generally well-meaning, but humanity is often sacrificed in hagiography. Since gods feel no pain, this process potentially belittles the extent of Madiba's personal sacrifice and that of those around him.[2] To look at an epic life through food cuts past the God mirage into the daily existence of a very real man: a man who has nourished South Africa and the world with his unstinting appetite for freedom.

OPPOSITE: MADIBA AT THE INVESTITURE OF HIS GRANDSON AS NKOSI ZWELIVELILE
Matthew Willman © Nelson Mandela Foundation

Like an onion, the life of Madiba has many layers. While the outer political layers have been much scrutinised, the domestic inner core has been overshadowed by the breadth of the public persona and consequently remains underexplored. A man can be assessed as much by his public as by his private behaviour, and to ignore the personal is to limit the analytical value of the record. For all the strengths of previous political and historical tomes, they tend to capture the bald facts without providing a sense of what those events felt like for those involved.

HISTORY REFLECTED IN A SOUP SPOON

While secondary sources have been analysed, this book has a focus on new interviews, first-hand memories, taste and, through taste, to feeling. The experience of eating is very visceral; it is a sensation that we can all share. To examine historical events through food allows the reader not merely to understand in an academic manner but also to get a sense of what it was like to be there.

To taste requires recipes. Those set out in the ensuing chapters are an accurate reflection of one man's table of life. Every effort has been made to ensure that the recipes have not been prettied up or modernised. Food being a form of material culture, the recipes provided here stand as archaeological evidence to capture the mood of the moment. They are an era as reflected in the bowl of a soup spoon. The ingredients and method for Winnie Madikizela-Mandela's spaghetti and mince are taken from contemporary descriptions of the dish as she made it when she was newly married in 1958. The recipe for the Nesquik and brown sugar birthday treat that Madiba made in his Robben Island cell in 1980 is taken directly from a letter describing the beverage as it was being consumed. As such, this book offers a taste of the times like no other.

FROM PROUST'S MADELEINE TO WINNIE'S *UMBHAKO*

It is important to acknowledge that memory is an imperfect record of the past. It is perforce filtered through contemporary perception and subsequent occurrence into a form in which the often confusing randomness of 'real life' is given the comfort of shape and meaning. With famous or much researched events, such as those discussed in this book, first-hand memories can be further distorted by interaction with previous researchers. There is a tendency for those who have been repeatedly interviewed to develop a standard script which can interfere with their ability to remember.

One of the strengths of this book is that it allows for the examination of the past in a manner that bypasses the standard responses. The success of this endeavour is due, in part, to the power of food as a prompt with which to rescue interviewees from the processed memories of their conscious minds and to place them in a more primitive site of memory within their own brains.

We all know that tastes and smells can transport us to times past. Whether it be the aroma of *umbhako* (pot bread) or a bite of Proust's madeleine biscuits, food has the power to call up the presence of that which and those who are gone, in an intuitive, unconscious and immediate manner. We have all experienced the sensation of having whole memories, complete with associated emotions, arrive uninvited by virtue of an action as simple as dipping a buttermilk rusk into a cup of coffee.

Recent neurological discoveries show that food has the power to evoke the unbidden and long-forgotten. Most of the research on this topic pertains to smell memory, but since over 90 per cent of what is perceived as taste is actually

smell, the research is equally prescient.[3] Humans respond in an involuntary manner to smell (and, by extension, to taste) because the olfactory nerves go first to a primitive region of the brain called the limbic system, which is situated beneath the cerebral cortex. The limbic system associates subconscious emotions with memory. Only after this limbic relay has occurred does the information arrive in the higher cortical brain regions for perception and interpretation. Thus it is that smell and taste are unique among the senses in that they have privileged access to the subconscious.[4] So, for instance, childhood trauma can reappear, as if from nowhere, with the scoop of a spoon or the stab of a fork. The bottom line is that in an extensively researched area, food provides a way into unexplored memories that have lain dormant.

JUSTICE IN A TEACUP

In the erroneous tendency to deify Madiba, the role of the broader political and social community into which he fits and fitted has been largely overlooked. A book of recipes is the ideal tool with which to demonstrate that while Madiba became a leader, he was never a lone agent.

Meals are almost always shared events. Even when we eat alone, we carry with us taste preferences learnt in a communal setting. In what we choose to eat, we express who we are and where we have

come from. In so doing we reveal our formative influences. There is no better way to see the young boy Rolihlahla as he once was than to share a bowl of *umngqusho* (samp and bean mélange) with the old man that Madiba became. Similarly, to drink tea from his mentor Gaur Radebe's teacups or to take a bite of a pastrami sandwich with his friend Nat Bregman allows the reader to experience the growth of greatness in its earliest hours.

Madiba himself said of the Nelson Mandela Centre of Memory and Dialogue (Nelson Mandela Foundation), under whose auspices this project was undertaken: 'We want the Centre to dedicate itself to the recovery of memories and stories suppressed by power. That is the call of justice.'[5] In giving voice to the lesser-known characters in Madiba's life, most notably the predominantly female cooks in the kitchens, this book subscribes to the concept of 'memory for justice'. From Barbara Waite's steak and kidney pies to Xoliswa Ndoyiya's sweet chicken, they were there, they provided a vital support role, and their contribution deserves to be acknowledged.

Cross-culturally, food is an invaluable social tool for communicating emotional messages. When we cook or serve meals for others, we make it clear what we think of them. Some of those who dined with or prepared food for Madiba are well known and either much acclaimed or heartily vilified.

in what we choose to eat, we express
who we are and where we have come from

cross-culturally, food is an invaluable tool for communicating emotional messages

But there were many previously unrecognised cooks in the kitchen. The culinary compassion of Thayanayagee Pillay (who brought curry to those awaiting trial for treason in 1956) is clear. The negative sentiments of swastika-tattooed warder 'Suitcase' van Rensburg, who throughout 1968 insisted on urinating next to the prisoners' porridge on Robben Island (and whose lunchbox the prisoners consistently refused to carry to the lime quarry), are as unmistakable as the joy expressed by Lillian Ngoboza, who served Madiba the rum and raisin ice-cream on the night of his eventual release from prison in February 1990.

South Africa is a complex, multi-cultural country. Its diversity is reflected in its freedom struggle and on the dinner plates of those involved. This book provides a delicious journey which travels in and out of Madiba's mother's *inkobe* (a porridge-like dish made from husked, dried mealies), through his first wife Evelyn Mandela's jelly and custard desserts, and on to George Bizos's oregano and lemon-basted lamb, Ray Harmel's chopped liver and Amina Pahad's chicken curry.

Ultimately, it is the man himself who makes the best case for looking at his life through food. In 1970 Madiba wrote to his wife Winnie from Robben Island prison: 'How I long for *amasi*, thick and sour! You know darling there is one respect in which I dwarf all my contemporaries or at least about which I can confidently claim to be second to none – healthy appetite.'[6]

ONIONS CAN MAKE YOU CRY

Be warned, peeling onions can make you cry. As you read this book and cook these dishes, you will encounter moments of seemingly unbearable suffering. But they were borne, and for all the heart-breaking sadness described below, what follows is ultimately a tale of triumph. In every recipe there is the taste of a freedom struggle that was deliciously successful.

Madiba's friend and comrade Tokyo Sexwale has said: 'Whenever Madiba calls people to the dinner table he declares, "Let's go to battle."'[7] So let's.

Chapter One

THE TASTE OF NAMES

THE ENSUING PAGES TRACK A CHILD'S JOURNEY through a series of hearths and homes. Early memories are often sketchy and Madiba's are no exception. While the sequence of events is clear, some of the exact dates are missing.

What is unambiguous is that in the childhood and youth of Madiba we see the visceral, instinctive, spiritual taste of the future. We also see the development of literal taste preferences that have lasted a lifetime. Every recipe that is given here resonates with the flavours of a multi-layered personality, formed in multiple childhood influences, all of which have a culinary component.

BEFORE NELSON WAS NELSON

Before he was anything else, Rolihlahla Mandela was a child of the Thembuland *terroir*. He was formed by the pastures of Mvezo district, on the banks of the Mbashe River, where he was born on 18 July 1918. He came to consciousness on the soils of Qunu, to which he moved with his mother in the winter of 1926. He matured from boy into man amidst the stately aloes and poplar trees of the Great Place at Mqhekezweni – the home of the Thembu King – into which he was absorbed in the aftermath of his father's death. This land carried not only the sunshine, rainfall, crops and cattle of his immediate family but also the history and culture of over five hundred years of the Thembu kingdom and the Madiba clan.

GOATS AT THE MVEZO BUS STOP, 2007

OPPOSITE: MBASHE RIVER AS SEEN FROM THE MANDELA HOMESTEAD IN MVEZO

In 1918 Mvezo was very different from the impoverished rural community it is today. Madiba recalled that his family was self-sufficient in matters of food production and that 'everything we ate we grew and made ourselves. My mother planted and harvested her own mealies … milk from our cows and goats was always plentiful.'[8]

Madiba's cousin Sitsheketshe Mandela grew up in the former President's household: his mother died in childbirth and Madiba's mother and his mother were sisters. Of this time he said: 'We boys had everything we needed from the cattle and fields. I was younger than him so he used to send me out to collect the cattle and then he used to milk the cattle himself and also take corn and grind it with a stone and we would eat it with *amasi*. There was *marhewu* and *imifino* … we very seldom bought anything edible but we lacked for nothing.'[9]

Although there was a trading store at Bashe Bridge owned by R.T. Wood (whom Madiba later described as 'the first white man I ever saw' and to whom we shall return in later portions of this chapter), consumer goods were luxuries that were served only on very special occasions.[10] Madiba recollected: 'Christmas was when we children tasted tea for the first time. Sometimes it was just hot water with sugar.'[11]

In rural communities, it is land and social support structures that feed families. The son of the chief of Mvezo, Nkosi Mphakanyiswa Gadla Mandela, and his third wife Nosekeni arrived at a time when the changing political and economic environment was having an increasingly negative impact on the ability of the Mandela family, and others like them, to maintain themselves off their lands.

In the wider world 1918 is generally thought of as the year in which the First World War ended, but Rolihlahla Mandela came into a family for whom the lament for lost land rights and political autonomy loomed larger than any foreign conflict. Thembuland had been annexed by the Cape Colony within living memory of the baby's elders, and though the annexation did temporarily allow for the development of a surplus-producing peasantry in the Eastern Cape, the Mandela family (as members of a traditional aristocracy) were not beneficiaries of the new social order. Nkosi Mphakanyiswa, like his forefathers, was in the business of indigenous governance; as such, the loss of autonomy and self-determination had a negative impact on his kraals and cooking pots. Thus it was that the bitter-sweet flavours of ancient rights and recent dispossession infused into and resonated for decades in Mvezo's most famous son.

THE MYTH, THE OX AND THE GRINDING STONE

Madiba's father, Nkosi Mphakanyiswa, was a chief by both blood lineage and custom and had been confirmed as such by the Thembu King Dalindyebo.[12] Despite his traditional legitimacy as a chief, the South African government accorded him the lower-ranking position of headman. Even this title required ratification at local level by the Chief Magistrate in Umtata (now Mthatha) and at national level by the Department of Native Affairs in Pretoria.

In 1926 Nkosi Mphakanyiswa was dismissed as 'headman' of the Mvezo district by the government authorities. In the 80 years since the incident occurred, the actual events that led to his dismissal have become shrouded in the mists of time. Legends have developed in which the chief's behaviour has come to be seen as prophetic of the subsequent heroism of his son. So entrenched are such myths that everyone in the district, including Madiba, retells the fable as fact. Because the tale is repeated in *Long Walk to Freedom*, it has become

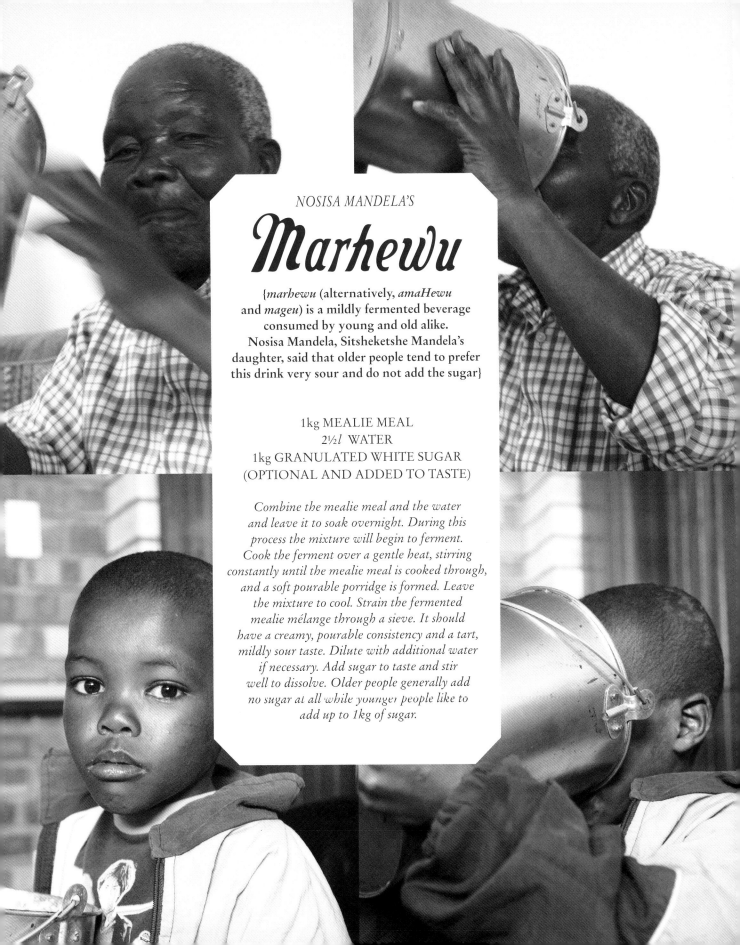

NOSISA MANDELA'S

Marhewu

{*marhewu* (alternatively, *amaHewu*
and *mageu*) is a mildly fermented beverage
consumed by young and old alike.
Nosisa Mandela, Sitsheketshe Mandela's
daughter, said that older people tend to prefer
this drink very sour and do not add the sugar}

1kg MEALIE MEAL
2½*l* WATER
1kg GRANULATED WHITE SUGAR
(OPTIONAL AND ADDED TO TASTE)

*Combine the mealie meal and the water
and leave it to soak overnight. During this
process the mixture will begin to ferment.
Cook the ferment over a gentle heat, stirring
constantly until the mealie meal is cooked through,
and a soft pourable porridge is formed. Leave
the mixture to cool. Strain the fermented
mealie mélange through a sieve. It should
have a creamy, pourable consistency and a tart,
mildly sour taste. Dilute with additional water
if necessary. Add sugar to taste and stir
well to dissolve. Older people generally add
no sugar at all while younger people like to
add up to 1kg of sugar.*

IN REPLY PLEASE QUOTE
IN ANTWOORD GELIEVE TE REFEREREN

No. 2/14/19

Bashee Bridge,
14ᵗʰ Sepᵗ 19??.

The Chief Magistrate,
          Umtata.

Dear Sir,

I am informed by Xam Ngandola
of Gadla's ward, Mvezo, that Headman
Gadla is still worrying him to move his
Kraal.

Some time last year – a year before, Xam
got me to write you or the R. M., and
Gadla failed in his attempt to shift him
Since then he has attempted to shift
Kulelo Msila, and one Vetine as well as Xam
There is a good deal of dirty work done
by Headmen at times and Natives look to
you for protection.

Selling of Sites by headmen is quite a
common thing – so I am told by Natives – &
a good Cow & the Headman will often
get a Kraal shifted.

I give you this information in the interest of
justice only – I have nothing against Gadla

I am, Sir Yrs faithfully,

[signature]

Ag. Magistrate.

[left margin, vertical:] I understand that Xam has been put to some expense to defend his Site – Gadla trying force to an attorney. R.B.

EFO

when the magistrate intervened he [sidestepped] the chief, the king and the kingdom

incorporated into all subsequent historical and political tomes.

However the dismissal occurred, the effect was to impoverish the family, through the confiscation of land and cattle. Over those 80 years the Mandela chieftaincy was usurped by those deemed more favourable to a series of political regimes starting with the Union government and ending with the Transkei Bantustan administration. In 2006, the Mvezo Mandela chieftaincy was restored to its rightful heir in the person of Madiba's grandson, Mandlesizwe Mandela, who governs the district under the official title of Nkosi Zwelivelile.

Of his great-grandfather's dismissal Nkosi Zwelivelile recounted the local legend thus: 'From what is often said, a certain man had impregnated someone's daughter without having paid dowry, so he was then summoned to my

great-grandfather's area and he was fined cattle for that and he felt it was a heavy sentence. So he went and appealed to the white magistrate, who in turn summoned my great-grandfather, who refused to come as he refused to acknowledge foreign rule in Thembuland because he only recognised the authority of the Thembu people and the king of the Thembu, and for this he was removed by the magistrate on a charge of insubordination.'[13]

As with all myths the truth is in the symbolism and not necessarily in the facts presented. The archival record shows that the reality, while different, was no less indicative of the tensions caused by competing authority structures and the pressure on agricultural land.

The trial documents dated 9 July 1926 suggest that Nkosi Mphakanyiswa's attempts to evict Xam Qandala and Kulelo Nsila (who he argued had

OPPOSITE: LETTER FROM THE TRADER R.T. WOOD TO THE CHIEF MAGISTRATE IN UMTATA (MTHATHA) ON BEHALF OF THE COMPLAINANTS AGAINST NKOSI MPHAKANYISWA GADLA MANDELA
ABOVE: MANDLESIZWE MANDELA WHO GOVERNS AS NKOSI ZWELIVELILE OF MVEZO

GLORIA NGCEBETSHANA'S

Imifino

{while this dish is often thought
of as a mélange of mealie meal and spinach,
the word spinach is a misnomer as
wild leafy vegetables such as the lemon-scented
umboso plant and the peppery *rhwabe* are
traditionally used in Thembuland. Gloria
Ngcebetshana is Madiba's niece;
her grandmother was Nkosi
Mphakanyiswa's sister}

500g EDIBLE WILD LEAVES SUCH AS
UMBOSO AND *RHWABE* (WASHED
AND FINELY CHOPPED)
1*l* WATER
1kg MEALIE MEAL
4 TABLESPOONS GRANULATED
WHITE SUGAR
1½ TEASPOONS SALT

*Cook the wild greens in boiling water,
until the vegetables are very soft, approximately
15 minutes. Add the mealie meal, sugar and
salt, and stir well to combine the vegetables and
the mealie meal and in order to avoid lumps.
Cover the mixture and cook until the mealie
meal is soft, approximately 30 minutes.*

illegitimately occupied communal land in Mvezo) resulted in a complaint by the land invaders, which included accusations of corrupt land dealings and misappropriation of oxen. The complainants got the trader at Bashe Bridge, R.T. Wood, to write several letters on their behalf to the Acting Chief Magistrate in Mthatha, T.M. Young.

Far from refusing to defend himself in front of the magistrate, Nkosi Mphakanyiswa's defence is comprehensive and is quoted verbatim in the trial record. He denied all accusations of wrongdoing and put forward a defence in which he stated that 'this story has been fabricated against me because I brought a charge against Xam Qandala and his elder brother for leaving a kraal site on the commonage. They also say I am responsible for getting the Messenger into the Location to seize for taxes … They were all favourable towards me until I brought the two cases against Xam and Kulelo.' The magistrate rejected Nkosi Mphakanyiswa's defence, and he was dismissed.

Whichever version of history one believes, the source of the conflict was essentially agricultural, culinary even, in nature, for in rural communities access to land and oxen is a vital component of food production. The dispute reflects a society in the midst of painful social, economic and political stress as traditional authority was increasingly undermined by the Union government administration. To attempt to farm on the commonage suggests that there was insufficient land in Mvezo and, moreover, that there was a breakdown in the Thembu traditional social structure, which had hitherto valued the collective over the individual. When challenged by Nkosi Mphakanyiswa, the response of those occupying the commonage indicates that the conflict was a result of the presence of two rival authority structures competing for control over the people and lands of the Eastern Cape.

In 2007 Nkosi Zwelivelile explained that 'the one complaining in this case was not without rights to appeal within Thembuland traditional law. Even now if you are not satisfied with a chief's decision, you are entitled to take it up with a higher authority. If people in Mvezo feel a decision of mine is harsh, they have a right to go to the king and put the matter before him, and so it was with my great-grandfather. When the magistrate intervened, he was saying it was acceptable to sidestep the chief, the king and the kingdom itself. When this man went to the magistrate he was breaking tradition and custom, and this was what was destroying the entire structure of the kingdom.'[14]

Nkosi Mphakanyiswa's response reflects how deeply entrenched in traditional culture he was. He defended his honour in so far as he attended the trial but he didn't appeal against his dismissal and chose instead to rely on the support bases offered to him within the Thembu royal house. He moved his wives from Mvezo back to their home areas in order to provide for their social and economic well-being. He stated in the trial that his health was poor and he used the time available to him to ensure that the Regent of Thembuland would care for his son after his death.

There is no archival record of a death certificate for Madiba's father. *Long Walk to Freedom* states that Nkosi Mphakanyiswa died in 1927, but this seems unlikely given that his grandson Nkosi Zwelivelile noted that Madiba's two youngest sisters, Leaby and Nokuthamba, were born in 1929 and 1930 respectively. Their cousin Nombulelo Ngcebetshana said in 2007 that she was older than both of them. In 1930 a child born in 1918 would have been 12. While it is unclear exactly when Madiba's father died, what is certain is that he died without seeing his lands and position restored. Thus it was that Nkosi Mphakanyiswa's youngest

© MuseuMAfrika

THEMBU HERDBOYS, 1920

son grew up not in the relative grandeur of his first home at Mvezo but in the considerably reduced circumstances of his mother's family homestead in Qunu.

Today, the huts of what was once Madiba's first home at Mvezo are in ruins, but fragments of the corn-grinding stone upon which his mother processed grain remains in position, an alimentary reminder of the family it once fed.

THE COMFORT OF A COMMUNAL DISH

At his mother's homestead in Qunu, Rolihlahla lived with his sisters in a set of three huts – one for sleeping, one for cooking and one for storing food. Madiba's sister Mabel recalled that *umphokoqo* and *umngqusho* were the family's staple diet and that they shared these meals from a communal dish.[15] This collective eating style and the Thembu customary table manners that Madiba learnt in

his mother's house marinated deep into his adult domestic preferences. As we shall see in Chapter 4, such social preferences were subsequently influential in building cross-cultural friendships, which in turn laid the ground for political alliances.

The politics of the 1940s and 1950s will be dealt with in later sections of this book. Here it is important only to note that for many years after its inception in 1912, the African National Congress (ANC) was an exclusively African political organisation. The cross-racial alliances and ultimate policy of non-racialism that characterise the modern Congress movement began in the affection and trust created in social interactions. Long before there were formal political alliances, there were friendships. Indeed, Madiba told his Congress Alliance comrade Ismail Meer that what had first attracted him to the households of members of the Transvaal Indian Congress was the social style he found there, the communal dishes and eating with hands reminding him of his own childhood food habits.[16]

THE HERDBOY AND THE STOLEN MEALIES

In addition to the formal family food sources, little Rolihlahla had access to the bounty of Thembuland through his culinary adventures as a herdboy. Herdboys are officially charged with the responsibility of looking after flocks of sheep and herds of cattle. They are also notoriously naughty, and Madiba was no exception. Much later in life, as a prisoner on Robben Island, he wrote to his sister of 'the unforgettable occasion when you scolded me for stealing green mealies from Rev. Matyolo's garden'.[17]

In addition to their reputation for naughtiness, herdboys are well known as indigenous food

Chicken

{although Mrs Toni was
no longer able to cook, she assisted with a
description of the chicken dish. This dish should
be made with an *umleqwa*, a free-range,
home-slaughtered chicken}

1 WHOLE CHICKEN
4 TABLESPOONS SUNFLOWER OIL
1 ONION FINELY CHOPPED
2 TOMATOES, GRATED
1 TABLESPOON FLOUR
1 CUP WATER
SALT TO TASTE

*Portion the chicken. Heat the oil and fry the
chicken pieces until they are well browned,
about 5 minutes. Add the onions and sauté them
until they are golden, about 5 minutes. Add the
tomatoes and the flour, mix well. Add the water,
cover the pot and simmer until the chicken is
cooked, at least 30 minutes. Season to taste.*

connoisseurs. Anyone who wishes to discover where the best wild mushrooms are or how to roast a cane rat to perfection should ask a herdboy. Of his herdboy days Madiba said: 'I was no more than five when I became a herdboy looking after sheep and calves in the fields … It was in the fields that I learnt how to knock birds out of the sky with a slingshot, to gather wild honey and fruits and edible roots, to drink warm, sweet milk straight from the udder of a cow, and to catch fish with twine and sharpened pieces of wire.'[18]

Mandlenkosi Ngcebetshana was a herdboy contemporary of Madiba's. Of this time he said: 'We used to know all the wild fruits and vegetables: real herdboy foods that adults do not eat. We used to be so full, just from the fields. Most of them are gone now. I remember there was something that used to look like a potato. It's not a potato or a sweet potato, rather it is wild, and as herdboys we used to dig them from under the ground, scrape off the dirt and eat it raw like an apple – its Xhosa name is *qhobozela*. I don't think it has an English name. Then there was a *nongwe*, which looks black when you dig it out. It's like a sticky root. It's hairy so you need to scrape it. It tastes like a carrot but it's not a carrot. We used to like those, too. Also I remember *gonsi* – it's delicious. It has a sour taste like *amasi* but it's also a root; you dig it out. There were *khowa* mushrooms that used to come out when it was raining (I think you sometimes still see those) and as young boys we would rush and collect them and eat them in the fields. And we liked a tree we called *mga*, I think the tree is called a mimosa in English. We would take the branches and cut and peel them because inside you find a softer sweet stem that we would like to chew like sugar cane. Most of these foods are finished now. They don't grow so well as they did when we were young boys. But the major thing is not that the crops are finished but that even the boys don't herd any more – it is the old men who are herding now

and the boys are all at school. And these are foods for herdboys, they aren't foods for men.'[19]

While there were pranks and minor culinary infringements, the relative freedom of his boyhood stored up an intellectual and emotional autonomy that served Madiba well during his long years of imprisonment. In 1970, writing to his friend Douglas Lukhele from Robben Island, he said of himself: 'I am essentially a rustic, born and brought up in a country village with its open space, lovely scenery and fresh air … throughout my imprisonment my heart and soul have always been somewhere far beyond this place in the veld and the bushes. I live across all these waves with the memories and experiences I have accumulated over the last half century – memories of the grounds in which I tended stock, hunted, played … It is only my flesh and blood that are shut up behind these tight walls; in my thoughts I am as free as a falcon.'[20]

WHEN NELSON BECAME NELSON

From the age of 8, Rolihlahla attended the Qunu school where his first teacher, Miss Mdingane, gave her pupils English names and insisted that they answer to them at all times. In this act of nominative imperialism Rolihlahla became Nelson – although his mother consistently pronounced it 'Nelisile' and his childhood friends shortened it to 'Nel' (a nickname he was still using to sign his prison letters in the 1960s and 1970s).

Although Madiba is remembered by his surviving contemporaries in Qunu as an able student, they reminisced that the lure of the fields and his herdboy companions was powerful. Mandlenkosi Ngcebetshana recalled: 'He used to school here above at Qunu Primary, and when he was supposed to go to school he used to bunk school and go to the fields and play with the herdboys there. And one time he was told, "Today there are exams and the inspectors are going to be at the school to see that they are done properly," and without preparing he just rushed to school and he wrote and passed. He was very in love with the fields and with what the herdboys were doing.'[21]

After his father's death Nkosi Jongintaba Dalindyebo, the Regent of the Thembu people, made good on his promise to Nkosi Mphakanyiswa by incorporating the young Nelson into his household at Mqhekezweni.

FROM THE TRAUMA OF CHICKEN WINGS TO THE PLEASURE OF SCONES

Whatever the reasons, layers of names became layers of consciousness. A series of anglophile habits – including food preferences – were superimposed on the first flavours of Thembuland. Initial attempts at Eurocentric culinary behaviour were tentative and not always successful. Mqhekezweni was more westernised than Qunu, and Madiba's first endeavours to impress a girl, Winnie Matyolo, were sabotaged when his lack of dexterity with a knife and fork caused a

WINNIE TONI (NÉE MATYOLO) IN HARDING, NOVEMBER 2007

chicken wing to fly off his plate, thus revealing his inexperience with these unfamiliar culinary tools.

When asked about this experience Madiba told the author: 'I was 16 and, you see, her older sister was in love with another Mandela and she felt that it wouldn't be right for both sisters to be involved with the same family, so she tricked me. That chicken was only half cooked and the wing went round and round on my plate and I could make no progress. Try as I might it would not be cut. And eventually I cast aside my knife and fork and I gave up and I ate nothing. And the older sister said to the girl I loved, "You see, he doesn't know how to use a knife and fork, he is not suitable for you." But I was in luck because the younger sister said, "It doesn't matter, I will teach him."'[22]

As is often the case with youthful romances, part of the problem seems to have been that Madiba failed to make the object of his affection aware of the nature of his feelings. Winnie Toni (née Matyolo) was a week from her 90th birthday when she was interviewed in her daughter's house in Harding in KwaZulu-Natal. A retired midwife who had married a Bizana lawyer,

Mrs Toni was understandably sketchy about the details of a love story that in her mind was over before it began.

Of their teenage friendship she said: 'Yes, I remember him when he was a boy – we were schooling together at Mqhekezweni. First, his home was in Qunu not Mqhekezweni, then he came over to school with us and then we became friends. We were both young, there was nothing wrong. Nothing to tell. People said later he was a bit in love with me but I don't think it was so. We were neighbours, so he came often to my father's house – my father was a Methodist minister. Sometimes, on and off, he would eat a meal at my house because we were sort of the same age. My sister, she was older than us, she cooked that chicken that he talks about. It was very plain – no spices, just salt. Then we stopped going to school together. We separated because I was schooling at Shawbury and he went to Clarkebury. I never went to his mother's house but I went to the Great Place. We used to play, eat – we ate samp, meat, drank *marhewu*, that's all. Then he went to Johannesburg and then he went over to the Island for some years and he came back after 30 years and he was well.'[23]

Subsequent encounters with European culinary genres were more rewarding. In 1934 Madiba enrolled at Clarkebury Methodist School. Mrs Harris, wife of the headmaster, the Reverend Cecil Harris, had a soft spot for the young student, which she demonstrated with tea-time gastronomic treats. All pupils were required to undertake manual duties on the school property and the schoolboy Nelson was assigned to work in Mrs Harris's garden. It was amidst the cabbages and hollyhocks that Madiba had his first contact with scones.

Mrs Harris's baking left such an impression that years later, as a prisoner on Robben Island, he wrote to the Harrises' daughter Mavis Knipe and reminded her that her mother had often brought him 'a buttered scone or bread with jam, which to a boy of sixteen was like a royal feast'.[24]

WHEN NELSON BECAME DALIBHUNGA

In 1935, the 16-year-old boy Nelson underwent the sacred rite of passage without which Thembu men are not considered to be men. As is the custom, he emerged from the circumcision ceremony with a new name, as the man Dalibhunga.

THE EARLIEST KNOWN PHOTOGRAPH OF MADIBA TAKEN AT HEALDTOWN WESLEYAN COLLEGE WHICH HE ATTENDED IN 1937 AND 1938. MADIBA IS IN THE BACK ROW, FIFTH FROM THE RIGHT

There was a meat-laden feast to mark the end of this process, but to reach the feast day the boy Nelson and 25 other *abakhwetha* (initiates) had to be prepared for manhood by their elders in an isolated lodge in the Tyhalarha Valley. Though such a time is intended to be one of relative privation, the initiates in Tyhalarha seldom went hungry thanks to the girlfriends of a fellow initiate, Banabakhe Blayi (whom Madiba described as 'the wealthiest and most popular boy at our

circumcision school'), who kept the youths supplied with delicacies.

It was thoughtful of Banabakhe Blayi's girlfriends to provide fine viands because the official sources of food available to initiates are punitive in the extreme. Nkosi Zwelivelile said of his time at circumcision school: 'The food that you get as an initiate is not like ordinary food in ordinary times. During the whole experience you are in an unknown state, you are not a boy, not a man. We always refer to initiates as animals. I know in my own instance, one of the king's sisters, Zikhona Dalindyebo, was cooking for me and she would make food that was just merely cooked, not well cooked and enjoyable. She did this to remind us that we were not part of normal society. It was half-cooked food and very dry – no meat. Maize half-cooked is symbolic of being between states. From this time you are supposed to gain a full understanding of what makes you be a man. Many people think that the act of circumcision is what makes you a man, but it is the ideology and principles that are put to the initiates through an educational process that do it. You go through the transition and become men, and the plain food helps you learn and remember that.'[25]

In 1995, 60 years after the Tyhalarha Valley circumcision school, then President Mandela encountered the Blayi homestead once again. He was clearly deeply demoralised by the fact that the family had been 'caught up in the poverty of this area. They once had 500 sheep and all that wealth has just disappeared.'[26]

as is the custom, he emerged from the ceremony with a new name, Dalibhunga

FROM PIG THEFT TO CHEAP ALCOHOL

While circumcision school was predominantly a time of lectures from elders and earnest philosophical discussions, there were also playful stick-fighting sessions and minor acts of naughtiness including the theft and roasting of a local farmer's pig. Such boyish pranks were not only tolerated in initiates but socially sanctioned as the last acts of childhood. While any future purloining of pigs would be regarded as a criminal act, in *abakhwetha* such behaviour was seen as a 'boys will be boys' act of high spirits.

Of the unfortunate pig, Madiba wrote: 'To lure the pig we took handfuls of sediment from homemade African beer, which has a strong scent much favoured by pigs and placed it upwind of the animal. It was so aroused by the scent that he came out of the kraal, following a trail that we had laid and gradually made his way to us … When he got near us we captured the poor pig, slaughtered it and then built a fire and ate roast pork underneath the stars. No piece of pork has ever tasted as good before or since.'[27]

Boyish pranks ended with the circumcision ritual and a community celebration and much feasting. Madiba later recollected that the high spirits of the event were somewhat

GOATS IN QUNU, 2007

dampened by the words of the keynote speaker Nkosi Meligqili, King Dalindyebo's son, who reminded his audience that manhood in a context of subjugation was 'an empty illusory promise that can never be fulfilled, for we Thembus and all black South Africans are a conquered people, we are slaves in our own country. We are tenants on our own soil … our initiates will go to the cities and live in shacks and drink cheap alcohol, all because we have no land to give them.'[28]

Thus we see that Madiba's childhood began and ended with a lament for lost land and the dignity of economic and social independence that goes with land ownership. The lament began with his father's dismissal and culminated in the speech at the circumcision ceremony. The message was clear: land makes you a man because it is through land that you feed your family.

While the youthful Dalibhunga resented the sombre mood that Nkosi Meligqili brought to what might otherwise have been a joyous feast, the leader's words stayed with him and became part of a gradual awareness of the hunger for freedom. There is no doubt that the 1955 Freedom Charter is resonant with Nkosi Meligqili's words when it states that 'restrictions of land ownership on a racial basis shall be ended and all the land re-divided amongst those who work it to banish famine and land hunger'.[29]

The sad reality of modern-day Thembuland is that both Nkosi Meligqili and Madiba's father Nkosi Mphakanyiswa were right to be concerned about the impact of outside governance of Thembuland. In the current conditions of impoverishment in Qunu, it is difficult to imagine the thriving community in which the young Madiba once lived. However, a comparison of Christmases past and Christmases present serves as a telling reminder that Qunu was not always as it is today. Madiba's reminiscences of his childhood include Christmas Eves in which adults would slaughter stock for the next day's meal. While the herdboys would go out to work with the livestock as usual, the adults 'would ask you to come back about one o'clock and then they would give you food … But in many villages and kraals, they don't actually give you a dish for yourself. What elderly people do, they eat and they keep on giving you pieces, and sometimes that is enough to feed you. But other villages and kraals were more generous. They would give the boys a dish. The meat for boys was normally from the neck or backbone, not the best type, with a lump of bone.'[30]

By contrast, Madiba spent Christmas Day in 1995 in Qunu walking the hillsides of his childhood home. At each homestead he would ask the householders: 'Are you going to slaughter an animal for your Christmas meal?' Very few householders had the means to do so. Those who did were slaughtering chickens, not the sheep and cattle that Madiba recalled from his childhood herdboy Christmases. The poverty of a once-thriving community clearly shocked and saddened the President, who said: 'I hold a party so the children can have some meat at Christmas but it is a forlorn attempt. They go back to their squalor and their misery. You have to see the way people live to really understand the evil of racial oppression.'

MADIBA AT A QUNU CHRISTMAS PARTY, 2000

Chapter Two

FIGHTING WITH FOOD

THE FOOD OF MADIBA'S RURAL CHILDHOOD was a source of emotional and physical sustenance throughout his life. But as the mealie-roasting Qunu herdboy grew up, he was increasingly confronted by the inequalities of the society in which he lived.

In the tales of student food protests, teacup racism and poverty-induced lack of food that follow, we shall see that the culinary context played a key role in stimulating Madiba's hunger for freedom.

TAKE-AWAYS, BALLROOM DANCING AND RYE BREAD

Madiba graduated from Clarkebury Methodist School and Healdtown Wesleyan College in Fort Beaufort, and in 1939 moved on to Fort Hare University. This educational route was unusual for young African men of his generation and reflected the fact that his regal benefactor was grooming him to become an advisor within the structures of Thembu leadership. It seems likely that the patrician youth who arrived in the university town of Alice saw education as a means to restore the economic and social standing of his mother. There were no obvious signs of the political dedication of later years. Indeed, his interest in politics was so limited that he did not join his fellow students at Healdtown when they protested against the 1936 Hertzog Acts, which disenfranchised African voters in the Cape Province and annulled black-owned land title-deeds.

Though surviving members of the class of 1939 are few and far between, Joe Matthews grew up at Fort Hare where his father Z.K. Matthews was an academic. Of this time he recalled: 'I knew everybody because I lived on the campus – I remember from about the time I was about 6 years old when Govan [Mbeki] arrived at the university. I remember all the students who came and left, came and left. The community was very small at Fort Hare; you are talking of a few hundred students. A tiny campus, church every morning, and even as a young boy you would see these people in all kinds of situations: sports, social and so forth. So as a young chap I remember them all.'[31]

Matthews noted that 'there were many students of royal descent amongst the student body and the arrival of Nelson Mandela caused little

OPPOSITE: MADIBA AND HIS FRIEND BIKITSHA, JOHANNESBURG 1941
Prof. Charles van Onselen personal collection
ABOVE: JOE MATTHEWS RECALLED FORT HARE UNIVERSITY

17

FORT HARE

Rye Bread

The Fort Hare rye bread recipe is lost, but the following
bread approximates to that described by
Joe Matthews.[32]

1½ CUPS RYE FLOUR
3 CUPS BREAD FLOUR
1½ TEASPOONS SALT
2 TEASPOONS INSTANT YEAST
1 TABLESPOON MOLASSES
2 TABLESPOONS BUTTER
1¼ CUPS WARM WATER

*Mix the flours, salt and yeast. Combine the molasses, butter and
water. Mix well then add the wet ingredients into the dry.
Mix until the dough forms a ball (add extra water if necessary)
and then knead the dough for approximately 10 minutes (adding
extra flour if necessary). Set the dough aside in an oiled bowl and
allow it to double in size. Turn the dough out of the bowl and
shape in a small, greased loaf tin or on a baking tray. Cover the
dough with a damp tea towel and allow the dough to prove until
doubled in size (at least 1 hour). Preheat the oven to 180°C and
bake for approximately 45 minutes. The bread is cooked when it
makes a hollow sound if tapped on the bottom.*

interest. It was another freshman who caused all the excitement at the start of 1939.' He continued: 'I was only 10 years old but the arrival of [Oliver] Tambo, now *that* was an event. I remember my father came into the house excited about two boys who were coming to Fort Hare who both had their matrics first class with distinctions. So this was the excitement of the term which began in 1939; not Mandela. Tambo and Joe Mokoena [who ended up as a Professor of Mathematics at Fort Hare] – they caused so much excitement; first of all at St Peter's School [for African boys in Rosettenville, Johannesburg] where the excitement at the excellent results was such that the principal held a meeting outside the City Hall to say, "There you are: two chaps at St John's [for white boys in Houghton] and two chaps at St Peter's all with distinctions, so blacks and whites have equal abilities." So it was quite a thing these two chaps, Tambo and Mokoena. Not Mandela.'

Madiba spent his first year at Fort Hare immersed in social and academic life. He liked ballroom dancing and he enjoyed outings to the Ramona restaurant in Alice with Oliver Tambo, whom he had met on the football field. Black students were barred from entering the restaurant through the front door but they could order take-aways at the back entrance. Of this social spot Joe Matthews recollected: 'The Ramona restaurant in Alice was owned by a chap called George Delis. His practice of not serving blacks through the front door was not peculiar to Ramona – in all the facilities around

MADIBA IN THE FORT HARE UNIVERSITY BLAZER, 2006

Benny Gool © Nelson Mandela Foundation

Alice in those days you would get discrimination. The student food at Fort Hare was often not of a high standard – not ingredients, rather how it was cooked, so when we had money we would prefer the Ramona. We even went into Alice to buy bread because Ramona had a bakery as well as the restaurant and we would go for that bread. The bread at the college, which was designed by the Church of Scotland chaps who held sway in the university administration, and they preferred rye bread – we called that bread *umqeqe*, which was a sort of derogatory name. People didn't like it because it was very dark and heavy. It looked too brown. Rye bread was standard at Fort Hare. It was a really dark rye – now you can buy it at Woolies [Woolworths], but then we didn't like it.'

Despite having been to circumcision school, Madiba was a man-child who said of himself that he 'yearned for some of the simple pleasures that I had known as a boy. I was not alone in this feeling and I joined a group of young men who engaged in secret evening expeditions to the university's farmland where we built a fire and roasted mealies. We would sit around eating the ears of corn and telling tall tales.'[33]

FORT HARE AND THE FOOD FIGHT

It was at Fort Hare that politics entered Madiba's life. And it came in via the dinner table. Though accounts differ as to the exact culinary circumstances of the student protest which led to Madiba's expulsion from Fort Hare, all agree that the struggle was gastro-political. An often-retold university legend has it that in June 1939 the Fort Hare debating team was invited to compete against its opposite number at the white university of Rhodes, in neighbouring Grahamstown. According to the story, the visit revealed to the youthful Madiba and his friends that the food available to students at Fort Hare was much worse than that eaten by the white students at Rhodes. The experience caused Madiba to stand as a Student Representative Council (SRC) candidate in the 1940 elections on the seemingly innocuous platform of a promise to improve the quality of student food. The campaign led to a food boycott, which in turn resulted in an SRC election boycott. Although the boycott was broken by only 25 of the 150 students on campus, Madiba found himself elected onto what he considered to be an illegitimate SRC. When the hapless student leader attempted to resign, he was informed by the Fort Hare principal, Dr Alexander Kerr, that he would face expulsion if he refused to participate on the SRC. His refusal to withdraw his resignation saw him expelled.[34]

Joe Matthews remembered the strike somewhat differently, however. 'The strike started because Mr Lundy, who was the boarding master, was accused of having kicked one of the women on the kitchen staff. That was the allegation. That's what the strike was about. The students wanted him to be removed for abusing the women in the kitchen. It was a protest in which students were showing solidarity with the kitchen staff. And Madiba had to sign some document agreeing that they wouldn't strike again, but he wouldn't, and so he left because he wouldn't sign.'[35]

There is nothing in Fort Hare's records to confirm or deny whether it was taste or kitchen worker abuse that sparked the strike. Whichever it was, we see that Madiba's first principled political stand was essentially a fight about food. His refusal to

condone injustice resulted in his expulsion from Fort Hare. When his guardian tried to insist that he return to university, the subsequent row between the two culminated in his leaving the Eastern Cape and heading for Johannesburg.

It is often said that the move to Johannesburg was occasioned by Madiba's unwillingness to enter into an arranged marriage. But the truth is that the marriage was only put on the table because he had been expelled from university and was hanging around at the Great Place without any plan for his future. The suggestion of an arranged marriage stemmed from the Regent's concern that his own health was failing and that, in the absence of a university degree, he would like to see his ward settled before his death.

THE HUNGER OF YOUTH

The sorry tale of how Madiba and his cousin Justice Dalindyebo arrived in Johannesburg in April 1941 has been often told and is not worth repeating in any detail. Suffice it to say that the inept half-truths that the two used to explain their presence in Johannesburg in defiance of the Regent's instructions offer a reassuring reminder that Madiba is a man, not a deity, and was once a callow youth.

Thus it was that the final transition from boy to man came not at circumcision school in the Eastern Cape but rather in the political maelstrom of Johannesburg in the 1940s. Madiba's ultimate coming of age coincided with that of urban black South Africa, and indeed of Johannesburg as a whole. When Madiba arrived in the City of Gold, he was 23 and Johannesburg itself had been in existence for a mere 55 years.

Mining the world's greatest gold fields had created considerable wealth in the new city, but very little of it had filtered down to the rapidly expanding African urban settlements and squatter communities into which the young runaway was absorbed. Although South Africa was in the midst of a spurt of industrialisation and urbanisation, poverty and unemployment fed by colour-bar laws restricted the economic prospects and life chances of African people. There was seldom enough food for the majority of urban Africans and there were many who paid for its lack with their lives. Between 1939 and 1940 the cost of the staple food, mealie meal, went up by 20 per cent and cooking fuel rose by 50 per cent while African wages remained static. The extent of the poverty is revealed most starkly in the statistic which shows that among urban Africans six out of every ten babies born in 1940 were dead by the end of their first year. [36]

While he came from patrician stock, Madiba's decision to run away had robbed him of the comforts and social contacts that the patronage of the Regent had hitherto granted him. He had left university without a degree, he had few friends in the big city, and had limited means with which to support himself. If the city was undergoing rapid transition, so was Madiba. Amid the slums and hunger of Alexandra township, the visible injustices of the society in which he lived soon became apparent to the hitherto apolitical, privileged young man.

Madiba lodged in a room at 46 Seventh Avenue, Alexandra, rented to him by John Madzeka Xhoma, a professional landlord with three properties and also a horse-bound transport business. He and his wife Harriet had arrived in Alexandra from Cradock in the Eastern Cape in 1908. By the time the family let a room to Madiba, John Xhoma was a deacon at St Michael's, the local Anglican church. The Xhomas had eight children (five daughters – Winnie, Didi, Bela, Eunice and Edith – and three sons – Daniel, Thabibi and Xadiga). Those members of the Xhoma family who remember the 1940s say that the patriarch was known to children in the community as 'Flytoppie', a name which implies that he buzzed around like a fly and was given to reporting those youngsters who had committed misdemeanours, to their parents. [37]

In 2007 the Xhoma family still lived at 46 Seventh Avenue and Madiba's backroom was still being rented out to tenants. The only surviving member of the Xhoma family who remembered Madiba's stay was Gladys Xhoma, who said: 'In 1941, I was 9 or 10; no, more like 7 or 8. My granny and grandfather, Harriet and John, owned this house. Winnie was my mother and I was the first granddaughter in the house.' [38] While they were not related by blood, Mr Xhoma acted in a fatherly manner towards Madiba, who in turn treated the Xhoma children and grandchildren as younger siblings. Gladys Xhoma remembered: 'By then Mandela was still studying and there was a time when he was arrested in town, in Johannesburg, and taken to Langlaagte police station (which is called Brixton now). I remember that he sent someone to report that he was arrested, and my father and my uncle went there to check on him. To this house he was like a brother. When we came

there was seldom enough food for the majority of urban Africans and many paid for its lack with their lives

late he used to beat us. If we did anything wrong he would discipline us. Our grandfather didn't mind when he beat us because he was showing us the right way. He used to send Eunice and me to buy milk for him and he loved peanuts (boiled not fried).'

Though hunger was a daily companion, Madiba was spared the worst effects by the kindly Mrs Xhoma, of whom he wrote: 'Every Sunday for all the time I lived on the property [she] gave me lunch, and those steaming plates of pork and vegetables were often my only hot meal of the week.'[39] The family told that Harriet Xhoma's Sunday special was pork head, so one can assume that this is the meal Madiba referred to.

Despite his lack of money, it seems to have been a happy time for Madiba. Gladys Xhoma remembered that 'he used to whistle, always whistling. He loved whistling; it was the first thing he used to do.' Madiba didn't forget Mr Xhoma's kindness, and years later Gladys Xhoma recalled that 'I did see him again after he left Alexandra. We went to his offices in Commissioner Street where he was working as a lawyer. I went there with my grandmother Harriet to see him. We went to him for an advice because after my grandfather John passed away, there was a family conflict where some male relatives wanted to take over this property, so he helped my grandmother to keep our home.'

THE XHOMA FAMILY STANDING OUTSIDE MADIBA'S ROOM, ALEXANDRA 2007

WALTER SISULU AND A MAN NAMED GARLICK

Thanks to the business connections of Walter Sisulu (to whom he had been introduced by his cousin Garlick Mbekeni), Madiba secured employment in 1941 as an articled clerk within the law firm of Witkin, Sidelsky & Eidelman, situated in the Old Mutual Buildings on the corner of Harrison and Commissioner streets.

Sisulu was an estate agent with whom the law firm dealt in the matter of African property transactions. Nat Bregman, who was also an articled clerk in the firm, recalled: 'Walter Sisulu was in the office almost every day. You see, Alexandra, Sophiatown and Evaton were areas where blacks could own property, and Sidelsky had formed a business with a chap called Muller and they were building houses in Alexandra. And this is where Walter Sisulu came into the picture because he was an estate agent and he used to bring people in and Muller's father arranged to lend people money on bonds. He brought people in who were wanting to build rooms, and those wanting to sell their houses. So Walter Sisulu was a good client, and because he was such a good client Mandela got hired.'[40] It is a mark of Walter Sisulu's perspicacity and generosity that at a time when no one, least of all Madiba himself, recognised that the rural runaway had any special qualities, Sisulu not only noticed but went out of his way to assist the young man's aspirations. Despite having a job, Madiba's early years in

OPPOSITE: GLADYS XHOMA PREPARING PIG'S HEAD FOR THE POT

HARRIET XHOMA'S

Pig's Head with Gravy

{Recipe supplied by Nomalizo
and Gladys Xhoma}

1 PIG'S HEAD
WATER (SUFFICIENT TO COVER THE HEAD)
1 TABLESPOON SALT
3 TABLESPOONS SUNFLOWER OIL

*Clean the pig's head carefully to ensure there is no dirt
in its ears, nostrils or mouth. Remove the ears and the brain (use an axe to chop the
skull in half to get at the brain), then cut off the meat from the head.
Rinse the meat well. Put the meat in a pot and cover with salted water. Simmer the head
gently for 1 hour. After 1 hour pour off any remaining water. Retain this water to
use in the gravy. Add the oil and allow the meat to brown gently over a medium heat.*

Mrs Xhoma's Gravy

{This recipe appears to be an early version of what South Africans today
commonly call chakalaka, which is a fusion of African and Indian culinary
styles that developed in Johannesburg}

1 ONION, FINELY CHOPPED
2 TABLESPOONS SUNFLOWER OIL
1 TABLESPOON MEDIUM-HOT CURRY POWDER
2 CARROTS, GRATED
1 TABLESPOON WHITE SUGAR
1 CUP OF STOCK FROM THE PORK BOILING WATER
6 GRATED TOMATOES

*Fry the onions in the oil. When the onions are golden, add the curry powder and
mix well. Add the carrots, sugar, grated tomato and pork stock.
Cook until a rich gravy is formed.*

Johannesburg were characterised by hunger rather than food. The young articled clerk enrolled to study by correspondence through the University of South Africa in order to complete his first degree and later at the University of the Witwatersrand for an LLB. He spent what little money he had not on food but rather on university fees and candles to study at night.

GAUR RADEBE AND THE TEACUPS

At the law firm of Witkin, Sidelsky & Eidelman, the young Madiba was ideally placed to watch and learn from those at the forefront of a new form of urban African protest. Ultimately he would participate in forging a new African National Congress (ANC) in which radical mass protest, rather than patient petitioning by and for an African elite, became the order of the day.

Gaur Radebe is recorded in history as the ANC and Communist Party leader who was involved in the formation of the African Mineworkers' Union and who organised the highly successful Alexandra Bus Boycott of 1941 (which is commonly held to be the first significant act of urban African protest action of the 1940s). To the young Madiba, however, Radebe was the colleague who stood up to racial inequality in the matter of teacups.

Radebe worked at the law firm as a clerk, interpreter and messenger. It was he who revealed to Madiba that the prevailing climate of racial prejudice was present even within the liberal environs of Witkin, Sidelsky & Eidelman.

WALTER SISULU IN HIS OFFICE, 1954

On Madiba's first day at the law firm, the secretary, Miss Lieberman, informed him that new cups had been bought for him and Radebe – the unstated message being that he was not to use the existing crockery from which white members of staff drank. When Gaur Radebe deliberately chose an existing cup rather than one of the new ones, his young colleague was initially more shocked and unsettled than impressed by this confrontation of racial inequalities in the workplace. Gaur Radebe must have been bitterly disappointed in the 23-year-old youth who, instead of joining his teacup protest, chose to say he wasn't thirsty and beat a hasty retreat. Madiba's subsequent response to the new crockery boycott was to take tea on his own in the kitchen.

In the social context of racial oppression, the story of racial discrimination amongst the teacups might

the young clerk spent what little money he had not on food but on university fees and candles to study at night seem minor in its importance. It is an example of petty, tiresome daily racism written in tea rather than a gross human rights violation scrawled in blood. But the refusal to share cups stands at one point of a spectrum that ends at the other with six out of ten African babies dying of poverty-induced malnutrition. The form that racism took in the offices of Witkin, Sidelsky & Eidelman reflected the conflicts within the ostensibly liberal environment of the law firm. In many other firms at the time there would have been tin mugs for Africans (or no mugs and no tea at all) and certainly no shared common room. The sorry tale of the teacups indicates the increasingly untenable position of liberals in Johannesburg in the late 1940s.

BOYCOTTING THE BUSES

© BAHA

THE SANDWICH THAT CHANGED THE WORLD

Not all those at Witkin, Sidelsky & Eidelman held Miss Lieberman's prejudices. Madiba shared an office with another young articled clerk, Nat Bregman, whom he later described as 'my first white friend'.[41] Despite his 86 years, Nat Bregman was still working in 2007 as a lawyer. He said of the former President: 'We were in adjacent desks

for about three years because we were both articled clerks. We both earned five pounds a month. He used to call me Naty. We used to joke and all the rest of it and have our laughs but he was quite a serious chap. He was very intent upon studying and doing his law. To give a classic example, when Sidelsky gave him a rise and Sidelsky said, "What are you going to do with your rise?" he said, "I'm going to buy more candles so that I can swot later at night." But it was a very natural relationship of two people working together and chatting. It was during the war and I had a map of what was going on and we would discuss the war and those sorts of things – how many planes were being shot down in the Battle of Britain and all the rest of it. I do remember that one day, we were sitting in the office and he said to me, "When I become the Prime Minister of this country, you will be my Minister of Justice." I don't remember why or how but I have it in mind that he said those words.'[42]

Though pastrami and pickles are unlikely political tools, it was through them that Madiba was first introduced to Communist social theory. In a world where the majority of restaurants were for whites only and black people were prohibited from buying alcohol, even sandwiches could be political. Nat

Bregman provided Madiba with his first example of culinary non-racialism. Madiba recalled: 'One lunch-time we were sitting in our office and Nat took out a packet of sandwiches. He removed one sandwich and said, "Nelson, take hold of the other side of the sandwich … now pull." I did so and the sandwich split roughly in two. "Now eat," he said … As I was chewing Nat said, "Nelson, what we have done symbolises the philosophy of the Communist Party to share everything we have."'[43]

Nat Bregman noted: 'I was 18 or 19 or something like that, and I think my mother must have made my sandwiches. I brought sandwiches every day and possibly we shared them on more than one occasion, but that one seems to have made a real impression on him. My family didn't keep kosher, not really, not in those days. I became kosher very many years after that, but it was probably pastrami or something like that. But I really can't remember so long after it was eaten. To me the more important thing was the friendship that he showed me after he came out of prison. In 1995 I was having a knee replacement, and the day I went into hospital he was the guest speaker at a fund-raising breakfast and a friend of mine came to him and said, "I'm a friend of Nat Bregman's," so he said to him, "Where's Nat, why isn't he here?" and this friend of mine told him that I was in hospital, so he said, "Which hospital?" and they told him that I was at Morningside Clinic. So he put down his knife and fork and he got up and he said, "You must excuse me, I've got a very good friend in

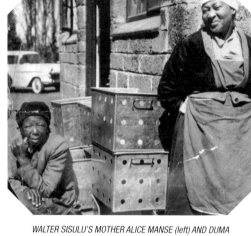

WALTER SISULU'S MOTHER ALICE MANSE (left) AND DUMA NOKWE'S MOTHER ORPAH NOKWE, AT FATHER HUDDLESTON'S FEEDING SCHEME, ORLANDO WEST 1950

Sisulu family collection

hospital." Oh well, I tell you, when he arrived with Zelda [la Grange, his executive personal assistant and spokesperson] and bodyguards and all the rest of it, everyone was agog with excitement and I was very moved that he came. To interrupt his day's programme to fit me in for a visit was very moving for me. It's something very few other people would do … to just put down your knife and fork and come to visit me in hospital. That's really special.'[44]

MA SISULU AND THE SERVANT OF THE PEOPLE

It is not clear whether it was the cooking of Walter's mother Alice Manse (known to all as Ma Sisulu) or her son's charisma that initially attracted Madiba to the Sisulus' home in Orlando West, Soweto. But Madiba soon became a regular dinner guest of the Sisulus at 7372 Magang Street.

Amidst the pots and pans of Ma Sisulu's kitchen, a political consciousness was born. Walter Sisulu exerted a strong influence on Madiba's decision to align himself with the African National Congress. Madiba recalled: 'I didn't know the name of the ANC until I was at Fort Hare, but even then I did not identify myself with the ANC until Comrade Walter recruited me. I tended to follow what he was doing … he was a man who made a tremendous impression on my thinking.'[45]
Six decades later, at his friend's funeral, Madiba acknowledged the crucial influence of Walter Sisulu on his life and work when he said: 'By ancestry I was born to rule but Sisulu helped me to understand that my real vocation was to be a servant of the people.'

Through Sisulu, Madiba came into contact with young ANC activists such as Anton Lembede, Peter Mda, David Bopape, Duma Nokwe and William Nkomo. He also became reacquainted with his Fort Hare dining companion Oliver Tambo. According to Joe Matthews: 'The interesting thing about the South African political struggle was that it was led by very close friends: Tambo, Mda, Sisulu, myself and so on. We were not only colleagues but very close friends.'[46]

© Jürgen Schadeberg

SISULU FAMILY MEAL

her son's friends entertaining. As Madiba said: 'She liked to investigate things. For instance she was very interested in what I was studying. I had to explain in great detail what it meant to be studying law.'[49]

Ma Sisulu played host to the young men as they debated what they saw as the inappropriate conservatism within the existing ANC leadership. Of her hospitality, Madiba noted: 'We had a lovely time at number 7372. The old lady treated us as her children, though sometimes she would find it difficult to provide enough food because we were so many and they were not a wealthy family.'[47]

Amid the breaking of *amadombolo* (dumplings) the young men came to the conclusion that a new era demanded a new course of action. According to Madiba, 'We in the Youth League had seen the failure of legal and constitutional means to strike at racial oppression; now the entire organisation was set to enter a more activist stage.'[48] Although the actual launch of the ANC Youth League took place at the Bantu Men's Social Centre in 1944, there is no question that it was at Ma Sisulu's table that the Youth League was born.

EVEN NICE BOYS EAT TOO MUCH

The founder members of the ANC Youth League were undoubtedly remarkable young men, and it seems that Ma Sisulu found the company of

However charming the young men were, the extent of Ma Sisulu's generosity becomes clear when one considers the degree to which their hunger for freedom was equalled by their capacity to eat her out of house and home. Others were less forgiving of Madiba's hungers.

In a letter from Robben Island to his wife Madiba described his voracious appetite in these words: 'I could polish off enormous quantities of food in any order. I could start with pudding backwards and feel just as happy and contented at the end of it. I well remember the painful remarks of a housewife who was also a medical student at the time. She and hubby had invited me for dinner one day. I had built quite some formidable reputation as a meat eater. After watching my performance for some time as the heavily laden dishes on the table rapidly vanished, she bluntly told me that I would die of coronary thrombosis probably in my early forties. I was foolish enough to challenge her statement and tried to support my argument with the sweeping declaration that thrombosis was unknown amongst our forefathers in spite of the fact that they were great meat eaters; whereupon she promptly produced a huge textbook out of which she read out emphatically and deliberately the relevant passage. It was a galling experience. I almost immediately felt a million pains in the region of my heart.'[50]

Chapter Three

THE FOOD OF LOVE

W HEN LOVE IS INVOLVED, HAPPINESS IS OFTEN OBLIVIOUS TO EXTERNAL HARDSHIPS. The amorous stories that follow are predominantly joyous and are remembered with a lightness that belies the bravery and very real human suffering of the period.

While in-depth socio-political analysis of the period will be left to others, the reader should be aware of the bitter-sweet backdrop to the events described below.

Every recipe was served in a context of racial oppression, which throughout the 1940s and 1950s was increasingly eating into the lives and loves of all South Africans. From 1948, colonial-style racial segregation was transformed into full-scale apartheid. Every culinary creation detailed in the ensuing pages was prepared, and eaten, in the rancid context of banning orders, the Bantu Education Act, the Group Areas Act, the Immorality Act, the Suppression of Communism Act, the Sharpeville Massacre and two major political trials.

No culinary decision is without roots in its time. It is possible to chart the changing

Eli Weinberg © Mayibuye Archives

political climate in dinner-party invitations and picnics. The reader will notice that even in the mid-1950s, when he was a successful lawyer and middle-aged man, Madiba was an enthusiastic picnicker – an indication of the limited number of restaurants that black people were allowed into. Similarly, the guest lists for weddings and social soirées of the period tell of a social life which by the late 1950s had been profoundly thwarted by the fact that almost every significant political activist was banned, jailed or in exile.

THE FIRST TASTE OF DOMESTIC BLISS

Evelyn Mase has often been written out of the Madiba story. In fact, so little attention has been paid to the historical role of the first Mrs Mandela that the wrong photograph of her has been used in almost all books, including *Long Walk*

OPPOSITE: MADIBA AND EVELYN MASE *(extreme left)* AT THE SISULU'S WEDDING, 1944
Sisulu family collection
ABOVE: MADIBA WITH BATSHAKA CELE

to Freedom. Madiba and Evelyn's daughter Dr Makaziwe Mandela was adamant that the widely used photograph of a plump smiling girl is not her mother. Indeed, the woman in question bears no resemblance to the heavy-lidded, oval-faced beauty in her own photographic collection.[51] The other woman was identified, in 2007, as Batshaka Cele, a relative of Winnie Madikizela-Mandela. Dr Mandela said: 'The right picture of my mum is the one in the Sisulus' wedding photograph.'

To write Evelyn Mandela out of the story is to grossly oversimplify Madiba's biography and the formation of his complex personality. Her support for Madiba was both financial and emotional. While he was training to be a lawyer, her nursing income largely supported the couple and her love sustained him through his twenties and early thirties. According to their mutual friend Phyllis Ntantala: 'It was during his years with Evelyn that he grew and blossomed politically into the national figure he is.'[52]

Eli Weinberg © Mayibuye Archives

MADIBA WITH HIS SON THEMBEKILE

through her cousin Walter Sisulu, with whom she lived while training to be a nurse. A whirlwind courtship, after their first meeting in 1943, resulted in their wedding a year later. Despite the painful and bitter divorce that was to follow, for a considerable period of time the couple and their children, Thembekile, Makaziwe and Makgatho, were happy. Of the early years of their marriage Dr Makaziwe Mandela said: 'My mother did have fond memories of that time. For example, when she had babies they shared equally the work … He was a man who was involved – when they were still in love – in taking care of the kids, changing diapers at night and telling her, "Don't worry, tonight I will take care of the children." That was before he was captured, and politics and the ambition of becoming a leader took hold. Before he was a politically involved person, he was very involved with us.'

Sitsheketshe Mandela lived with Madiba and Evelyn when he was a teenager in the early years of their marriage and recalled that

Evelyn Mandela died in 2004 but her daughter said: 'When my parents were still together I was young. I was 4 years old when we left but I know what my mother said about that time. Let me start with the hard part. My mum believed that she was responsible for supporting his education to become a lawyer, and then when he did that, my father told her to "get you gone".'[53]

Like so many significant events in Madiba's early adulthood, Evelyn Mase came into his life

they were happy, gregarious times. 'There would be parties – the old man used to be a socialite and the house was always full of ANC people: Duma Nokwe, O.R. Tambo, Walter Sisulu and others. They used to have a meal, and after the meal there would be a drinking session and I would wait until they had left and I would drink the bottom of their glasses but I never liked my cousin's glass because he liked very sweet liquor – and I liked strong liquor – brandies and whiskies. I used to prefer Dr [Diliza] Mji's glass because Dr Mji [President of the

EVELYN MANDELA'S

Jelly with a Twist

{recipe supplied by
Dr Makaziwe Mandela}

1 PACKET POWDERED JELLY
(ANY FLAVOUR IS POSSIBLE BUT EVELYN
MANDELA FAVOURED STRAWBERRY)
1 CUP OF BOILING WATER
4 EGGS (SEPARATED)
4 TABLEPOONS WHITE SUGAR
2 CUPS MILK

*Sprinkle the jelly powder over the boiling water,
stirring constantly until all the crystals have dissolved.
Allow the jelly mixture to cool. Make custard by
mixing the egg yolks and sugar together (beat well until
light and fluffy), then slowly add the milk and cook
gently over a low heat until a custard forms. Allow the
custard to cool and then fold it into the cool but still
liquid jelly. Beat the egg whites to stiff peaks. Put the
custard and jelly mixture in the fridge, and when the
mixture is almost set, fold in the beaten egg whites.
Pour into a jelly mould to set.*

Transvaal ANC Youth League] used to have strong glass whereas my cousin drank sweet liquor. Not at all to my taste.'[54]

EVELYN'S JELLY WITH A TWIST

For a man who clearly got such pleasure from children, domesticity and the joys of being a good host, it is tragic how little of these pleasures Madiba enjoyed. Throughout the late 1940s politics increasingly ate into his domestic time. In later years he would say with regret: 'I enjoyed relaxing at home, reading quietly, taking in the sweet and savoury smells emanating from the pots boiling in the kitchen. But I was rarely at home to enjoy these things.'[55] When questioned about what was in her mother's cooking pots, Dr Makaziwe Mandela commented: 'My mum was a very good cook. We all learnt, me and even her grandchildren, we all learnt to cook from her. When we were children my mother cooked the regular food: *pap* with spinach, *boerewors* and *umngqusho*, and also jellies and custards, sago pudding, trifles, a whole lot of things. I remember especially a jello with milk and egg. But most of all, my mum cooked the traditional foods of the Eastern Cape. This is what my father loved and still loves – samp and the like. On Sundays she would do rice, chicken, mutton and everything. What my mum liked passionately was real traditional dishes – all the things my father likes. It's the same food that we still cook – when we go home to Qunu, we are not looking for *foie gras* – tripe and steamed dumplings, that's what we all like in my family.'[56]

EVELYN AND THE TOUGH MEAT

Political involvement was a significant bone of contention between Madiba and his first wife. By 1947, he had been elected to the Regional Executive Committee of the ANC proper, a fact that reflects the changing nature of the organisation and his growing political profile. Evelyn Mandela was uncomfortable with Madiba's increasing assumption of the mantle of leadership within the ANC, which she felt had a negative impact on their family life. One gains some sympathy for her position upon hearing the story of how the Tobruk squatter protest disrupted her home life and undermined her faith in her own cooking skills. The Reverend Michael Scott was a white clergyman who had been campaigning against the government's intention to forcibly remove the people of the Tobruk squatter camp on the outskirts of Soweto. In 1946 he accused other members of the Tobruk Action Committee of embezzling money from the campaign funds. The accusation, which subsequently turned out to be well founded, resulted in death threats, and the Reverend Michael Scott and a co-worker, Reverend Mr Dlamini, fled their homes and took refuge with the Mandelas. While Scott was a charming house guest, Dlamini complained constantly about Evelyn Mandela's cooking. 'This meat of yours is very hard and lean, not properly cooked at all … Mandela, you know your wife just cannot cook.'[57] Whatever Reverend Mr Dlamini might have said, it seems likely that the small portions and inexpensive cuts of meat reflected the Mandelas' limited means and overloaded hospitality budget rather than Evelyn Mandela's domestic prowess.

CHRISTMAS AND THE CLASH OF WORLDVIEWS

Joe Matthews, who stayed with the couple at the very end of their marriage, commented: 'I remember Evelyn. She was in her own right a strong woman, with strong views, and I think that eventually caused the break-up. She was sort of unusual because at that time the average African woman went along with what the husband wanted, but she didn't. She was quite incredibly strong. She was a Jehovah's Witness and her church taught that she shouldn't participate in politics. I think a great deal of conflict occurred because she didn't like the politics. He was a nice daddy; always, always a good dad to the children, but I think myself that he may have been unkind to her because she was so immersed in that church of hers … Eventually it became impossible to live with because she didn't like his friends – we were all political and very far away from her ideology, which she took very

seriously. There was a clash of worldviews on a very fundamental level.'[58]

Madiba and his wife's divergent attitudes to Christmas parties provides a simple culinary example of the distance between the two. Amina Cachalia recollected that she 'went to Madiba's house for two Christmases. The one was very early on when Evelyn was still there – I think 1951 or so. We sat in the little garden and the kids were playing around and Evelyn had cooked a real feast; there was chicken and rice and salads and custard afterwards. I remember the custard so clearly. It was just a lovely meal. Evelyn was a very reserved sort of lady, so she cooked the dinner but she kept to herself in the kitchen and then after lunch we walked up the road without Evelyn to Walter [Sisulu]'s house to wish them happy Christmas, and the kids were in the street shouting "Happy, happy, happy".'[59]

© Alf Kumalo

MADIBA'S MOTHER, MRS NOSEKENI MANDELA

Jehovah's Witnesses do not celebrate Christmas, and Madiba's enthusiasm for inviting friends to mark this ritual suggests that the cultural and ideological gap was deep and wide from relatively early on in the marriage. For Madiba to expect a member of such a sect to cater for Christmas functions might charitably be described as insensitive. And yet concessions to her religious persuasion were not an option for Madiba, as Jehovah's Witnesses are opposed to participation

XOLISWA NDOYIYA'S

Qunu Amasi Recipe

1*l* UNPASTURISED MILK
1 HOLLOWED-OUT CALABASH (ALSO KNOWN AS AN *ISELWA*)
WITH A STOPPER AT THE TOP AND BOTTOM

Put the milk into the calabash. Ensure that the stopper is not in too tight
as the fermentation process will release gas, which can cause the calabash to burst. Leave
the milk to separate into curds and whey. In summer this will take 3 to 4 days; in winter
it can take up to 10 days. Remove the bottom stopper, which allows the whey to
run out. Scoop out the curds that are left behind. (According to Xoliswa Ndoyiya:
Some people remix the whey and curds, but Madiba likes you to discard the
whey and just eat the curds.')

in secular political activism, and to have conceded would have required him to deny what had become the very essence of his personality and life's purpose. By the mid-1950s the marriage was beginning to collapse under the weight of Madiba's increased political commitments and Evelyn Mandela's religious dedication. But none of this should diminish the fact that it was Evelyn who provided him with his first experience of adult domestic stability and that, despite their separation in 1956 and divorce in 1958, for a while his home life with his wife gave him great happiness. For the first time in his life, Madiba had a home at 8115 Orlando West, Soweto, of which he subsequently said: 'I finally had a stable base and I went from being a guest in other people's homes to having guests in my own.'[60]

MAMA MANDELA AND THE CALABASHES

During the latter years of Evelyn Mandela's tenure, Madiba's mother and sister Mabel came to stay. While this created further constraints on space in the small house, it resulted in a blossoming of the African culinary arts. According to Joe Matthews, who was living with the Mandelas when Mrs Mandela senior arrived: 'People think you just do anything and that's an African meal, and of course that's not true. Madiba was a real gourmand in his appreciation of the traditional foods of the Eastern Cape. And he would know whether it was good stuff or not. For example, the calabash is crucial for getting a really good sour milk. And it becomes thick and then you can remove the whey from under the curds by removing the cork at the bottom of the calabash. You see, that's what he wanted, the real thing. Whereas if you came to him and said, "Here's a milk that has become sour in a canned fruit jar," now that's not right. With sour milk you can tell if you are loved at home by what the lady does. And you've got to be able to do it because our current generation now go to the supermarket. Even *amasi*

is bought at the supermarket, there are no calabashes anymore. But what they gain in speed they lose in taste. Now Madiba, you see, would never go to a shop to buy *amasi*. It has to be genuine and he would know that this is genuine stuff.'[61] The passion for *amasi* as described by Joe Matthews is reflected in a letter that Madiba wrote to his wife from jail after subsisting for six years on a diet without soured milk. 'I long for *amasi* – the food for which I loved to sharpen my teeth and to stretch out my tummy, the act that I really enjoyed, went straight into my blood and into my heart and that produced perfect contentment.'[62]

The significance of the calabash in Joe Matthews's description is explained by Madiba's relative Monde Ngcebetshana. 'Inside the actual calabash itself there are the veins and they give the milk that you put inside a nicer, richer taste – sourer, with a distinctive fragrance and flavour.'[63] Xoliswa Ndoyiya, Madiba's chef from 1990, concurred. 'When I am in Qunu I always use a calabash. It separates the milk solids from the whey much better, so you get a much more sour taste. You can really taste the difference between *amasi* made in a calabash and that made in a glass jug. Madiba would always know the difference. You must never make it in a plastic container or a milk carton as the taste is totally wrong. The real skill with *amasi* is to know when it's ready – the best thing is to have several sets of *amasi* on the go at any one time so that you make sure that there is always some that is done and some that is still busy souring. Patience is the thing. If I try and give Madiba *amasi* that isn't ready, he will say to me, "Why are you rushing me to eat this when it's not ready yet?" Often he will ask me to bring him the *amasi* and we look at it together and he will decide whether it's ready.'[64]

Mrs Mandela senior's culinary skills were not confined to *amasi*. Joe Matthews recorded: 'His mother was first class in that sort of field because

OPPOSITE: LUCRECIA NGCEBETSHANA HOLDING A CALABASH, QUNU 2007

she didn't modernise the things. For example we have a mealie bread – we call it *isonka sombhako* – and Madiba's mother made it very well. She didn't buy tinned mealies – it was fresh corn, so it was nice and fresh. It's not the way the modern lady would do it. It was like this with the kind of *umngqusho* that she did too. There was real love in the preparation. And the *isopho* – soup – she didn't go and buy samp at the shop; she did it with freshly crushed mealies and the beans were drawn from her lands. She didn't grow in Orlando but she would get them at home in Transkei. She only used really good stuff.'[65]

ABOVE: MADIBA AND K.D. MATANZIMA

Eli Weinberg © Mayibuye Archives

Almost half a century later Madiba was to tell Ella Govender, Household Comptroller in the Presidency: 'You don't just cook for my stomach, you cook for my blood: it's the way my mother used to feed me,' implying that Govender's food nurtured and supported him on many levels.[66]

Despite his admiration for traditional African food, Madiba seems to have been somewhat wary of serving it to those from other cultural backgrounds.

Rica Hodgson recalled telling Madiba in the mid-1950s: '"I've never eaten a real African meal. I would like to eat a real African meal." He said, "Okay, you're invited. Come to my home next Sunday and have lunch with us." So we duly went, and what was prepared for lunch? Roast chicken and roast potatoes, and peas, and tinned peaches and cream. I mean, the same lunch that I would have given them almost. So I said, "So where's the African food?" Nelson said, "What do you want me to do? Go and grub for roots for you? What do you want me to give you?"'[67]

FROM MEALS WITH MATANZIMA TO CURRY WITH MADIBA

The first Mrs Mandela moved out of 8115 Ngakane Street (corner of Vilakazi Street), Orlando West, in 1956 and the following year Madiba met Nomzamo Winnie Madikizela. Unbeknown to both parties, the woman who was to become the second Mrs Mandela had eaten at his home long before she met its owner. In 1953 Winnie Madikizela, then a social work student, was courted by Madiba's nephew and Fort Hare friend

... on 10 March 1957 Madiba took Winnie Madikizela out to lunch

OPPOSITE: SITSHEKETSHE MANDELA EATING UMNGQUSHO, QUNU 2007

NOSISA MANDELA'S
Umngqusho

400g SAMP
300g SUGAR BEANS
WATER
SALT TO TASTE

Soak the samp and the beans overnight in cold water. Rinse the soaked samp and beans well, and place them in a large pot. Add sufficient fresh water to ensure that not only is the mixture covered but that there is at least 2cm of water above the level of the samp and beans. Bring the water to the boil then reduce the heat and simmer until the samp and the beans are soft, about 2 hours. Add extra water if the mixture gets dry. When the samp and beans are soft drain excess water and season to taste.

I would take one spoon, swallow
and drink Coca-Cola, then attempt another

Kaiser Matanzima. Though his admiration was unrequited, Matanzima's ardour was such that he frequently travelled to Johannesburg to see her and would stay in Madiba's house. On one such occasion, when Madiba was away, Matanzima invited Miss Madikizela to dinner. He fetched her in Madiba's green Oldsmobile and fed her at 8115 Ngakane Street. As the owner was away, Winnie was left with the impression that the house belonged to Matanzima. It seems likely that Evelyn Mandela cooked the meal with which Matanzima tried, and failed, to woo the beautiful student.

Accounts of Madiba and Winnie Madikizela's first meeting differ. In *Long Walk to Freedom* Madiba wrote that they were introduced in Oliver Tambo's office when she came with her brother to consult the legal practice. Adelaide Tambo's recollection was that they were shopping in the Park Station delicatessen and bumped into Madiba browsing among the shelves of delicacies. In 2007 Winnie Madikizela-Mandela herself commented: 'All these stories, I don't know where they get them from. I was simply at a bus stop. I was a medical social worker at Baragwanath Hospital. And in those days the Johannesburg General Hospital was right up the hill. The bus used to leave from there to collect doctors and nurses. I would stand there every day at the same time and he would be driving up to the Fort because he would be going to what was then Number 4 [prison at the Old Fort] where he had lots of clients that he was defending, and one day the bus didn't pitch, so he offered me a lift.'[68]

However it happened, on 10 March 1957 Madiba took Winnie Madikizela out to lunch. Again, the exact details are sketchy. He said that the venue was Azad's restaurant while she remembered it as Kapitan's, but since both were Indian restaurants on Kort Street, the divergence is of little significance. What is more interesting is their distinctly different perceptions of the success of the occasion. The 22-year-old woman found the experience less than satisfactory. Of their first date she recalled: 'I had never eaten curry in my life before and I drank gallons of Coca-Cola because it was burning – this hot, hot food that I had never tasted before. It was such a culture shock for a girl from Pondoland. I would take one spoon, swallow and drink Coca-Cola, then attempt another. By the time we finished eating I had tears in my eyes and was sneezing. I had taken such care with my appearance and then there was my nose running and my eyes watering! It was actually a dreadful experience at the time, but of course he never even noticed the discomfort of me eating like that. He was having spoon after spoon and I just could not believe that anyone could eat such dreadful food. It was chicken curry and mutton curry and I ate this funny bread for the first time – *roti*, flat bread: I had never seen that before. I was from Pondoland. I was a country girl. I didn't know such things. I had been in Johannesburg since 1953 and I just never moved in such circles. I was an ordinary social worker and my case load was in the townships. I worked with what was then Site and Service, there wasn't Soweto as it is today;

WINNIE MADIKIZELA AT THE 1953 SCHOOL OF SOCIAL WORK CHRISTMAS PARTY

it was Site and Service, shacks. You can imagine, you want to impress this person and there you are sneezing and choking – it was horrible and I didn't want him to see that I had never eaten this type of food before. I was just watching him enjoying. I never told him. To think of it, that it was a disaster!' Conversely, Madiba was charmed by her inexperience in matters culinary, and that same day asked her to marry him.

While Winnie Madikizela did not take this initial proposal seriously, she did gradually fall in love with him over the ensuing weeks. When news of their courtship got back to her erstwhile beau, Matanzima, he rushed to 8115 Orlando West to deal with his amorous rival. There was one final confrontation in which the two suitors asked Winnie Madikizela to wait in the dining room while they engaged in heated argument. She hovered for a few minutes, and then became irritated by the notion that they could decide

her fate without her and she left. Though neither gentleman told the tale of how the conflict was resolved, from then on Madiba had no rivals for the object of his affection.

LATE FOR LUNCH … AGAIN

While her dramatic beauty first caught Madiba's attention, it was Winnie Madikizela's willingness to learn about and participate in politics and her eagerness to meet his friends and comrades that ultimately made her a more suitable partner for the man who was rapidly moving to the centre of the struggle for racial equality.

Later, as President, Madiba was very careful to be punctual. He was determined to contradict the reputation of black leaders for keeping 'African time' and was very censorious of his younger comrades' attitude to timekeeping. When Thabo Mbeki arrived late at his daughter Zindzi's wedding in 1992, he received a stinging reproof. And yet it was not always thus. In the 1950s Madiba and Winnie Madikizela were frequent lunch guests at Michael and Ray Harmel's Gardens home in Johannesburg. Ray was a garment worker and Michael was a writer and the principal of the Indian Central High School in Fordsburg and both were significant members of the Communist Party. Their daughter Barbara Harmel recalled: 'They were delightful lunch guests and I adored them, but they would drive my mother insane because they would be invited for one o'clock but they would seldom arrive before three. We would be waiting and waiting and then they would finally come and they would be in gorgeous clothes and glamorous cars and my factory worker mother would be muttering into the chopped liver in the kitchen about "damn bloody bourgeois".'[69]

RAY HARMEL'S

Chopped Liver

{recipe supplied by Barbara Harmel}

20g SHMALTZ (RENDERED CHICKEN FAT)
1 ONION, ROUGHLY CHOPPED
250g CHICKEN LIVERS
SALT AND PEPPER
2 HARD BOILED EGGS

Gently melt the schmaltz and fry the onion until it is soft and golden, about 5 minutes. Add the chicken livers to the pan and cook through, about 5 minutes. Allow the mixture to cool and then blend the livers with one of the boiled eggs. Season to taste and allow the mixture to cool before garnishing with the second egg chopped fine.

For all her eagerness to learn about politics, lunch almost invariably ended with Madiba and Michael Harmel in the garden engrossed in in-depth, confidential political discussion, Ray in the kitchen washing up, and 22-year-old Winnie and 16-year-old Barbara curled up on Barbara's bed paging through photo albums and re-reading letters from Barbara's pen pals. Of this friendship Barbara Harmel said: 'Winnie was part glamorous big sister and part surrogate mother to me. They only came to lunch about once a month but she phoned me at least twice a week to see that I was okay. She was very sensitive to how hard it was for me to grow up in those times and under those circumstances. She was quite simply the best thing that had ever happened to me, and I adored her.'[70]

RAY, BARBARA AND MICHAEL HARMEL

Eli Weinberg © Mayibuye Archives

With the benefit of adult eyes Winnie Madikizela-Mandela remembered the occasions slightly differently. 'She cooked very well, Ray Harmel. I remember those chopped livers, lots of onion in the liver. But they weren't really social functions … Of course we hardly ever had lunch at home because we would go for these lunches, which were a cover for the political meetings, that was their real purpose. At these lunches they wouldn't be there, they would often be in meetings right through the meal. That is why I had so much time with Barbara because I was being taken as a cover actually to make it look like a social occasion. So I was waiting for the political meetings to be finished. Barbara was such a lovely little girl but so troubled. She was a young girl and I was a brand-new social worker. I listened to her problems. I had been trained to understand that no problem is too small to solve. Someone will come with a problem – "my shoes pinch me" – and the next one comes and says, "I have just lost my husband and I can't bury him. I haven't got money." We were trained to see all problems as valid.'[71]

Of the food that was served at these lunches Barbara Harmel said: 'My mother came to South Africa from Lithuania as a very young woman and so she cooked in a way that was part Yiddish traditional and part white South African standards, and that is what she fed everyone including the Mandelas. We would start the meal with herring or clear chicken soup with matzos balls and then move on to roast beef and roast potatoes. And then end up in trifle or cheese blintzes. We had the most marvellous plum tree, and while we children used it to have pip-spitting contests from the front stoep, my mother turned what fruit we left her into wonderful, almost English-style desserts – so there were trifles, stewed plums with boudoir biscuits.'[72]

NUMBER ONE SOCIAL ANNOUNCEMENT

Madiba's courtship of Winnie Madikizela coincided with the strains of the Treason Trial. This was accompanied by a banning order which limited his freedom of movement and his right to attend public gatherings. Despite the hardships, there were plenty of pleasant culinary interludes. On 10 March 1958 (exactly a year from their first date), after they had been on a picnic on a farm on the Evaton Road, Madiba told her that Ray Harmel was an excellent dressmaker and that she should commission her to make a wedding dress.

The *Golden City* Post of 25 May 1958 recorded the upcoming engagement. 'It's this week's no. 1 social announcement. Attorney Nelson Mandela and social worker Miss Winnie Madikizela are holding a party today to announce their engagement.' The social columnist Arthur Maimane went on to note that 'Mandela will be the first bridegroom I know of who won't be able to make the usual – and often boring – "my wife and I" speech at the wedding reception since he is banned from addressing public gatherings!' The champagne-laden engagement party was held at the bride's aunt Phyllis Mzaidume's home in Orlando West.

The next day the story of the engagement was also covered in glowing terms in the social columns of *The World* newspaper. While the Mandelas' relationship is often viewed as a political union, it is important to recognise the depth of passion involved. Amina Cachalia remembered: 'I went to Christmas with Winnie and Nelson in 1959. I remember it so clearly because that was the last Christmas we ever had in Soweto, because after 1960 it was just impossible. Roast and *phutu* and rice, vegetables, Christmas cake. It was a lovely lunch. Winnie was very young and absolutely beautiful. They were exceptionally happy. I think Nelson was completely besotted. She used to glow – there was something about her – even when she was not dressed up she still glowed, and he was transfixed in her presence.'[73]

Whereas the relationship blossomed and grew into a marriage that withstood three decades of hardship before it ended, the lunch dates at the Harmels were not so tenacious. Barbara Harmel remarked: 'I finished matric in 1960. It was the first state of emergency and my father was on the run. The lunches came to an end because even those people who weren't in jail or in hiding were banned and not allowed to talk to each other.' Despite this, 'Winnie and I went on meeting – I would meet her for lunch in her office – we brown-bagged, ate sandwiches from the OK Bazaars [supermarket], because there were very few restaurants where white and black people could sit together.'[74]

RANSOMING THE BEST MAN FOR AN OX

Madiba's second marriage was celebrated on 14 June 1958. There were traditional festivities at the bride's father's home in Mbongweni, Bizana, followed by a ceremony at the local Methodist church and a reception at the town hall. Though the town hall was technically reserved for whites only, the bride's father, Columbus Madikizela, applied for and was given permission to hold the reception at the venue.

Columbus Madikizela saw to the traditional ceremony, which was accompanied by the slaughter of several beasts and the brewing of sorghum beer. Aunt Phyllis Mzaidume was in charge of the Eurocentric culinary portion of the meal which was served at the town hall.

The Madikizela family went through the traditional ritual of 'kidnapping' best man Duma Nokwe, who was a Johannesburg advocate and

© BAHA

DUMA NOKWE (second from left), 1960

Secretary-General of the ANC, and demanding the ransom of an ox to release him. The ox delivered, Nokwe was free to rejoin the groom's party. His release was just as well because the number of guests from the groom's side was considerably reduced by the politics of the day. Ahmed Kathrada recalled: 'I was invited but I couldn't go. Madiba had to get special permission to attend himself. Most of the people he invited from Jo'burg (the Slovos, the Harmels, Walter and others) were banned, and some of us were not only banned from attending meetings but also confined to the Johannesburg municipal area.'[75] Barbara Harmel remembered a more prosaic reason for her failure to attend: 'It was during term time and my parents wouldn't let me miss school.'[76]

THE MELTING BRIDE AND GROOM

While all previous biographies of Madiba describe a 14-tier fruit cake as part of the proceedings, the bride, when asked about what would have been an astonishing gastro-architectural structure, told a different tale. 'Who on earth wrote that? There was nothing like that, my dear. No, to my memory it was five tiers. My aunt Mzaidume arranged for the cake, which was made in Johannesburg and transported to Pondoland. It had white icing and the two little figures, a bride and a groom.'[77]

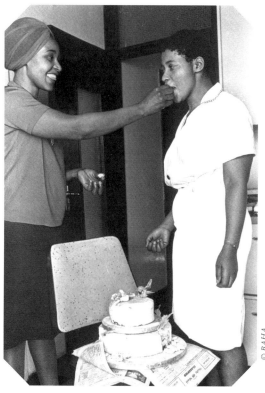

WINNIE MANDELA (left) AND A NEIGHBOUR WITH THE WEDDING CAKE, 1970

It was the bride's intention to take a portion of the cake to the groom's ancestral home but time caught up with them. Despite the fact that festivities continued for a week at the Madikizela home, Madiba, who had been granted a six-day relaxation of his banning order, was legally required to return to Johannesburg, and the top tier of the cake returned with the couple. The tier was packed away and kept in anticipation of a party that was never to be. As it turned out, the cake spent considerably more time with the bride than the groom ever did. In 1978 Winnie, who had been without her imprisoned husband for over 14 years and was at the time banished to the desolate rural settlement of Brandfort, said of the cake: 'The day Nelson comes out of prison, we must go and complete the second part of our ceremony. I still have the wedding cake, the part of that cake we were supposed to have taken to his place. I brought it here to Brandfort. It crumbled a bit when they dumped our things. It is now in my house in Orlando, waiting for him.'

Asked about the cake in 2007, Winnie Madikizela-Mandela's eyes welled with tears. 'For me, it became a symbol of our love. I kept it in memory of our wedding and in hopes of a life that never was. There I was, the most unmarried married woman. I had never lived with him. Even for our wedding he had to get permission from the Chief Magistrate and was only given a few days. And for those few days we were normal people. When we got back from the wedding, even before he went to jail, we didn't have a normal life because the routine at home was that he would get up and go to Pretoria every day to the Supreme Court for the trial. The only time that we had a normal life was just that week of our wedding. That week was to me a whole lifetime, because it symbolised what life might have been. The cake was really all I knew about marriage … I clung to the cake because it was in memory of a life I still dared to hope would happen when he came out of prison.'[78]

Their daughter Zindzi was only 18 months old when her father went to jail but the cake became a feature of her childhood. 'I remember that tier – wherever we went, we went with it. It was always there – as children it was more of an irritant than anything else because we were curious, we were like "what does it taste like?" I do remember that it still smelt good and I thought, "Gee, why can't we just keep half for him?" She kept it in a little box – it was all white, there wasn't another colour; all the little decorations were white. And some of it started to fall apart. The piping around the edges started to fall off.'[79]

Sadly, the cake, which Winnie Madikizela-Mandela

WINNIE, MADIBA AND THEIR SECOND CHILD, ZINDZI

© Alf Kumalo

protected for over 20 years, was destroyed in 1988 by a fire at her home in Soweto. The bride and groom figurines melted into the ashes. In 1989 she sadly noted: 'We have never had the opportunity to celebrate out wedding anniversary together.'[80]

EVEN CHICKENS LONG FOR FREEDOM

The cake did not lack for company on its return trip to Johannesburg. In a prison letter to his wife sent in 1970, Madiba recalled their return from her Eastern Cape home village after the wedding: 'You remember how we carried a calabash of *amasi* all the way back from Mbongweni village. What a lovely trip!'[81] In addition to the cake and the *amasi*, there were also two live chickens in the vehicle. As they were packing to leave, the bride's father attempted to give the couple a large assortment of cattle and sheep, which the groom politely refused as impractical in the urban environment to which the couple were returning. In order to spare his new father-in-law's feelings Madiba consented to take two live chickens. The chickens clucked and squawked as far as Pietermaritzburg where the couple stopped for a roadside picnic. During the stop the chickens escaped, and despite the couple's best efforts the fowls resisted all attempts to recapture them. There was much chasing and lunging at the birds followed by considerable hilarity when both bride and groom conceded that they were now so urbanised that they no longer knew how to catch chickens. Amid much laughter, they decided to grant the fowls their freedom.

On their return to Soweto, there was a second ceremony awaiting them, prepared by Madiba's mother, relatives and friends, in which a sheep was slaughtered at 8115 Orlando West, and a second wedding feast was consumed. Soon afterwards, a delegation of Madiba's clansmen arrived in Soweto and officially welcomed his new bride into the Madiba clan. She was given the name Nobandla by the Madiba elders.

YOUR FATHER DID TRY AND WARN YOU …

At the Bizana wedding Columbus Madikizela had warned the bride that the groom was already married to the struggle against apartheid and that if she wanted to be happy she must adapt to his lifestyle and political commitments. 'If your man is a wizard, you must become a witch.' Once back in Orlando, the new bride was often reminded of these words when yet another family meal was interrupted by a telephone call about politics or by a visitor alerting Madiba to the need to bail out or represent a comrade who had been arrested.

Almost immediately, the second Mrs Mandela's marriage was subsumed in strategy meetings for the Treason Trial, which would go on long into the night. And during the day her husband spent his time in the dock as an accused.[82] As she recalled: 'When he was on trial, when he did come home he would disappear around half-past eight and he would come home to change and he would rush straight to Pretoria. They would be having National Executive Committee meetings, planning every night. The ANC had to live and he was literally the life of the organisation.'[83] Though she missed him in his absences, when he was at home his

gregarious nature often proved extremely trying for his new wife. 'I am still cross with him to this day. The things he used to do; always bringing people home without warning. You know, he is so generous when it comes to that. It's from his traditional upbringing … We have a saying that you cook for strangers who are friends that you do not yet know. So my pots were always fuller than they needed to be for the immediate family … He would pitch up with something like ten people, without any warning. It was nothing to him and he would actually be surprised that you did not have enough food to feed all these people! He would be like, "What's wrong with you? Why didn't you cook?" And he would bring all nationalities and there are times when we do not eat the same – sometimes vegetarians, sometimes kosher. It was very difficult.' Their daughter Zindzi said: 'We learnt early that the cleverest thing to do is eat your meat first in case somebody comes and you have to surrender it.'[84]

Despite the pressure of political commitments there were moments of domestic pleasure. The first thing that the new Mrs Mandela did was learn to make curry. 'Now, I learnt to cook curry because he enjoyed it so much on our first date. I thought, my God, let me at least do something that will please him – because he is very unassuming, he's not fussy and at the time he was not fussy at all … When I started cooking these curries for him, the first attempts were a disaster. He actually said, "You see, darling, you must add a lot of water in the curry" – only for me to learn later on that you don't add any water at all!'[85] Indeed, Winnie Madikizela-Mandela was later famed for her curry-making skills but these were techniques that she acquired from her friend and comrade Adelaide Joseph after her husband went to jail. In the late 1950s it was the second Mrs Mandela's innovative pasta creations that Madiba most admired. Many years later, he wrote to her from Robben Island: 'Do you remember the wonderful dish you used to prepare for supper? The spaghetti and simple

Winnie's spaghetti and mince is an idiosyncratic dish which reflects her husband's tastes

mince from some humble township butchery! As I entered the house from the gym in the evening that flavour would hit me full flush in the tongue.'[86]

Winnie Madikizela-Mandela's spaghetti and mince is an idiosyncratic dish which reflects her husband's tastes more than an Italian origin. Part mince curry, part lasagna, it is the Mandela family comfort food deluxe. Of her recipe she said: 'I invented it. I would curry the mince meat (by then I was a professional in making curries) and put it in a casserole, boil the spaghetti separately, drain it and put it on top of the mince meat as a layer. Put it in two layers, one layer at the bottom and one in the middle. Mince meat, spaghetti; mince meat, spaghetti. Then grate cheese and put it over the spaghetti and then put the yellow of half an egg over the cheese. Put that in the oven, bake it. Such a lovely dish. I never made it after Brandfort. It had painful memories for me so I deliberately stopped cooking it at a certain point. But I must make it this Sunday.'[87] According to her daughter Zindzi: 'You could feed an entire village on one mouthful, it was so filling.'[88]

SWEETENED TONGUES AND THWARTED LOVE

Romance has been given short shrift in previous histories of Madiba. But in his darkest moments of despair as a prisoner on Robben Island, it was to the memory of his first date with his second wife that he turned for sustenance. The supportive role of Winnie Madikizela-Mandela as a romantic icon in Madiba's life was very significant.

In a prison letter to his wife, Madiba wrote: 'Perhaps, no I am sure, the good old days will come when life will sweeten our tongues and nurse our wounds. Above all remember March 10. That is the source of our strength. I never forget it.'[89]

Madiba's love and passion for his wife radiates from every photograph of them together and every letter that he wrote to her when they were apart. The tragedy of what was one of the greatest African love stories was how little time they actually spent together. From the time of their first meeting to that of his sentence of life imprisonment, he spent considerable periods away from his family at various trials, in meetings, in prison, on the run and on overseas missions.

The subsequent complex role of Winnie Madikizela-Mandela in the history of South Africa's liberation struggle can, at least in part, be attributed to the fact that a young woman who had, prior to meeting her husband, lived an extremely sheltered and relatively privileged life, was left with the huge responsibility to speak for the Mandela name in conditions of extreme stress, isolation and ill health. At his daughter Zindzi's wedding in 1992, Madiba reflected: 'I have often wondered whether any kind of commitment can ever be sufficient excuse for abandoning a young and inexperienced woman in such a pitiless desert.'[90] Whether Mrs Madikizela-Mandela succeeded or failed in meeting the challenge of her circumstances has been much debated elsewhere. What is clear is that for 27 years it was the dream of returning to his wife and their kitchen that kept her husband strong.

WINNIE MADIKIZELA-MANDELA'S

Spaghetti and Mince

3 TABLESPOONS SUNFLOWER OIL
1 ONION, FINELY CHOPPED
2 TEASPOONS FRESH GARLIC AND GINGER MIX
2 TABLESPOONS MASALA (CURRY SPICE)
1 SMALL DRIED RED CHILLI, CRUSHED
½ TEASPOON TURMERIC
500g MINCED BEEF
4 MEDIUM TOMATOES, GRATED
5 CURRY LEAVES, ROUGHLY CHOPPED
250g SPAGHETTI
150g CHEDDAR CHEESE, GRATED
1 EGG YOLK
SALT AND PEPPER TO TASTE

Preheat the oven to 180°C. Simmer the onions in the oil until soft and pale golden, about 5 minutes. Remove the onion pan from the heat and add the masala, dried chilli, turmeric, and ginger and garlic mixture. The pan is off the heat so that while it is still hot, the spices will cook but will not burn. Allow the spices to cook off the direct heat until they begin to give off an aroma, about 2 minutes. Return the pan to the heat, add the mince and brown well, about 5 minutes. Add the tomatoes and the curry leaves, and allow the mixture to simmer for 10 minutes. Season to taste. While the sauce is cooking, bring a pan of salted water to the boil. Add the spaghetti and cook until al dente, about 5 minutes, then drain the pasta and set aside. In a casserole dish, put a fifth of the mince at the base, then top with a quarter of the spaghetti. Repeat the layering until there are five layers ending with a layer of mince. Mix the grated cheese and the egg yolk together and then sprinkle the mixture on top of the last layer. Bake in a hot oven until a golden-brown crust forms, about 30 minutes.

Chapter Four

THE FOOD OF FRIENDSHIP

IN ADDITION TO THE FOOD OF LOVE, the dinner tables of the 1940s and 1950s saw numerous meals cooked and served in friendship.

Many of these friendships were made with people with whom Madiba shared broad political convictions but whose cultural backgrounds and organisational allegiances were initially very different from his own. The role of these friendships in building the trust that formed the basis for subsequent political alliances should not be underestimated. The friendships discussed below were formed at a time when the ANC Youth League (ANCYL) was opposed to alliances with non-African organisations. Despite the shared opposition to the increasing racial oppression of the times, formal co-operation with political groupings representing South Africans of Indian origin or members of Communist organisations of any hue was rejected. The 1944 ANCYL's Manifesto stated: 'Africans must develop independent of foreign domination and foreign ideologies.'

LESSONS IN CURRY

Madiba might have been wary of official political coalitions, but he had no such hesitation about cross-cultural dining. In 1943, having completed his first degree, he enrolled at the University of the Witwatersrand for a Bachelor of Law degree and rapidly became friends with fellow law students Joe Slovo and Ismail Meer. Although it was several years before they were to work within allied political organisations, a non-racial consciousness emerged in the young law student, who enjoyed the company and respected the political conviction of his classmates. As Madiba said, it was at Wits that he 'discovered people of my own age, firmly

ABOVE: DAVID BOPAPE, WALTER SISULU AND MADIBA ADDRESS AN ANCYL MEETING, 1944

aligned with the liberation struggle who despite relative privilege were prepared to sacrifice themselves for the cause of the oppressed'.[91]

Ahmed Kathrada remarked of the politics of Madiba and the Youth League in the early 1940s: 'At that time they were exclusivist but not racialist, never racialist. Madiba always had strong social contacts with everyone. I met him in '44/'45 at the flat of Ismail Meer when I was still at school. They were friends. He ate there all the time and he even stayed there.'[92] Ismail Meer's autobiography, *A Fortunate Man*, quotes a letter he received from Madiba in which he wrote, 'I am eternally grateful that you taught me to eat curry.' One cannot over-stress the long-term significance of this lesson in both culinary and political terms.[93]

For all his enthusiasm, Madiba was initially quite unfamiliar with Asian flavours, a fact revealed

OPPOSITE: WINNIE MANDELA WITH KING SABATA, 1963
© BAHA

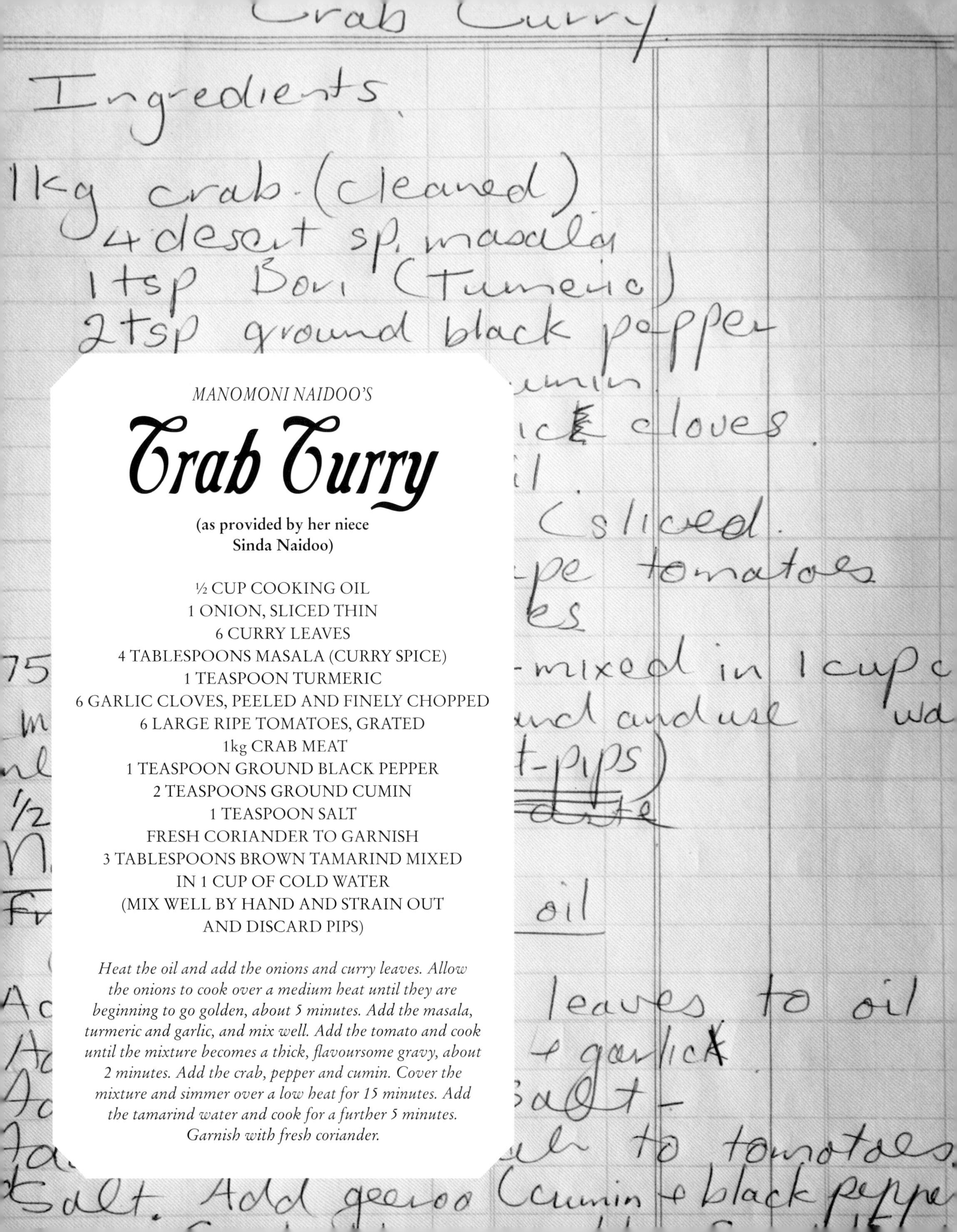

Crab Curry.

Ingredients.

1kg crab. (cleaned)
4 desert sp. masala
1 tsp Bori (Turmeric)
2 tsp ground black pepper
... ... umin
... ... ice cloves.
... ... l.
... (sliced.
... pe tomatoes
... es
... -mixed in 1 cup c
... and use wa
...t-pips)

75
m...
n...
½
N...
Fr...

A...
A...
A...
Fa...
Salt. Add geeroo (cumin + black peppe...

... leaves to oil
... + garlicA.
... salt.
... to tomatoes

MANOMONI NAIDOO'S

Crab Curry

(as provided by her niece
Sinda Naidoo)

½ CUP COOKING OIL
1 ONION, SLICED THIN
6 CURRY LEAVES
4 TABLESPOONS MASALA (CURRY SPICE)
1 TEASPOON TURMERIC
6 GARLIC CLOVES, PEELED AND FINELY CHOPPED
6 LARGE RIPE TOMATOES, GRATED
1kg CRAB MEAT
1 TEASPOON GROUND BLACK PEPPER
2 TEASPOONS GROUND CUMIN
1 TEASPOON SALT
FRESH CORIANDER TO GARNISH
3 TABLESPOONS BROWN TAMARIND MIXED
IN 1 CUP OF COLD WATER
(MIX WELL BY HAND AND STRAIN OUT
AND DISCARD PIPS)

Heat the oil and add the onions and curry leaves. Allow the onions to cook over a medium heat until they are beginning to go golden, about 5 minutes. Add the masala, turmeric and garlic, and mix well. Add the tomato and cook until the mixture becomes a thick, flavoursome gravy, about 2 minutes. Add the crab, pepper and cumin. Cover the mixture and simmer over a low heat for 15 minutes. Add the tamarind water and cook for a further 5 minutes. Garnish with fresh coriander.

in a nostalgic letter that he wrote to his wife from Robben Island. In it he recalled a youthful culinary encounter with his friend and comrade Naranswamy Naidoo: 'When we reached the Naidoos' Doornfontein residence we were hungry and tired. Amma, wearing that free and easy smile of hers, presented us with a meal of crab and rice. It was my first time to see these creatures cooked and merely the sight of them made me feel sick and everything inside me – my gizzard included – began protesting violently. You know, darling, that I never give up easily on such matters. I tried to be as graceful as was possible in the circumstances and even dared to chew 1 leg or 2. It was a delicate adventure. Thereafter I became much attached to the Naidoos and enjoyed crabs very much.'[94]

Naranswamy Naidoo (also known as 'Roy') and his wife Manomoni (known to all as Amma, 'mother') lived with their five children at 18A Rockey Street in Doornfontein. He was the delivery man for a bakery and a stalwart of the Transvaal Indian Congress. Of the crab curry, their daughter Shanthie Naidoo remarked: 'They were river crabs. In those days a man used to come round the houses selling them and my mother made that recipe a lot. My father was known for popping in with people. I don't think she was expecting Madiba that day. I think she had just made the crab curry for the family and we all shared … People used to come often. Whenever people came they joined the family for lunch or supper; it wasn't a special invited thing – very much open house. It became

NARANSWAMY AND MANOMONI NAIDOO

© Naidoo family collection

difficult at a later stage because I was banned, and even when Indres, my brother, was released from jail he was under house arrest – he had to go and sit in his room so everyone else could still pop in.'[95]

The culinary education provided by Ismail Meer, Naranswamy Naidoo and others was comprehensive and the student was extremely eager to learn. By the late 1940s Madiba was recognised by all his friends as a connoisseur of Indian food. Joe Matthews recollected: 'Sisulu and I were always amused by Madiba's interest in good food and how eclectic his tastes were. Of course none of us had a lot of money, but, for example, Walter Sisulu and I would go to Mr Moretsele's restaurant because there, for what was then one shilling and sixpence, you got a plate of soft porridge and meat. But not Madiba. Madiba would be at Kapitan's (which is up the road) having chicken or lamb *biryani* [rice, saffron and lentil mélange]. Sometimes he would invite you to come along to share the *biryani* with him but not always. Sometimes he would go on his own for the food, not for the social occasion, and he knew all about the food. You could see in his ordering that he was not someone who was just picking up the menu and ordering at random. He was choosing with care and skill and knowledge. He would say, "I want this, you must bring that and that and that" … he often stayed at Kholvad House with Ismail Meer and J.N. Singh, so he knew all your authentic Indian foods with the correct names and so on.'[96]

CHICKEN CURRY AND THE LAND ACT

It wasn't only the crab curries and *biryanis* that impressed Madiba. In 1946 the Smuts government passed the Asiatic Land Tenure Act, which restricted Indian land ownership and access to trading areas. In response the South African Indian Congress organised a Passive Resistance Campaign under the leadership of Dr Monty Naicker and Dr Yusuf Dadoo. The campaign lasted two years and saw several thousand South Africans of Indian descent imprisoned for deliberately breaking racist laws. Madiba and his comrades in the ANCYL were profoundly influenced by the unity of mass action demonstrated in this campaign. Compared with the quiet petitioning style of the ANC leadership at the time, the militancy of the Indian Congress struck them forcibly. Indeed, the Passive Resistance Campaign was very influential in later ANC mass action campaigns (such as the Defiance Campaign) and was central to the subsequent decision of the ANCYL to abandon its hostility to cross-racial political alliances.

While Manomoni Naidoo's crab curry opened the kitchen doors for Madiba to a world of new flavours and political strategies, it was in Amina Pahad's home that his taste for such flavours and strategies matured. Her table rivalled Ma Sisulu's for the generosity of its portions and the power of the political debates that took place around it. Like Ma Sisulu, Mrs Pahad was an excellent cook with a talent for making a small number of ingredients go a very long way. The emotional warmth and generosity that filled her chicken curry was a Johannesburg culinary legend. Barbara Harmel remembered: 'She was an astonishing woman: part behind-the-scenes domestic goddess, part political activist. When she was at home she cooked for but never ate with the men. Even if my mother and I were sitting and eating with the men, she wouldn't. But when she was in her political role she could not have been stronger or more assertive.'[97]

Ahmed Kathrada commented: 'Many people, myself included, considered her to be their second mother. The flat at number 11 Orient House was

© Pahad family collection

AMINA PAHAD WITH HER SON ESSOP, 1946

Dry Chicken Curry

{as provided by her daughter-in-law Meg Pahad}

1 LARGE CHICKEN
1 TABLESPOON SUNFLOWER OIL
1 ONION, CHOPPED
1 CUP YOGHURT
2 TABLESPOONS LEMON JUICE
2 TABLESPOONS CORIANDER LEAVES,
CHOPPED
2 CLOVES
5 PEPPERCORNS
1 CINNAMON STICK
2 PODS CARDAMOM
3 GREEN CHILLIES, SLICED
LENGTHWISE
1 TEASPOON GINGER, GRATED
2 TEASPOONS GARLIC, CRUSHED
½ TEASPOON CHILLI PASTE
1 TEASPOON CUMIN SEEDS, GROUND
1 TEASPOON SALT
½ TEASPOON SAFFRON
5 MEDIUM POTATOES, PEELED AND
QUARTERED

Portion the chicken into 6 pieces. Skin each piece and discard the skins. Fry the onion in the oil until translucent, about 5 minutes. Mix the yoghurt, lemon juice, coriander, cloves, peppercorns, cinnamon, cardamom, ginger, garlic, chilli, cumin, salt and saffron and the fried onions. Marinate the chicken in the yoghurt mixture for one hour. Place all the ingredients (including all the marinade) in a pot and cook over a low heat until the chicken is cooked through, about 45 minutes. Stir the mixture occasionally and add a little water or chicken stock only if it is in danger of sticking on the bottom of the pot. While the chicken is cooking, deep-fry the potato pieces until they are golden on the outside and al dente in the centre, about 5 minutes. Add the potatoes to the pot when the chicken is almost cooked (about 30 minutes). Cook the chicken and the potatoes together until both are completely cooked and serve with roti.

where we all ate. I ate there whenever I felt like it. Just pop in unannounced and there was always food. *Biryanis*, *dhal* and rice, wonderful meat dishes. She was always cooking, to the extent that at some stage she even lost the use of her arms for a while from the stress of it all.'[98]

As Joe Matthews recalled, 'There was always food at Mrs Pahad's. Always. She was a fantastic woman. Whenever you were really down and out and had no money and whatever, you would make your way up to her and the first thing she would ask was, "Have you had food?" I used to feel sorry for Goolam, her husband, who must have been spending an absolute fortune on feeding us all. And we could eat – we were young chaps with healthy appetites!'[99]

Mrs Pahad's ability to combine political bravery with domestic warmth greatly impressed Madiba. He recalled: 'I often visited the home of Amina Pahad for lunch, and then suddenly this charming woman put aside her apron and went to jail for her beliefs. If I had once questioned the willingness of the Indian community to protest against oppression, I no longer could.'[100]

During the Passive Resistance Campaign of 1946 Amina Pahad left five small sons and a husband in Johannesburg and joined scores of other Indian women in occupying a plot of land in Durban. She was injured when the group was set upon by a group of white vigilantes and subsequently spent a month in jail.

RUSKS AND AFFECTION

Madiba's interest in cross-cultural eating was not confined to a love of Indian food. As Joe Matthews commented: 'You can link Madiba's interest in specific foods with individuals and friends. Through his Jewish friends he would know all about what is kosher, what is not. He knew about Afrikaans food from Bram and Molly Fischer. He always wanted to explore the culture of others by way of their foods.'

The Fischer household saw more than its fair share of social interaction because, as George Bizos remembered, 'Molly Fisher was not only a first-class cook but they were also the only family that had a swimming pool.'[101] Bram Fischer was an Afrikaner advocate who defended leading anti-apartheid activists. In later years he was to lead the defence team for the Rivonia Trial and in 1966 he was himself sentenced to life imprisonment for contravention of the Suppression of Communism Act and conspiracy to commit sabotage. His wife Molly taught at the Indian Central High School. In *Long Walk to Freedom* Madiba described Molly Fischer as 'a wonderful woman, generous and unselfish, utterly without prejudice'.[102] What he did not mention was that her generosity often extended to rusks and meatballs. Her daughter Ilse Wilson recalled: 'My mother was a very good cook. She had Elizabeth David in the late 1950s or early 1960s, long before anyone else I know, but my parents kept the kind of household where you weren't formally invited.

Madiba wanted to explore the culture of others by way of their foods

MOLLY FISCHER'S

Rusks

{as taken from her handwritten notes in the back
of Molly Fischer's cookbook which indicate that the recipe
came originally from Ouma Fischer, Bram's mother}

1kg CAKE FLOUR
225g BUTTER
1 EGG
225g GRANULATED WHITE SUGAR
500ml BUTTERMILK
10g BICARBONATE OF SODA
1g CREAM OF TARTAR
PINCH OF SALT

*Preheat the oven to 200°C. Grease two large tins.
Combine the flour, bicarbonate of soda, cream of tartar
and salt. Rub the butter into the dry ingredients until
the mixture resembles breadcrumbs. In a separate bowl
beat the eggs, sugar and sour milk together. Add
the wet ingredients into the dry ingredients and mix well
to form a dough. Break off 100g pieces of dough and shape
them into balls. Place these balls close together in the sprayed
tins in two rows. Bake the rusk loaf at 200°C for 10
minutes, then reduce heat to 180°C and bake until cooked
through, about 45 minutes. Turn the rusk loaf out on to a
cooling rack. When cool, break the rusks into neat portions
and allow to dry out in the oven at 100°C.
Drying out will take at least 1 hour.*

You just dropped in and were fed pot luck
– Mandela, Sisulu, [Moses] Kotane, everyone.'[103]

CHINESE FOOD WITH THE SECURITY POLICE

George Bizos spent two years as Madiba's classmate in the part-time, late-afternoon law classes of 1948 and 1949. 'We used to meet during the day in the late '40s whilst we were student clerks delivering papers to the court, and because of our friendship at the university we would hang around together. There were only a couple of restaurants that we could go to together. There was an underground (because you go down the stairs) Chinese restaurant near John Vorster Square and conveniently close to the magistrate's court. It had an entrance filled with porcelain and bottles of ginger and it was owned by a Chinese family who didn't really mind if black people and white people ate together. We did go there but it was tricky because it was also frequented by the security police.'[104]

AMINA CACHALIA AND ROBERT RESHA
(WITH MADIBA IN THE BACKGROUND), 1953

© BAHA

NOT ALL SOIRÉES ARE A SUCCESS

Not all such cross-cultural meals were so successful. Ahmed Kathrada recalled an occasion from the late 1950s. 'There came a time when cheese and biscuits and wine became very fashionable in white homes. Madiba and Winnie and I went to one such home and we were served the cheese and biscuits and there was the usual

chat. But we were used to a meal being served and none came, and we couldn't say, "Give us food, we are hungry," and afterwards, in the car, Madiba said to Winnie, "When we get home, you must please cook us something. We need proper food."'[105]

Sometimes Madiba was not so much the recipient of poor cooking as its architect. Amina Cachalia recalled that in 1950 Madiba and Yusuf Cachalia (who later became her husband) cooked her a spectacularly unsuccessful birthday dinner. She remembered the meal with enormous affection for the people involved but was adamant that the actual food was a disaster. 'On my 21st birthday, we were at Aggie Patel's flat in Lilian Road [Fordsburg] (opposite where the Plaza is now), me, Nelson, Yusuf, Arthur Goldreich and Robert Resha. Yusuf got it into his head to cook 21 pigeons – he thought it would be a treat for my 21st birthday – but I took one look at those poor little things, so tiny and pathetic, and I said, "No, what are they?" You see, I was a really good little Muslim girl and, poor little things, I didn't know if we should be eating them. And anyway they looked awful – the meat was so dark. Anyway, Yusuf roped Nelson into helping with the kitchen duties and they got all excited about making this my birthday treat. Nelson couldn't cook to save his life, Yusuf was a good cook but neither had any experience with pigeons. So Yusuf did the cooking and Nelson cleaned the rice and so forth. He was trying to be helpful. In the end they sort of curried the birds. I was told not to come into the kitchen

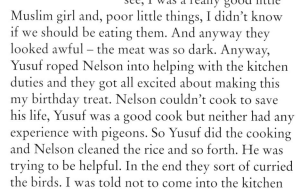

because this was their day in the kitchen. They spent the whole afternoon cooking those pigeons. And by the time they came to the table, I was even less keen to eat those pigeons, so I just had the rice and the sauce, but I couldn't bring myself to eat the birds. Nelson says that that was the day he first realised that Yusuf and I were more than just friends, and it was because he saw the care [Yusuf] was taking with those pigeons. There was such a lot of effort going into those pigeons.'[106]

TEA AND DEFIANCE

As a result of the combination of increasing social and political intimacy and the changing times, the 1951 ANC National Conference in Bloemfontein took a formal decision to embark on a joint, cross-organisational, non-racial programme of passive resistance and civil disobedience. This programme of action, officially known as the Defiance Campaign for the Defiance of Unjust Laws – referred to by all as the Defiance Campaign – began on 26 June 1952 with Madiba as Volunteer-in-Chief responsible for national recruitment.

His role was to travel the country in order to explain the aims and objectives of the campaign and to encourage participation. The 1952 Defiance Campaign, like the 1946 Passive Resistance Campaign before it, was designed to disrupt the fledgling apartheid state by clogging up prisons with those who defied the unjust, racially discriminatory laws. It saw participants undertaking such acts as using the 'whites only' section of the post office, walking through 'whites

only' entrances to train stations, breaching curfews and infringing pass laws. Over the next five months, eight thousand people nationwide went to jail for engaging in acts related to the campaign.

The Defiance Campaign provoked a rapid security crackdown from the apartheid state. In July 1952 police conducted a series of raids on the homes and offices of key Defiance Campaign leaders. Once again, food and drink came to the rescue of the anti-apartheid forces. Amina Cachalia remembered: 'When the police raided our offices at the TIC [Transvaal Indian Congress] they were going through a ton of our papers, and so my husband Yusuf told me in Gujarati, "Make some tea for these people: it will distract them." It wasn't my initiative, I must tell you, because I hated making tea for those guys. But it worked very well because one of them, a policeman called Helbrecht, he was already having a headache, so I said to him, "Mr Helbrecht, can I give you some Aspirin and a cup of tea for your headache," and he said, *"O, dit sal baie lekker wees, Amina"* [Oh, that would be very nice, Amina]. So I got tea and sandwiches going for them, which seemed to do the trick because while they were eating, Kathrada got out with all sorts of documents. How he did it I don't know, right under the noses of these policemen who were busy drinking tea. They were there for hours going through all our stuff, but eventually they didn't take very much away because all the stuff that mattered, the stuff that they should have taken away, Kathy had already taken while they were having tea.'

Sitsheketshe Mandela recalled a similar incident at Madiba's home in Orlando during a police raid when Evelyn Mandela served tea while 'he asked the children and me to hide the documents in the house'.[107] But there is only so much that a sandwich and a cup of tea can do. On 30 July 1952 Madiba and 20 other Defiance Campaign leaders were arrested for violating the Suppression of Communism Act.

While they were awaiting trial, TIC activist Adelaide Joseph smuggled messages to the prisoners interleaved between *roti* flat breads. Ilse Wilson recalled that 'her technique was to put messages between each layer of a stack of *rotis* and then she would say to the policeman on duty, "Please ask them to send back what they don't eat because we've got a dog and we're poor," and that's how the messages would come out again.'[108] The resultant trial ended with Madiba being sentenced to nine months' imprisonment with hard labour, suspended for two years.

MADIBA WITH HIS DOG GOMPO

© Alf Kumalo

In December 1952, Madiba was issued with a six-month banning order which forbade him to attend any meetings, leave Johannesburg or talk to more than one person at once. But the banning order proved a mixed blessing: it meant that he was legally required to eat at home, which pleased Evelyn Mandela and their young family.

COOKING UP THE CONGRESS OF THE PEOPLE

The Freedom Charter is a bill of social and economic rights that came to represent the mission statement of the Congress movement. The original idea derived from Madiba's mentor at Fort Hare, Professor Z.K. Matthews. His son Joe Matthews recollected: 'What happened is this: a number of organisations, the Institute of Race Relations and so forth, in the aftermath of the Defiance Campaign, were saying that there should be conferences and meetings to try and bridge the gap between the races and so forth, and we were

Adelaide Joseph smuggled messages to the prisoners interleaved between roti flat breads

all discussing that over lunch. I don't remember exactly what we were eating but my mother was cooking and her style was quite spare, simple food. So it would have been that sort of food. My mother was a great believer in no condiments, no additions and so on. The foods must be plain and that was her style. And my father said, "Can't we do it differently? Everybody is inviting people to a conference. Shouldn't we make it a mass participation thing and have a campaign thing in which people are requested to tell us what their demands are and what they feel their future should be like instead of having a conference of invited guests?" And I had been reading a whole lot of Chinese literature and I said, "Alright, the Chinese called their thing a Congress of the People. Let's call a congress of the people," you see, and there was a nationalist in what was then British Honduras who had called for the adoption of a freedom charter, so we said, "Let's get a campaign which will culminate in the adoption of a Freedom Charter."[109]

By the time the lunch dishes were cleared, a plan had been drawn up to gather all races in a Congress of the People to produce a non-racial proto-constitution. The idea of a Congress of the People was subsequently endorsed by the 1953 ANC National Conference in Queenstown, and a series of meetings and door-to-door canvassing was undertaken across South Africa to collect suggestions from a very broad cross-section of the population. The resultant document, espousing fundamental social and political rights, was entitled the Freedom Charter, and it was intended that this document would be discussed and ratified at the Congress of the People.

Ahmed Kathrada said of the planning of the Congress: 'I was on a committee, I think it was called the General Purposes Committee. Rusty Bernstein was the head of the committee. We were tasked with making sure the practical details happened – water, electrical generators, food, plates, mugs, etc. I remember I went to Industria [in Johannesburg] to collect the metal dishes and tin mugs for the soup. I always tease people now when they want to jump into a car for the slightest thing. For the Congress of the People we had one car allocated to us, so I had to go to Industria on a horse and cart to pick up the dishes.'[110]

SOUP WITH MEAT AND SOUP WITHOUT MEAT

The Congress of the People ultimately took place on 25 and 26 June 1956 at Kliptown in Soweto. Three thousand delegates of all races were present. Progress towards ratification of the Freedom Charter was slow because of the need to provide a trilingual translation before each clause could be adopted. On the afternoon of the second day the police swooped on the gathering before all the clauses had been adopted. The meeting was disrupted and the police confiscated a host of documents, many of which were used in the subsequent Treason Trial, which began in December 1956.

SOUP PRODUCTION AT THE CONGRESS OF THE PEOPLE, 1955

The extent to which the ANC had moved from its initial position of racial exclusivity into a mass-based, non-racial political alliance was illustrated in the catering arrangements that were made for the Congress of the People. Two signs that were confiscated by the police from the delegates' catering tent and handed in as evidence by the prosecution at the Treason Trial showed that the vegetarian Hindu delegates were provided for. The signs – 'Soup with meat' and 'Soup without meat' – illustrate the diversity and cross-cultural tolerance of the Congress movement. In soup there was an edible embodiment of the Freedom Charter, which declared 'South Africa belongs to all who live in it, black and white'.

Chapter Five

MANDELA AND TAMBO
AT LUNCH AND AT LAW

IN THE AFTERMATH OF THE 1948 NATIONAL PARTY ELECTION VICTORY, apartheid oppression began to take its toll on every aspect of South African life.

The economic prospects of black workers were substantially damaged by increasingly restrictive job colour-bar laws and constant attacks on the progressive trade union movement. Group Areas legislation evicted many black people from their homes and also prevented them from being able to conduct business in areas that were reallocated for the use of whites only. Bantu Education policies were introduced with the explicit intention of equipping black children for nothing but menial jobs, and independent church schools were suppressed. Amid the growing oppression, Oliver Tambo and Nelson Mandela formed a legal partnership with offices at Chancellor House in Fox Street, Johannesburg.

FOOD, DRINK AND LAND AT THE FOREFRONT OF SURVIVAL

Of the firm, George Bizos said: 'Mandela and Tambo had an almost nationwide practice. Oliver was the office man and Nelson did

most of the trials, and they also briefed young advocates like me, Joe Slovo, Duma Nokwe and others. To be defended by a black firm of attorneys was a matter of pride, particularly to people who felt the oppression of apartheid, both rural and urban, and there was always a full waiting room.'[111]

Ruth Mompati joined the firm as Madiba's secretary at the beginning of 1953, just after the Defiance Campaign. 'Clients came from the villages. Chiefs would come because they had been removed by the so-called Native Commissioners for not agreeing with them or resisting being pushed around … some of the people he represented had very little schooling but Mandela made them realise they were right to defend themselves, that it was their right as human beings not to allow anyone to disrespect them.'[112]

Food, drink and land being key elements of survival, many of the cases taken on

OPPOSITE: MADIBA IN NATALSPRUIT CONSULTING CLIENTS ARRESTED AS A RESULT OF A DEMONSTRATION TO PROTEST THE BANTU EDUCATION ACT, 1955
© BAHA
ABOVE: MADIBA IN HIS OFFICE AT MANDELA AND TAMBO ATTORNEYS, CHANCELLOR HOUSE FOX STREET, JOHANNESBURG 1952

by Mandela and Tambo had a gastronomic or agricultural aspect. From the peasant farmers in Sekhukhuneland who were being removed from their land by apartheid legislation and the women in Cato Manor who were arrested for brewing and selling beer, to prison labourers exploited on potato farms and other people who had committed 'crimes' such as using a water fountain designated as 'whites only' – wherever there were apartheid-engendered attacks on the livelihood and dignity of the oppressed, there were Mandela and Tambo.

MADIBA ON THE HARMEL'S STOEP, 1958

SPAGHETTI SWITCHBOARDS

Despite appearances to the contrary, it was not all smooth-sailing professionalism at Mandela and Tambo. Barbara Harmel, who worked in the offices in her school holidays, recalled: 'I was supposed to be working the switchboard – we called it a spaghetti switchboard because there were so many wires – but I was only 15 and I'm still not very good at technical things and I constantly lost calls. Oliver would come out of his office with a face like thunder and say, "Barbara, what happened to my call?" but Nelson would always come out grinning, no matter how many times I cut him off.

*MADIBA OUTSIDE THE
BANTU EDUCATION BUILDING, 1955*

Years later, after his release from prison, I was at Shell House [ANC head office] and I wanted to say hello to him, and his staff were reluctant to let me see him because he was so busy; and when he heard my name he came rushing out and he said, "But I must see her. She is a former colleague from Mandela and Tambo!" which was very kind of him, given that I was really a kid who lost his calls more than I was a colleague.'[113]

FROM THE FRUITS OF EDUCATION TO FISH AND CHIPS IN THE CAR

In addition to their lives as legal advocates for the rights of the oppressed, Mandela and Tambo were men about town, enjoying the fruits of their endeavours as young professionals. They had succeeded against great odds, and while their fees were not high, the large number of clients brought relative prosperity for both men. This allowed Madiba to buy a new car, and indulge in his taste for tailored clothes, fine food and glamorous social events. From opening nights at the musical *King Kong* to stylish evenings at Matlaku's, the stylish Soweto shebeen – if it was hip and happening, Madiba was part of it.

At the same time the social and professional space

Phutu Pap

{the actual Moretsele recipe has been lost but what follows is a reconstruction which approximates to that served at the restaurant and is based on the descriptions of those who dined there}

1 CUP WATER
3 CUPS MEALIE MEAL
SALT TO TASTE

Bring the water to the boil and then pour in the mealie meal (all in one motion without stirring). Lower the heat and simmer the mixture until the mealie meal is cooked through, about 20 minutes. Stir the mealie meal with a fork until the texture is crumbly. Season to taste.

Beef Stew

3 ONIONS, FINELY CHOPPED
4 TABLESPOONS SUNFLOWER OIL
1kg BEEF BRISKET OR CHUCK, PORTIONED
2 CUPS WATER
2 LARGE RIPE TOMATOES, GRATED
4 CUPS *MOROGO* (WILD SPINACH)
SALT AND PEPPER TO TASTE

Sautée the onions in the oil until soft and golden, about 5 minutes. Add the meat and brown well, then add the water and boil until it is cooked and soft, about 20 minutes. Add the tomato and the morogo and simmer gently until all the vegetables are cooked through. Season to taste.

Umhluzi Wetamatisi ne Anyanisi
(Tomato and Onion Relish)

3 TABLESPOONS SUNFLOWER OIL
3 ONIONS, FINELY CHOPPED
3 GARLIC CLOVES, FINELY CHOPPED
2 TEASPOONS HOT CURRY POWDER
10 TOMATOES, GRATED
SALT AND PEPPER TO TASTE

Heat the oil and sauté the onions until they are soft and golden, about 5 minutes. Add the garlic and the curry powder and mix well. Add the tomatoes and cook until a thick relish has formed, about 5 minutes. Season to taste.

there were very few restaurants open to African customers

Eli Weinberg © Mayibuye Archives

MORETSELE'S RESTAURANT, 1956

in which the black elite operated was being increasingly attacked by apartheid. In an unjust society even the restaurants reflect broader patterns of oppression. Ahmed Kathrada recalled that in Johannesburg, 'There were very few restaurants open to African customers. There was Moretsele's, where you could get a cheap, filling plate of *pap* and stew, and the owner Elias Moretsele had been

a past President of the ANC in the Transvaal [Moretsele was also a Treason Trialist]; the Blue Lagoon at 10 Von Wielligh Street: and the two Indian restaurants, Azad's and Kapitan's in Kort Street. I remember them all with affection as warm, generous people.'[114] Madiba's affection for the restaurateurs of the 1950s is evident in his subsequent prison letters. Writing from Robben

OPPOSITE: TREASON TRIALISTS, 1956
Eli Weinberg © Mayibuye Archives

TREASON TRIAL

The ACCUSED

DECEMBER 1956

Island to Sanna Teyise, the *chef-patronne* of the Blue Lagoon, in 1970, Madiba said: 'Your café was an institution around which people's lives turned. We were all intimate members of the Lagoon family.'[115]

The lack of restaurants open to black customers impacted on Madiba's professional and personal life. As a newly qualified advocate, George Bizos often worked with Mandela and Tambo. 'When I went with Oliver or with Nelson anywhere, particularly cases in the small towns, the inevitable lunch was fish and chips wrapped in newspaper and eaten in the car because you couldn't sit anywhere together. You couldn't even take sandwiches and sit together on a bench in the park.'[116]

In Johannesburg, Kapitan's (founded in 1887) was widely acknowledged as Madiba's favourite restaurant. By the early 1950s its *chef-patron* was Madanjit Ranchod, grandson of the original owner. It was extremely hard to pin down the chef to talk about Mandela and Tambo (his preferred topic of conversation was his trips to Brazil to catch deep-sea fighting fish or how he had cooked for the Sultan of Brunei on his yacht) but after much pressing he did concede that 'Mr Mandela liked mince curry with ginger pickle'.[117] Until his death, Madanjit Ranchod kept a letter from Madiba taped to the wall of his restaurant. Written in 1987 from prison in response to Ranchod's purported decision to close shop, it read: 'I learn with sorrow that your famous oriental restaurant on Kort Street is closing down. During the last 27 years we have lost so many dear friends and so many noted buildings that I sometimes fear that by the time I return, the world itself will have disappeared.' What Madiba could not have known was that since the mid-1970s, Madanjit Ranchod had threatened to retire every year, and by 1987 very few paid his threats any heed. The restaurant finally closed in 2007 the day after the octogenarian *chef-patron's* death.

DO NOT FEED THE ANIMALS

In December 1956, Madiba's professional and personal milieu was further damaged by a series of simultaneous dawn raids on the homes of 140 activists nationwide. Those arrested were brought to the Old Fort jail in Johannesburg. The prisoners were a diverse assortment of old and young, male and female, black and white, professionals, trade unionists, traditional leaders and factory workers. A second series of raids brought the total of those arrested to 155 and the charging of the *Guardian* newspaper meant that there were 156 accused.

The food supplied by the prison authorities was not to the prisoners' liking. Trialist Professor Z.K. Matthews wrote to his wife Frieda (who was at their home in the Eastern Cape): 'Breakfast is at 7 am and consists of porridge only. We just can't get it down … Lunch is at 11 am and consists of *inkobe* mixed with awful beans.' Fortunately the prisoners were not reliant on the food supplied by their captors because 'the people of Jo'burg have been so good to us. They send us breakfast and lunch – a separate parcel for every single person. Think of all the trouble those people have to go through writing out our names. The regulations allow for only individual parcels. They send us so much food that we do not need to eat the prison food.'[118]

According to Ahmed Kathrada: 'While the 156 were awaiting trial at the Fort, a formidable group of women took it upon themselves to provide food. I think it was organised under Mrs Pahad, who got different neighbourhood groups, many houses and volunteers, to cook. But they sent so much food that we had to send a message saying that "We don't need breakfast, lunch and supper. One meal a day will do."'

Once the case proceeded to trial, it was found that there was not a court large enough to accommodate so many defendants. The Drill Hall in Twist Street

*you had to be a very quick drinker
so that if there was a police raid
they found only empty glasses*

was, therefore, converted into a makeshift court. The accused were charged with high treason on the basis of a range of statements and documents issued during the Defiance Campaign and by the Congress of the People. The Freedom Charter was even cited as evidence of a Communist plot to overthrow the state by violence. At the Drill Hall a massive, ten-foot wire cage was constructed and 156 chairs for the accused were put inside. In the words of Ahmed Kathrada: 'We were very surprised by that wire structure. And I think it was Syd Shall or perhaps Ronnie Press who hooked a sign to the bars saying "Dangerous, do not feed". But our lawyers said, "We refuse to consult our clients through these bars," and by our next appearance the cage was gone.'[119]

MOUTHS STUFFED WITH SWEETMEATS

The prosecution's case was based on raiding so many houses and confiscating documents with so little discrimination that the weight of irrelevant information threatened to render the case incoherent. Included among the evidence were signs from the Congress of the People stating 'Soup with meat' and 'Soup without meat' and a Russian recipe book. For Ismail Meer, the prosecution's lack of discrimination in collecting evidence 'reminded me of the Gujarati proverb ... "they had stuffed their mouths with such big *ladoos* (sweetmeat balls) that they could neither swallow them nor spit them out".'[120]

A Treason Trial Fund established by the Bishop of Johannesburg ensured that the trialists were rapidly released on bail. While most of the defendants went home to enjoy Christmas with their families, Madiba found that in his absence Evelyn had packed up the house, taken the children to her brother's house and left him.

COMMUNISTS MAKE THE BEST COCKTAILS

Despite his sorry domestic situation, Madiba joined in the mood of abandon and devil-may-care that took over many of the defendants. Though the state's case seemed weak, the death penalty was always a looming possibility and wild partying was a common response of the defendants. Joe Slovo and Ruth First gave dance parties where everyone drank and jived the nights away. But even getting drunk was not as simple as it might seem. George Bizos recollected: 'Even for the unbanned people, you had to be a very quick drinker so that if there was a police raid, they only found empty glasses. Because it was illegal for black people to have intoxicating liquor, so we served short tots.'[121]

Gillian Slovo remembered that: 'The parties that my parents gave during that time were wild, rumbustious drunken affairs. I can't remember food being served. I think the point was to drink, although occasionally my father would make his speciality, of which he was very proud – salad

Besan Ladoos

4 CUPS *BESAN GRAM* FLOUR (CHICKPEA FLOUR)
1 CUP *GHEE* (CLARIFIED BUTTER)
2 CUPS ICING SUGAR
1 TEASPOON CARDAMOM SEEDS, FINELY CRUSHED
½ CUP ALMONDS, PEELED AND FINELY CHOPPED

Gently heat 1 tablespoon of ghee and sauté the nuts, then set them aside to cool. In a separate pan, heat the remaining ghee and add the flour. Mix it over a low heat stirring continuously till golden brown, about 3 minutes. Once it is browned, remove from the pan and let it cool. Once it is cool, add the cardamom, nuts and sugar. Mix well. Shape into pingpong-ball-sized ladoos (with the help of a little ghee if necessary).

TREASON TRIALISTS EATING LUNCH IN REVEREND NYE'S GARDEN (Madiba is third from the left), PRETORIA 1958

dressing. Tomatoes were banned from the salad, so it was really only leaves and dressing. And he used to get George Bizos to cook a lamb on a spit.'[122]

George Bizos's culinary talents were widely heralded by his colleagues and comrades. According to Joe Matthews: 'You know that the fame comes to Bizos, not as a lawyer but as the best chap for organising a nice braai in the evening – which he took extremely seriously. Everybody loved those braais. When he did a braai, he would come along and he would be so dead serious about the whole thing, making sure the coals were all nice and hot. And digging. I can never remember what he was digging for but he would be digging and digging. Especially outside in the garden at Joe Slovo's house in Roosevelt Park. When they got a house in Roosevelt Park, that they were very embarrassed about – for two prominent Communists it was rather a grand house but it had a fantastic garden for braais!'[123]

Alexi Bizos, George Bizos's son who was initiated into the ways of barbecuing lamb Hellenic-style when he was 11 years old, said that digging was his father's way of retaining the fire's heat and allowing it to radiate from the side. This method was later superseded in the Bizos household by the arrival of a deluxe Jet Master spit. George Bizos lamented the new-fangled methods: 'My sons took over the lamb years ago and they actually shove me away because they think that they know better these days. Even now that it's mechanised, it's still quite a business putting it up, and you have to wire it down, so that when the spit turns, it stays on.'[124]

Whether it be the traditional dig-a-hole method or the Jet Master version, the formula for calculating how many people a Bizos sheep will feed has remained constant since it was first calculated in the Slovos' garden more than half a century ago. In 1957, when he was asked how many people a sheep would feed, Bizos replied: 'Twenty Greeks

JOE SLOVO'S

Salad Dressing

{recipe supplied by Gillian Slovo}

½ CUP CORN OIL
¼ CUP WHITE WINE VINEGAR
PINCH OF SALT
PINCH OF WHITE PEPPER
¼ TEASPOON GARLIC, CRUSHED
PINCH OF SUGAR
DROP OF TABASCO
PINCH OF ENGLISH MUSTARD

Combine all the ingredients and mix well.

or 50 Anglo-Saxons.' To which his friend Nathan Lokoff added: 'Correction, George: 20 Greeks, 30 Jews or 50 Anglo-Saxons.' The Bizos formula doesn't say how many patrician Thembu elder statesmen such a lamb might feed, but given that Madiba had an unprecedented two helpings at his friend's recent birthday party, it seems likely that he is an honorary Greek in the matter of lamb consumption.

PEACHES, MRS PILLAY AND PEANUT BUTTER

In early 1957, soon after the Christmas recess, the Treason Trial was moved to Pretoria. This proved a burden for the trialists, who were predominantly Johannesburg-based, as they now had to undertake long and expensive daily commutes. Thus it was that Madiba, Robert Resha, Stanley Lollan and Helen Joseph travelled to court together in Helen's car, which they referred to as 'Treason Trixie'. 'The Peach Club' (as they dubbed themselves, after the fruit they bought along the roadside each day) whiled away much of 1957 and 1958 commuting and telling jokes. Helen Joseph recollected that 'we joked about our future and sometimes I would complain, "It's alright for you chaps, you will be together in jail, but I'll get the husband poisoners, because they are the only white women who get long sentences."'[125]

Once the trial was under way again, 'the feeding of the accused was divided equally amongst the Transvaal Indian Congress women and the white Congress of Democrats and Liberal Party women,' said Ahmed Kathrada. 'One week Indian, one week white women. But I must say the accused looked forward to the Indian weeks because they cooked substantial food: curries and rice and so forth. The white ladies made peanut butter sandwiches. I sound very ungrateful, and at the time we all acknowledged that, from a nutritional point of view, it was a healthy diet, but we had so much peanut butter in those weeks. So, so much peanut butter.'[126] Whatever the menu, lunch for the defendants was served under the jacaranda trees in the nearby garden of the Reverend Mark Nye. This inspired Mary Benson's remark that they were 'occasions which resembled garden parties'.[127]

In her autobiography *Side by Side*, Helen Joseph wrote that the 'the treason lunches were indeed nourishing, but not always my favourite diet. I enjoyed "Indian" week with its savoury curries, but faltered sometimes over "African" week with its meat and mealie meal. To bring my own packet of eggs, tomato and cheese was unthinkable, so I ate and then fought a losing battle at weekends with my encroaching poundage.'[128]

There were many culinary stars in the Treason Trial firmament. But if one shines brightest it is Mrs Thayanayagee Pillay, a stalwart of the Transvaal Indian Congress, having been repeatedly arrested during the Passive Resistance Campaign. Her long-time friend and comrade Mrs Thanga Kolopan recalled: 'We were arrested in 1946 in Umbilo Road and again in 1952 when we spent 14 days in the Germiston cells.'[129] According to her niece Shanthie Naidoo: 'We come from a political family that goes back over five generations. My grandfather was involved in the struggle even before Gandhi came to South Africa. He actually started the Indian Congress, him and a man called Mr Ali. And Gandhi fitted in and they built things up together.'[130] Ilse Wilson recalled: 'Mrs Pillay was an amazingly dedicated trial cook. Even when her husband died during the Treason Trial she didn't cook for three days but she ensured that one of her family members did, so that the trialists were still fed. I remember going to the funeral with my parents and hearing her say, "I will never be able to wear the dot again," but throughout her own misery she made sure that the trialists never went hungry.'[131]

OVERLEAF: ALEXI BIZOS (left, with the author on right) WAS INITIATED INTO THE HELLENIC STYLE OF BARBECUING LAMB AT 11 YEARS OLD

73

GEORGE BIZOS'S

Lemon and Oregano Lamb

{Alexi Bizos recommended a lamb that 'has some fat. Not too much but not lean' and his father favoured cold pressed *koroneiko* olive oil which 'comes from the kalamata district, khaya of the Bizoses'. Both father and son agreed that the marinade should be brushed onto the lamb using a pine tree branch as a brush. Alexi said this is important 'because my father and grandfather did and it does give a slight pine taste'}

1 WHOLE LAMB (GRADE AAA222)
1*l* LEMON JUICE, FRESHLY SQUEEZED AND FREE OF PIPS
3*l* SUNFLOWER OIL
1 CUP EXTRA VIRGIN OLIVE OIL
3 CUPS GREEK DRIED OREGANO
2 TEASPOONS OF SALT PER kg OF LAMB
1 TEASPOON GROUND BLACK PEPPER

Rub the lamb with the squeezed-out lemon wedges. This will clean the lamb of any blood clots (in particular those at the neck) and infuse the meat with citrus flavour. Make a marinade by combining the lemon juice, 1 litre of the sunflower oil and all the olive oil, oregano, salt and pepper. Wire the lamb to the spit firmly so as to ensure that the stomach cavity is facing upwards. To help the lamb stay in position, start wiring up the lamb from the back legs. Use the slit in the shank ligament of the hind left forequarter and slot the right leg into the cavity this creates, and secure with wire. Put 2–3 pieces of wire between the ribs, the vertebrae and the spit. Tie the neck and front legs to the spit. Make sure the lamb is secure as any limb coming loose in roasting becomes unmanageable. Massage the outside of the lamb with marinade, putting salt from the bottom of the marinade into the fatty parts, and then pour half the remaining marinade into the belly cavity, making sure all the lemon juice at the bottom of the marinade is used. Sew up the belly cavity and secure the spit so as to leave the belly facing up. Use a blanket stitch with crochet cotton and needle to sew up the belly. Cover with silver foil and leave to marinate overnight at ambient room temperature. Retain the remaining marinade, making sure a minimum of lemon is left in it to baste the lamb while cooking. Add additional sunflower oil to the remnants of the initial marinade for the basting. When you come to cook the lamb ensure that two fires are made, at each end of the lamb (fore and hind legs). The middle or flank does not need as much cooking so the heat from the two fires is sufficient to cook this portion. Seal the lamb initially on a very hot heat, using wood and lots of charcoal. After this initial phase the fire can gradually reduce. Add logs to each end as you progress. Depending on the size of lamb and your spit mechanism or firebox set-up, cooking should take 4–5 hours. Brush the marinade on to the lamb while cooking to keep it moist. Ensure that the lamb turns constantly. The Bizos's suggested that the cook places a pan under the middle of the carcass (between the fires) and puts some bread on the spit to toast so as to create what Alexi called 'a delicious snack replete with lamb fat drippings.' Test for readiness by inserting a carving fork into a hind leg, and pressing against the leg with the back of a carving knife. Lack of blood means that it is ready. While it may seem polite to chop up the lamb on a board Alexi Bizos argued that 'carving it slowly whilst on the spit and coming back for more is the Bizos way.'

Mrs Pillay was so dedicated that she undertook culinary duties even in weeks that were technically allocated to others. Shanthie Naidoo recounted: 'People were coming from Jo'burg all the way to Pretoria and they often didn't have breakfast, so she made it her duty to make tea, coffee and sandwiches and took it every morning. She did breakfast even if someone else was doing lunch that day.'[132] Daughter Vasugee Moodley remembered: 'Lunches we dished from pots, but breakfasts would be individually portioned each in a brown paper bag with the trialist's name on it. We put tea and coffee in big milk churns and poured it out into cups when we got there.'[133]

The whole Pillay family was involved in feeding the Treason Trialists. Elder daughter Sinda Naidoo said: 'When the trial started I was 15 or 16 and when my mother used to wake us up at four-thirty or five to make food for the trialists, I used to get so mad. We had a green station wagon which she would load with food and send my father's brothers to go and deliver it all.'[134] Vasugee Moodley remembered 'as a little girl going with my mother to give out the coffee and sandwiches in the morning. Father Nye was the priest there

and trialists would congregate in his garden and have meetings and lunch. He had a room there with wooden toys and I was so fascinated with it – dolls and little cars and all, but wooden. I used to go and play there while my mother distributed the food.'[135]

The culinary and political commitment of Mrs Pillay did not go unnoticed. The trialists sent her a signed thank-you letter and held a tea party in her honour. At the party, they presented her with a dinner service and a sari in the black, green and gold colours of the ANC.

TEA AND MASSACRES

On 21 March 1960, the Treason trialists were sipping on tea brewed by Mrs Pillay and biscuits care of the Congress of Democrats, when they learnt that in the township of Sharpeville, south of Johannesburg, the police had disrupted a march arranged by the Pan Africanist Congress (PAC). They had shot and killed sixty-nine people (including ten children and eight women) protesting against pass laws. Most of the dead had been shot in the back. Despite their criticisms of the PAC's campaign strategy, which they saw as an

ABOVE: MADIBA AND WALTER SISULU BURNING THEIR PASS BOOKS
OPPOSITE: MADIBA WASHING UP DURING THE TREASON TRIAL, PRETORIA 1958
© Mayibuye Archives

76

the state responded to the pass-burning campaign by declaring a state of emergency and detained hundreds of activists

attempt to usurp an ANC campaign planned for May, the ANC leadership felt that a rapid response was essential. ANC leaders began an immediate public burning of pass documents and launched a national stayaway campaign. Photographs of the event show Walter Sisulu burning his identity documents and letting the ashes fly into the night sky. The ever-fastidious Madiba burnt his pass in an aluminium cooking pot and carefully discarded the cinders.

The state responded to the pass-burning campaign by declaring a state of emergency and detained hundreds of activists. The ANC leadership decided that for the survival of the movement, some activists should go into exile while others remained behind in South Africa. Oliver Tambo was sent into exile (where he ensured the survival of the ANC over the ensuing three decades) while Madiba (who was out on bail but still appearing as a defendant in the Treason Trial) was arrested. After 36 hours in detention he was taken out of prison to attend the Treason Trial in Pretoria. From thenceforth he attended the trial during the day and was returned to prison at night. On 8 April 1960 the ANC was banned as an organisation.

FLASKS OF COFFEE AND COLLAPSING BUSINESSES

The Treason Trial eventually lasted almost five years, stretching into March 1961. While the state ultimately failed to convict the accused, it kept all those involved away from earning an income for such an extended period of time that many businesses (including the law firm Mandela and Tambo) collapsed. Both partners tried hard to keep the firm afloat, but with one member of the partnership in exile and the other missing for long periods of time, the loss of billable hours was ultimately crippling. Amina Cachalia recalled: 'When Nelson was in the Treason Trial he used to come back from the trial and go straight to his offices to do a couple of hours' work and I used to take him sandwiches or whatever I had at the house, curry or whatever we were eating, and a flask of coffee. In the afternoons I would rustle up a parcel. He was trying to keep his business going. He had to earn a living, so he would come straight from the trial to the offices. Even though they were given lunch in Pretoria he would call at 4 or 5 and say, "Won't you bring me a cup of tea" or "Won't you bring me something to eat".'[136] Despite the obvious demand for their services and their numerous court victories, the firm of Mandela and Tambo ultimately collapsed in 1961 under the pressure of political commitments and apartheid oppression.

OPPOSITE: AMINA CACHALIA, 2007
OVERLEAF: TREASON TRIALISTS' LETTER TO MRS PILLAY, 1961

AMINA CACHALIA'S

Mutton Curry

1 ONION, FINELY CHOPPED
2 TABLESPOONS *GHEE* (CLARIFIED BUTTER)
700g CUBED LAMB
¼ TEASPOON TURMERIC
1 TEASPOON GROUND CUMIN
½ TEASPOON GROUND CORIANDER
1 TABLESPOON OF A PASTE MADE FROM 2cm FRESH
GINGER, 2 CLOVES GARLIC, 3 CHILLIES CRUSHED TOGETHER
IN A MORTAR AND PESTLE WITH A PINCH OF COARSE SALT
3 LARGE POTATOES, PEELED AND CHOPPED INTO CUBES
1 TOMATO, ROUGHLY CHOPPED
1 CUP WATER
FRESH CORIANDER LEAVES FOR GARNISH

Sauté the onion in the ghee until the onions are golden, about 5 minutes.
Add the meat and braise until well browned, about 5 minutes.
Add the turmeric, cumin, coriander and the ginger, garlic, chilli paste.
Cook for 5 minutes to allow the spices to mature into the meat.
Add the potato, tomato and 1 cup of water. Cover and cook over a
medium heat until the potatoes are soft, about 20–30 minutes.
Add additional liquid if it looks in danger of drying out.
Serve with rice and garnish with fresh coriander.

1st August, 1960.

Mrs T. Pillay and Family,
PRETORIA.

Dear Friends,

          We have realised that today August the 1st it is
a whole year since you first started to bring us coffee in
the mornings - a whole year since you first decided to do
this, on your own, and a whole year that you have continued
doing without missing even one day!   Even during these
 difficult months of detention when we are no longer able
to see you, you have still maintained this thoughtful service
to us, and indeed increased it by sending us extra food to
replace the lunches.

          We only wish that today we could arrange a special
party so that you could be our honoured guest, and then we
could really express ourselves properly and show you how very
much we value your wonderful kindness to us during the past
twelve months.   We can't have that party now but we are
looking forward to having it as soon as we are free.

          All we can do now is to say "thank you" and assure
you that you hold a special place in our thoughts and in our
hearts.

                    Yours in the struggle for Freedom,

MRS PILLAY'S

Chicken Curry

{Mrs Pillay's recipe was kindly supplied by her longstanding comrade Mrs Thanga Kolopan, who says of her friend: 'Because of her family's involvement with Gandhi she didn't eat meat – she wouldn't even eat cake from the shop because it had an egg in it – but she cooked it for her husband and her children and the trialists'}

1 ONION, FINELY CHOPPED
½ CUP SUNFLOWER OIL
2 TABLESPOONS *MASALA* (CURRY SPICE)
½ TEASPOON TURMERIC
1 TABLESPOON GARLIC AND GINGER MIX
1kg CHICKEN, SKINNED AND PORTIONED INTO SMALL
ENOUGH PIECES TO BE PICKED UP IN A HAND
1 LARGE RIPE TOMATO, GRATED
10 CURRY LEAVES, ROUGHLY CHOPPED
1 CUP GREEN PEAS

Fry the onions in the oil until golden, about 5 minutes. Remove the pot from the heat and add the masala, turmeric and the ginger and garlic (take off heat so that while the pot is still hot, the spices won't burn). Add the chicken pieces and mix well. Return the pot to the heat and add the tomato. Allow the mixture to simmer until it begins to form a gravy, about 2 minutes. Add the curry leaves. Turn down the heat and put a lid on the pot and simmer until the chicken is cooked through, about 30 minutes. Add the green peas and simmer until they are cooked through, about 2 minutes. Mrs Pillay served the curry with rice and beetroot salad for the trialists.

Chapter Six

MAZAWATTEE TEA ON THE RUN

ON 29 MARCH 1961 JUDGE FRANZ RUMPFF found that the state had failed to prove that the African National Congress was a communist organisation and that there was no evidence that the defendants in the Treason Trial had planned the violent overthrow of the government.

When the judge announced that 'the accused are accordingly found not guilty and are discharged', the trialists cheered and there was a good-natured rush towards the courtroom exit.

Despite the victory, Madiba felt certain that he was a marked man and that the police would be coming for him again. He celebrated his acquittal by briefly embracing his wife and then spent the night in a Johannesburg safe house while she went home to Soweto alone. His caution proved wise as that night the police arrived at 8115 Orlando West and attempted to serve him with a banning order. When they couldn't locate him, a warrant was issued for his arrest. So it was that on 30 March 1961 Madiba began what was the first of 494 days as an underground operative.

His initial brief was to travel across the country visiting ANC branches and preparing them for a nationwide stayaway planned for the establishment

of the Republic on 31 May. In order to remain undetected, an underground agent needs to blend into the background of any social setting. Madiba's height, regal bearing and social prominence made a disappearing act difficult but he exchanged his elegant suits for blue overalls and wore round rimless glasses known at the time as 'Mazawattee Tea glasses' after the advertising image used to market a popular brand of tea. The granny glasses notwithstanding, the fugitive was christened 'the Black Pimpernel' by the media.

THE COMMANDER-IN-CHIEF'S *AMASI* ON THE WINDOW-SILL

Madiba stayed at a series of safe houses, ranging from a sugar plantation in KwaZulu-Natal to the servant's quarters of a doctor in Cyrildene, Johannesburg. His longest stay was at the flat of Communist Party activist Wolfie Kodesh in Yeoville, Johannesburg.

DELICIOUS 'MAZAWATTEE TEA

"Old folks at home."

OPPOSITE: WINNIE MANDELA AND ALBERTINA SISULU (WOLFIE KODESH IS BETWEEN THEM) OUTSIDE THE TREASON TRIAL, 1961
© Alf Kumalo
ABOVE: MAZAWATTEE TEA COMPANY ADVERTISEMENT

Of this time Ahmed Kathrada recalled: 'When he was hiding at Wolfie's place, I remember I went there a couple of times and cooked him a curry: mince, mutton, you know. My curries are only good for prisoners but Madiba seemed to enjoy it.'[137] Curry was not the only thing lacking from Madiba's diet and he decided to remedy things. 'While I was reading in the flat during the day, I would often place a pint of milk on the window-sill to allow it to ferment. I am very fond of this sour milk, which is known as *amasi* amongst the Xhosa people and is greatly prized as a healthy and nourishing food … One evening I overheard a conversation going on near the window. I could hear two young black men speaking in Zulu … "what is 'our milk' doing on that window ledge?" one of the fellows said … The sharp-eyed fellow was suggesting that only a black man would place milk on the ledge like that and what was a black man doing living in a white area? I realized then that I needed to move on. I left for a different hide-out the next night.'[138] The message was clear: in a divided a society an observant eye could tell the ethnicity of a tenant by the bottle of milk on a window-sill.

It was during this time that Madiba, as an individual, and the ANC, as an organisation, finally decided to abandon their longstanding policy of non-violence and to establish a military wing. This radical departure from established ANC policy was an immensely difficult transition for all involved. There were several secret meetings of the National Executive Committee at which Chief Albert Luthuli, the ANC President, expressed grave reservations about the use of violence, as did Natal Indian Congress members who had been raised on Gandhi's philosophy of passive resistance. Ultimately the organisation and its alliance partners agreed that the military might of the apartheid state could best be opposed by a campaign of acts of sabotage, and a military wing of the ANC was set up to carry out operations. Known as Umkhonto weSizwe (Spear of the Nation, or MK), with Madiba as Commander-in-Chief and Walter Sisulu, Govan Mbeki, Joe Slovo, Andrew Mlangeni and Raymond Mhlaba serving as the MK High Command, it was launched on 16 December 1961.

SELLING LILIESLEAF VEGETABLES TO THE POLICE

After the window-sill *amasi* incident made it clear that it was no longer safe for him to stay with Wolfie Kodesh, Madiba moved on to Liliesleaf Farm in Rivonia, then on the very outskirts of Johannesburg. Ostensibly the home of Arthur Goldreich, his wife Hazel and their three children, the property had in fact been surreptitiously bought by the Communist Party and made available to the ANC as a secret meeting place. So it was that in October 1961 the Goldreichs acquired a new 'houseboy' and chauffeur, David Motsamayi, aka Madiba, who moved into the servants' quarters behind the main house.

Courtesy Historical Papers Wits University

LILIESLEAF KITCHEN USED BY MK HIGH COMMAND

In addition to being a family home, Liliesleaf was a functioning agricultural smallholding. As Ahmed Kathrada recalled: 'Thomas Malifane was the foreman. He had been a member of the Communist Party in Sekhukhuneland before it was banned, and he brought some chaps from Sekhukhuneland to farm there. He grew vegetables: potatoes, onions, tomatoes and so forth. And Thomas used to go around on his bicycle selling these onions and potatoes to neighbouring houses. In fact his main customer was the Rivonia Police Station. Later, [Percy] Yutar, the prosecutor in our case, complained at the cheek of us to sell to the police. But they were Thomas's very good customers! When they discovered Liliesleaf, Thomas was arrested and severely tortured and he gave evidence, truthful evidence, and when he was finished, he asked the judge: "I just want to know, after I gave all the information to the police, why did they assault me after that?" and the judge said he would investigate but he never did.'[139]

STEAK, PEAS AND WALKS IN THE ORCHARD

Compared to the social isolation that had gone before, the early months of hiding at Liliesleaf seemed idyllic. Winnie Mandela visited, and while her daughters played with the Goldreich children in the orchards, Madiba revealed to his wife the extent to which his life as an underground operative had brought about culinary growth. 'Before, he had never so much as made me a cup of tea. In fact, I think the only time he ever cooked for me was at Liliesleaf. He was underground, so he had to cook for himself. I knew he did not know how to cook, but it seems he had subsequently learnt how to cook underground because he couldn't take the risk of having people cook for him. And that day when I came to Liliesleaf he made me a fat steak and mashed potatoes and green peas and lots of lettuce salad. And then he brought

a whole basket of fruit. I was shocked to see he even knew how to lay out the fruit. More than shocked, I was very suspicious. At first I didn't think he could have made it. I thought perhaps he had a girlfriend. I actually made suggestions: "Was so-and-so here?" I had people in mind, knowing him. But he told me what he had done and I saw that he really had made it himself.'[140]

The Mandela children so enjoyed their visits to Liliesleaf Farm that for years after, Zenani Mandela (who was 3 and a half years old when her father was arrested) believed her father was still living at Liliesleaf and would ask when they were going to visit him there. Despite the fond memories, such family moments were to become few and far between. The police kept the family under constant surveillance and the majority of Madiba's time was taken up with plans for MK's declaration of the armed struggle, which had been set for 16 December, a date of historical significance to Afrikaners as it commemorated a Boer victory over the Zulu.

MADIBA AS THE LION'S LUNCH

At the end of 1961 the ANC was issued with an invitation to a conference of the Pan African Freedom Movement for East and Central Africa in Addis Ababa, Ethiopia, in February 1962. The MK High Command decided that Madiba should attend in order to lobby for political, military and financial support for the ANC. Though he lacked the necessary travel documents, he crossed the border into Bechuanaland (now Botswana), and over the next six months journeyed through 12 African states. The trip culminated in eight weeks of military training in Ethiopia.

Travelling without a passport or visas was a complicated and illegal undertaking, but by the early 1960s the state of repression in South Africa was such that people opposed to the regime escaped without travel documents or were forced to accept one-way 'exit permits', which did not allow them to return to the land of their birth. Had he attempted to leave South Africa by legal means, Madiba, as an underground operative of a banned political party, would have been arrested or issued with an 'exit permit'.

Joe Matthews was given the task of ensuring that Madiba made it through Bechuanaland without arrest – a mission that almost ended in tragedy. As he recalled: 'We landed at Chobe airstrip and we had to drive from Chobe to Kasanga to the hotel in a Land Rover and on the way the driver said, "We have a puncture." Oh my God, there we were in the middle of the jungle and we had a puncture! So we got off and started the process of changing the wheel, and in the middle of that the driver, speaking to me in Tswana (which of course Madiba didn't understand), said, "There's a lion looking at us from behind that bush." And I looked and it was there! And I knew we were in trouble because this chap had told me that he was from Kanye in the south of Botswana, so he was not used to animals the way the chaps from the north are. You see, my tribe are the Bamangwato and we are great hunters, so we are used to wildlife. But not these chaps from Kanye. So I said to this chap, "No, no, no, just keep absolutely calm and carry on." Then I told Madiba, "Man, don't look, but behind the bush next to the road there is a lion staring at us." And Madiba almost jumped into the Land Rover and he said, "No!!!!!" and we had the Land Rover on a jack – and I realised, My God, this chap is going to frighten the lion. You see, so we were nearly the lion's lunch! But, in the end we changed the wheel very calmly and the damn thing was just like this, staring at us the whole time. And we got into the Land Rover and drove off.'[141]

This may sound like a tall tale but in Madiba's travel diaries from this period there is an entry for 19 January 1962 which says: 'arrived in Chobe, saw lion by roadside'.[142]

FUFU AND PARTY GIRLS

During the trip Madiba and Matthews enjoyed several interesting African culinary experiences, but as a fund-raising and contact-building mission it was not terribly successful. By 25 January 1962, the two had made it to Lagos, Nigeria, where Madiba recorded in his diary: 'I eat *fufu* for the

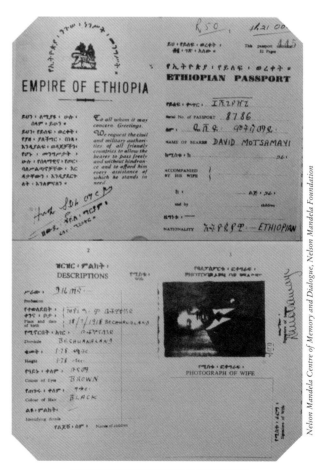

Nelson Mandela Centre of Memory and Dialogue, Nelson Mandela Foundation

MADIBA'S ETHIOPIAN PASSPORT AS ISSUED UNDER THE NAME OF DAVID MOTSAMAYI first time.' On the same page, he recorded the date and time for a meeting with the Congolese Foreign Minister, Justin Bomboko, next to whose name he penned the word 'arrogant' but there is no discussion as to what provoked such a remark. Joe Matthews was more forthcoming on the matter of the Foreign Minister. 'We scheduled to meet at a conference in Lagos that was a precursor to the formation of the OAU [Organisation of African Unity]. He gave us an appointment, and when we got to the appointment the place was full of French and Belgian white girls and so on. And we never got anywhere – he invited us in and everyone was having a whale of a time, but in that atmosphere no meeting was possible. Then we saw the President of Liberia and he lectured on the Bible and Christianity and we didn't get far with our lobbying. We got nowhere. And then we met the leader of Somalia (who was a medical doctor, that's all I can remember): that was in the days when there was a democratic Somalia. And he pointed out that Somalia had no money, so that all he could give us was moral support. So that was the most successful.'[143]

From Nigeria, they travelled on to the conference in Ethiopia where Joe Matthews recalled a visit 'to see the Emperor [Haile Selassie] in the old palace. We got such a fright when we went to see the Emperor – there were live lions as you come into the palace. And then we were ushered into the Emperor's presence and there were all these chaps shouting – poets and I don't know what. We were confused by it all – so much so that when the Emperor asked what he could do to help us, even Madiba was overawed and seemed to be in a bit of a daze. Despite his being a chief himself, he was still overwhelmed by the situation.'

The pair had an unsatisfying experience of authentic Ethiopian food with the imperial military attaché. As Joe Matthews recalled: 'I didn't like it.

I don't know how Madiba felt but there were frogs and raw meat and this and that. And honey wine. I wasn't used to it. And after that we ate in the Ras Hotel.'

Despite failing to bring in any significant donations, the trip was a chance for Madiba to reunite with his friend, comrade and former business partner Oliver Tambo. On 7 May 1962 he jotted down in his diary: 'OR arrives at lunch time. We meet head of Algerian mission.' On 16 May 1962 he noted that the pair were treated to a 'lovely dinner at Cuban Embassy'.

THE LAST SUPPER

A brief trip to London allowed Madiba to catch up with old friends and to report back to London-based comrades. After this, he returned to Ethiopia and enrolled in what was intended to be a six-month military training course. But it was not to be. After only a few weeks he received a telegram from the MK High Command, eager to commence its campaign of military action, and was instructed to return to South Africa.

Madiba re-entered South Africa via Bechuanaland and went straight to Liliesleaf farm. Here he was debriefed and briefly reunited with his wife. The next day, disguised as his comrade Cecil Williams's chauffeur, he drove to Natal in order to report back to Chief Luthuli, the ANC President, and the MK's regional command. He then went on to a dinner party at the Sydenham, Durban, home of his friend the photographer G.R. Naidoo and his wife Naga. At the table Madiba, Ismail and Fatima Meer, Dr Naicker and J.N. Singh tucked into a feast of chicken curry with double beans, mutton curry with potato, split pea *dhal*, lamb kebabs and carrot salad. Of the evening Naga Naidoo recalled: 'My children were small and I was busy looking after them and doing the cooking, so I didn't spend

Kitfo

{this Ethiopian form of steak tartare is what Joe Matthews was referring to from his Ethiopian travels with Madiba}

500g LEAN BEEF GROUND, OR FINELY CHOPPED
½ ONION, FINELY CHOPPED
¼ CUP VEGETABLE OIL
JUICE OF 1 LEMON
1 *MELUGUETA* PEPPER (OR OTHER HOT CHILLI
FINELY CHOPPED)
1 TEASPOON CUMIN, GROUND
1 TEASPOON CINNAMON, GROUND
1 TEASPOON CORIANDER, GROUND
1 TEASPOON PAPRIKA, GROUND
SALT AND PEPPER TO TASTE

Combine all the ingredients and eat immediately.

Fufu

{*fufu* (also spelt *foo-foo, foufou, foutou, fu fu*) is the most widely consumed starch in Western and Central Africa. It is almost always eaten as an accompaniment to soup or stew. In West Africa *fufu* is generally made from puréed yams and is sometimes blended with plantain cooking-bananas. In Central Africa the term *fufu* is generally used to describe mashed cassava or boiled cassava flour (in which case it is often known as *gari fufu*)}.

2kg YAMS
1 TABLESPOON BUTTER (OPTIONAL)
SALT AND PEPPER TO TASTE

Peel and dice the yams. Boil the yams until they are very soft, at least 1 hour. When they are soft, drain the yams and mash with the butter. Season to taste. To eat, break off small handfuls of fufu with your fingers and use them to scoop up and absorb the sauce of your choice.

too much time with the guests, but I know he said to me, "Ooh, this is really lovely," and I know he enjoyed every bit of it because it all got finished and there was a lot of food. The pots were empty when they were finished.'[144]

On Sunday, 5 August 1962, Cecil Williams and his 'chauffeur' set off for Johannesburg but were arrested by the security police outside Howick. Madiba was charged with inciting workers to strike and leaving the country without a passport and the case was referred to Johannesburg on remand. As he wrote in *Long Walk to Freedom*: 'My arrest had been discovered by my friends; Fatima Meer brought some food to the jail and I shared it with the two officers in the car.'[145] When asked about this, Fatima Meer commented: 'He's mistaken: it wasn't me who brought the food, it was Mrs Motala in Pietermaritzburg.'[146] When quizzed in turn, Mrs Motala, widow of the Treason trialist Mohamed 'Chota' Motala, thought perhaps the woman in question was Phoebe Brown, wife of the Liberal Party leader Peter Brown. After this the trail runs cold but someone brought snacks.

In the aftermath of the arrests, numerous accusations were made that Madiba had been betrayed by someone at the dinner party, and several diners were cast in the role of Judas. Whatever the gossip of the day, the innocence of all those present at the Last Supper seems to be confirmed by Joe Matthews. 'Years later when I was Deputy Minister, I called the people who arrested him and I said, "How did you fellows do it?" and they said, "No, Minister, it was easy: we just drew a circle around Johannesburg and we put people at all the exit points and he passed through our chaps on the way to Durban and so we waited for him at Mooi River." In those days you had to pass through Mooi River to come into Jo'burg from Durban. There were so many accusations about who had betrayed him, but it was nothing like that. They followed him from Jo'burg and they couldn't miss him. And there were so many stories afterwards about who betrayed him, but it was just police work and organisation that did it.'[147]

THE LAST SPAGHETTI AND MINCE

As awaiting-trial prisoners were allowed to receive food from their families, Winnie Mandela set to work on her famous baked pasta. Her daughter Zindzi recalled: 'I was 18 months old but I swear I remember my mother making that spaghetti and mince dish and taking it to my father. I remember it so vividly because we went with her to deliver it. It seemed to be very late at night to me and Zeni. We were left in the car and my mother went into the police station to give my dad the food. She had this dish that she always made the spaghetti and mince in – you know those old-fashioned green casserole dishes, quite heavy, almost cast-iron, and it was in this thing, and she was there for quite a while. I have never forgotten that because we were outside a police station where we should have been feeling safe but, on the contrary, we were quite scared, and she seemed to be taking so long and she had taken so much trouble making it that afternoon and we always knew that this was what my dad liked to eat. And because she was preparing this thing we knew where she was going.'[148]

memory was also sharpened by the times. She's right. I always took that to him. I would put it in that green casserole dish and take it to him and it would keep him for at least for a week. There was this kind warder who would put it in the fridge for him.'[149]

THE FIRST TASTE OF ROBBEN ISLAND

MRS NAGA NAIDOO'S

Lamb Kebabs

½ kg MINCED LAMB
1 ONION, FINELY CHOPPED
½ TEASPOON GARLIC, CRUSHED
½ TEASPOON TURMERIC POWDER
2 TABLESPOONS FRESH CORIANDER, CHOPPED
1 EGG
4 GREEN CHILLIES, FINELY CHOPPED
SALT TO TASTE
SUNFLOWER OIL FOR FRYING

Blend all the ingredients in a food-processor. Make into balls and either grill or shallow-fry until firm and brown, about 3 minutes on each side.

On 7 August 1962 Madiba was charged with inciting a strike and leaving the country without a valid travel permit. After a two-week trial he was sentenced to five years' imprisonment. He spent seven months at Pretoria Central Prison and was then transferred to Robben Island.

At that time, conditions for prisoners on Robben Island, always harsh, were at their most extreme. The notorious Kleynhans brothers, prison warders, conducted a sadistic reign of terror and assault, and food rations were even more dangerously sparse than in the years after 1964 when Madiba returned to Robben Island with his Rivonia comrades.

According to Philemon Tefu, an inmate with Madiba on his first Robben Island stint: 'You were eating right on sandy soil … and when the wind comes, if you are still having a dish of porridge you'll simply take, you know, sand on to your dish of *pap*, and after that wind there'll be a black layer on your *pap*, and you've got to remove that and eat because otherwise nothing.'

Despite never having heard her daughter describe this memory before, Winnie Madikizela-Mandela confirmed the event took place and said of the astonishingly early childhood memory: 'She was always an unbelievably bright child – it's true. She had this amazing mind for a child and I think her

As in later years, prisoners were not passive victims of their fate, and protest actions to improve conditions were commonplace. While the 1966 hunger strike has received the most attention in the history books, it was the 1963 strike, which lasted 21 days, that was probably the longest and most damaging to prisoner health. Philemon Tefu again: 'It was a terrible strike in that we were very much undernourished, and that strike I remember of all the strikes I participated in was the most physically painful. *Ja*, very painful because our bones here, you know, could feel that it was affecting the bones, *ja*. And what made it worse was that there was no time when we stopped working. So it was very, very painful.'[150]

Though he only arrived on Robben Island after the 1963 strike, Michael Dingake remembered being told of prisoners collapsing on duty at the limestone quarry and of stronger prisoners having to 'push the collapsed comrades in wheelbarrows back to gaol'.[151]

CHOCOLATE IN THE DOCK

On 11 July 1963, police raided Liliesleaf farm and captured almost the entire MK High Command. They also discovered sufficient evidence to link the already imprisoned Madiba to the activities at Liliesleaf and immediately transferred him from Robben Island back to Pretoria to stand trial.

On 8 October, after a considerable struggle, because prison authorities initially refused to allow a consultation of black and white clients simultaneously, lawyers Joel Joffe, George Bizos, Arthur Chaskalson and Bram Fischer met with their prospective clients for the first time. Even in serious moments Madiba had time for a food-related joke. The room that was allocated for legal consultations with prisoners had a high counter and metal grilles with bar stools. Prisoners were required to sit on one side of the grilles and lawyers on the other. Upon his arrival in the room Madiba greeted the lawyers with the words 'What will it be today, gentlemen? Chocolate or ice-cream soda?'[152]

Because Madiba had been in jail and the other accused had been in solitary confinement for almost three months, the meeting was at least as much a social gathering and political catch-up session as it was a legal consultation. Madiba's co-accused immediately noticed the effects of the 1963 hunger strike on him; he had lost over 12kg in the short period that he had been jailed. At the initial arraignment fellow-trialist Denis Goldberg recalled his shock when Madiba joined them for the first time in the dock. 'He had lost an enormous amount of weight in prison. I had a small slab of chocolate with me and I nudged him. He looked round below the level of the barrier of the dock and he nodded his head and I broke off a couple of blocks of chocolate and put them in his hand. He sort of

he had lost over 12kg in the short period that he had been in jail

wiped his hand across his face and the chocolate ended up in his mouth with a sharp corner sticking out of this very sunken cheek.'[153]

George Bizos also noticed the radical weight-loss. Fortunately he had more than a piece of chocolate to hand as he was working on several other cases during the Rivonia Trial, one of which was a case brought by a Greek delicatessen and bakery owner and this provided an elegant solution to Madiba's dietary needs. As Bizos recalled: 'Making French loaves was illegal in South Africa at the time. It was as a result of a war measure that stipulated the shape of the loaf baked and that it not be baked on the floor of the oven (as a French loaf is) but in a sandwich tin of one or two pounds. I think that *kitke* was exempt for religious reasons. And I was actually fighting a number of cases for Taki Xenopoulos

© BAHA

WINNIE MANDELA WITH HER DAUGHTERS
OUTSIDE THE PALACE OF JUSTICE DURING THE
RIVONIA TRIAL, 1963

of Fontana Holdings, who was seeking to invalidate the legislation that prohibited the making of French loaves. So every day I would bring what the English call cold cuts or cold meats and some salad, and we would spread out on the table at about 11.30 (you must remember they had breakfast very early). Initially, we had a problem, that it was unlawful for a convicted prisoner to eat food brought from outside, and much as we tried to persuade Nelson to partake of this food, he refused to do it because he said this was the regulation and he was going to obey it. Until one day we were all eating and he asked Chief Warder Breedt in Afrikaans, *"Meneer Breedt, wat doen 'n man as daar kos op die tafel is en hy is honger?"* [Mr Breedt, what does a man do if there is food on the table and he is hungry?] and Breedt (who was a very conservative Afrikaner but on a personal level he was fine) immediately, and without ever turning to look at him, said, *"Hy eet, Mandela"* [He eats, Mandela], so Nelson started eating and enjoyed it very much and I continued to bring the French loaves and cold meats. Eventually we won the case – it was about the big bakeries not wanting small confectionary shops to produce quality bread … it was the case that allowed me to take the Rivonia Trial for next-to-nothing, because there were no funds available, but the odd days that I took off in order to do the bread case made up for it to a certain extent, and the accused were also the beneficiaries.'[154]

LIQUID REFRESHMENT AND THE RIVONIA TRIAL

On 9 October 1963, the accused were taken to the Palace of Justice in Pretoria to begin the trial technically entitled *The State* versus *Nelson Mandela and Others* but more commonly known as the Rivonia Trial. The accused were charged with planning guerrilla warfare and acts of sabotage.

At the end of February 1964, the prosecution closed its case. There was so much evidence against the main accused that a guilty verdict was not in question. The only substantive issue yet to be decided was whether they would get the death sentence. The accused were determined to take the stand in order to demonstrate that, even if they were guilty in a technical sense, their actions were morally justified. Thus it was that

the defence case came to include Madiba's famous four-hour statement from the dock in which he argued that his involvement in planning acts of sabotage was the result of 'a sober assessment of the political situation that had arisen after many years of tyranny, exploitation and oppression of my people'.[155] Albertina Sisulu was in court for Madiba's speech and recalled that 'Walter was sitting next to him. After an hour Walter passed him a glass of water and he went on describing our history and our struggle. By the time he had reached the end of his address we were moved beyond words. And the women! The women were all in tears. When he said, "I am prepared to die," I did not realise that tears were pouring down my face.'[156]

A week before the verdict, George Bizos was told by the British Consul-General, Leslie Minford (who was known to have reliable contacts with both the South African and British secret services): 'George, there won't be a death sentence.'[157] Bizos said of this revelation: 'I did not ask him how he knew. For one thing he had downed a number of whiskies.'[158] On 12 June 1964, two days before Madiba and Winnie's sixth wedding anniversary, all the accused, with the exception of Rusty Bernstein, who was acquitted, were sentenced to life in prison. Madiba was 46; his wife was 30; his oldest child 19 and his youngest just 3.

Chapter Seven

ROBBEN ISLAND
SOLDIERS MARCH ON
THEIR STOMACHS

ROBBEN ISLAND IS SITUATED approximately ten kilometres off the Cape Town coast amidst the wild, icy waters of the Atlantic Ocean.

A site of incarceration for over four hundred years, the Island has played grim host to a plethora of imprisoned South African heroes including the 17th-century Khoikhoi leader, Autshumato, Malay political and religious opponents of the Dutch East India Company such as Sheikh Abdurahman Mantura (whose *kramat* or shrine is located on the Island) and 19th-century Xhosa warrior Makana. Between 1960 and 1991 it was used as a place of banishment for thousands of black political prisoners from southern African liberation movements including the African National Congress (ANC), Pan Africanist Congress (PAC), Black Consciousness Movement (BCM), South West Africa People's Organisation (SWAPO) and South West Africa National Union (SWANU).

ROBBEN ISLAND PRISON

As an apartheid prison, Robben Island was undoubtedly an abomination. The relative emphasis that almost all former Island inmates insist on placing on the rare good times bears witness to collective decisions to foster reconciliation through a consistent refusal to be bitter. The magnanimity of the victims should not be confused with the perpetrators' compliance with internationally accepted codes of acceptable prison practice. Such decisions notwithstanding, there is no foodie story in the world that can or should diminish the pain of beatings, the humiliation of strip-searches or the sorrow of being helpless to protect loved ones from persecution, banishment and impoverishment. There is not a recipe below that can compensate the Mandela family and others like them for the psychological cruelty of decades of censored letters and no contact visits. Gastronomy has no response to the misery inflicted on children who grew up without fathers, and fathers who were denied the right to guide their children into adulthood.

Just as food conditions for prisoners on Robben Island reflected the injustices of the wider apartheid society from whence they sprang, the prisoners' fights to improve their gastronomic fate mirrored those of their broader struggle. Whether it was the physical pain of a hunger striker's empty stomach or the emotional pain of love letters filled with culinary metaphors, Madiba and his Robben Island comrades used food, real and imagined, to reflect their hunger for freedom *in extremis*.

OPPOSITE: MADIBA'S CELL ON ROBBEN ISLAND

GROANING WITH CRAYFISH, LOADED WITH ABALONE

Prisons are never gourmet destinations. Even within the most civilised of penal systems, cost constraints and the problems of mass catering make the provision of food complex. But Robben Island was no ordinary prison. It was situated amidst an astonishing abundance of land and sea.

Robben Island Prison was closed in 1991 and became a museum in 1999. To this day, game runs wild, guinea fowl scuttle across every path, and the seas burst forth with crayfish and snoek. The children of the warders who lived on the Island in the 1960s report that they used to groan at the mere idea of yet another seafood-laden dinner. According to George Bizos: 'When you went there as a lawyer there would be a break in your consultation at twelve o'clock for Mr Mandela to go for lunch … and in the mid-'70s I was privileged to be invited to lunch at the officers' club on the island where the speciality was *perlemoen* [abalone] as starter and lobster as a main meal with a glass of wine.'[159]

Marcia Kriek is the daughter of the late General Wessels, the commanding officer of Robben Island when Madiba arrived there on 12 June 1964. 'From my young memories, it was a magnificent place, an environmental heaven. There were so many birds that at certain times of year we couldn't walk on the island because there were just nests everywhere. My father stayed in a beautiful old residence. It was a guest house and officers' mess along old British standards. The tables were set with white starched tablecloths and the cutlery was silver with starched napkins. The beds in the room I stayed in were very long and had been specially made for the then President Swart, who was well over two metres tall. The chef was in for manslaughter or murder or something but he was a magnificent cook. I remember that he would slice *perlemoen*

(in English it's called abalone) very thin and serve it fried in butter.'[160]

The seafood didn't stop at *perlemoen*. Marcia Kriek recalled: 'There were *alikreukel* too (I don't know their English name but they are found in shallow waters and they have a little sucker, periwinkles perhaps). Sometimes he cooked the abalone and *alikreukel*, minced them with a meat mincer, with a wooden handle, into a sort of crumbed mince-like texture. Then he fried them lightly in butter and served it on top of rice with lemon. To this day, my mouth waters at the thought of it.'

NO BREAD FOR MANDELA

Though white political prisoners were never housed on Robben Island, racial subdivisions among black prisoners were strictly enforced in all areas of prison life, including food. According to Madiba's fellow prisoner Michael Dingake: 'Our food was poor, unappetising and discriminatory. Coloured and Indian prisoners got what was known as D diet. "Bantu" [African] prisoners were on F diet. "Bantu" prisoners were denied bread. Breakfast was a plate of porridge with one spoon of sugar for "Bantu" prisoners and two spoons of sugar for Coloured or Indian prisoners. We also got a cup of dreadful black coffee – no milk.'[161]

In theory, D diet lunch consisted of mealie rice and vegetables while F diet prisoners lunched on porridge or boiled mealies and a yeast drink known as *phuzamandla*. The third meal of the day was porridge and a mug of thin 'soup' for F diet prisoners while D dieters were given bread spread with white margarine. So unpleasant was this bread and margarine mélange that it was universally known as a *katkop* (cat's head). Four days a week, D dieters were supposed to receive 110g of meat and F diet 60g. As fellow prisoner Indres Naidoo remarked: 'That is how it was: apartheid inside

Perlemoen

1kg *PERLEMOEN* SHELLED
½ CUP MILK
PINCH OF SALT
3 TABLESPOONS CAKE FLOUR
2–3 EGGS BEATEN
BUTTER FOR PAN-FRYING

Clean the perlemoen and cut each one into 4 thin strips. Beat each perlemoen briefly with a mallet in order to tenderise the flesh. Soak the beaten perlemoen in milk for 30 minutes to further tenderise the flesh. Drain off and discard the milk. Season, dip in flour, dip in egg and again in flour. Pan fry in butter until golden (2 minutes on each side).

MARCIA KRIEK'S

Sautéed Alikreukel

500g *ALIKREUKEL*
1 ONION, FINELY CHOPPED
2 CLOVES OF GARLIC, FINELY CHOPPED
2 TABLESPOONS PARSLEY, FINELY CHOPPED
½ CUP CREAM
BUTTER FOR PAN-FRYING
SALT AND PEPPER TO TASTE

Cook the alikreukel (periwinkle) in sea water until the plug shell comes loose. Discard the shells. Remove the dermpies and then mince the meat. Melt the butter, and then fry the onion and garlic until golden, then add the seafood mince. Cook the mince for 1 minute, then add the cream and cook for a further 2 minutes. Add the parsley, and season to taste. Serve with rice.

apartheid, even in the heart of the prison.'[162]

When those allotted the F diet complained about the food, Madiba recollected that the warders replied: 'Ag, you *kaffirs* are eating better in prison than you ever ate at home!'[163] When those allocated to D diet complained about the racist meal planning, they were threatened with reclassification.[164] Ahmed Kathrada commented: 'When we first got there, instinctively we wanted to reject this, but when we came together Madiba said, "Look, chaps, you don't reject this; our fight is for equality on a higher level."'

Though the prison diet was technically de-racialised in 1979, it was late in 1980 before the changes actually appeared on the tin plates of Robben Island prisoners because, as Dingake recollected: 'In 1979 we were told that a non-racial diet had been approved in principle by the policy-makers. But they were not sure when it would be implemented. When we complained about the slowness of the process, we were advised to "have patience" because the dietician was "very, very busy".'[165]

THE WEAK DRINK OF STRENGTH

However Spartan such descriptions of the diet sound, the written regulations understate the horror of the actual rations issued. Madiba recalled

that 'the meat was usually mostly gristle … coffee was actually ground maize roasted black and brewed in tepid water'.[167]

The 'soup' was oily liquid in which the meat had been boiled. Similarly, the *phuzamandla* was so weak that it had none of the strength-giving powers which give it its name. Of this brew Madiba commented that 'for lunch we often received *phuzamandla*, which means "drink of strength", a powder made from mealies and a bit of yeast. It is meant to be stirred into water or milk and when it is thick it can be tasty, but prison authorities gave us so little of the powder that it barely coloured the water. I would usually try to save my powder for several days until I had enough to make a proper drink, but if the authorities discovered that you were hoarding food, the powder was confiscated and you were punished.'

Furthermore, kitchens were staffed from the general (criminal) section of the prison and smuggling, theft and corruption were rife. Because warders and gangsters guaranteed preferential treatment and protection for members of the kitchen brigade in exchange for presents of food, the plates that arrived in front of the political prisoners seldom reflected the amounts and variety of food listed in the official dietary regulations.[168]

TABLE OF DAILY FOOD RATIONS FOR 1970 BY RACE CLASSIFICATION [166]

White prisoners at this same period received 500g vegetables, 80g gravy powder, 30g fat, 125ml milk, twice daily coffee, 30g salt and 80g of sugar. In 1976 F diets were awarded a single slice of bread, and in 1978 D diets started to receive 125ml of milk (in line with what was issued to white prisoners at this time). *Survey of the South African Institute of Race Relations.*

Item	Coloured and Asians	Africans
Mealie meal / mealie rice	400 g	350 g
Mealies	N/A	250 g
Bread	250 g	N/A
Meat or fish (4 x weekly)	110 g	60 g
Dried beans (meatless days)	125 g	125 g
Vegetables	250 g	250 g
Protone / gravy powder	20 g	20 g
Fat	30 g	15 g
Milk	N/A	N/A
Coffee or tea	Twice daily	Once daily
Phuzamandla	N/A	55 g
Salt	15 g	15 g
Sugar	60 g	45 g

BLEEDING GUMS AND SQUASHED BUTTERFLIES

Anecdotal evidence suggests that, regardless of category, the diet was deficient in key nutrients and was inadequate to meet the needs of adult men engaged in hard labour in the Robben Island lime quarry. Laloo Chiba recalled that 'my gums bled, I think from a lack of vitamin C'.[169] Former inmates Lombard Mbatha and Martin Ramokgadi both described being given prison clothes that were far too small when they arrived but were soon too large. Similarly, when Fatima Meer visited Madiba on Robben Island in 1975 she noticed that he 'looked terrible – emaciated, overworked in the prison yard. I knew Mandela as a strapping fellow; but now he was like a face in a pane of glass, or a squashed-up butterfly in a museum … He sat there looking sallow, emaciated. I said, "You've grown so thin," but he retorted, "But you've grown fat."'[170]

EATING ROCKS AND BROWN CABBAGE

Moreover, techniques of food preparation and conditions of ingredient storage were poor. Billy Nair remembered that 'as Indian and Coloured prisoners we would have mealie rice, which used to be boiled at 2 or 3 in the morning, so by the time we had it at 12 we were eating rocks'. According to Laloo Chiba: 'As far as the food is concerned, the preparation was horrible. To give you an instance, when it was summer season, plenty of cabbage, they loaded you with cabbage for a whole month and by the end the cabbage was brown and going off. Or if it was carrots, they would have secondary roots growing off them.'[171]

URINE, SUITCASES AND SPARE DIETS

During Madiba's first term of imprisonment on the Island there had been several sympathetic coloured warders who had smuggled food and cigarettes to the prisoners. But by 1964 such people had all been removed and replaced with white supremacists who used food as a weapon of abuse towards the prisoners. Warder Van Rensburg was, in Madiba's words, 'vindictive in large ways and small. When our lunch arrived at the quarry and we would sit down to eat … Van Rensburg would inevitably choose that moment to urinate next to our food.'[172] Van Rensburg was widely known by the prisoners as 'Suitcase' because like all prison warders he carried his lunch to work with him in a small cardboard suitcase. While the prison warders who worked in the criminal section got prisoners to carry their lunch cases, the political prisoners refused to do so for Van Rensburg and gave him the nickname 'Suitcase' because he was forced to carry his own lunch.

Officially, regulations allowed the Chief Warder to send prisoners to the isolation wing of the prison and to be placed on what was known as a 'spare diet'. The reality was that lower-ranking officers often had prisoners sent to the isolation wing. Madiba recalled that 'a man might lose his meals for a sidelong glance'.[173] Of the spare diet Laloo Chiba noted: 'If a prisoner is found guilty of infringing prison regulations you are locked up in an isolation cell, one day, three days, even six days, and you are given a mug of rice water (they boil the samp in water and then they drain the water and that's all you get, that starchy water). But you know, when you are in that position, lousy as it is, you still look forward to the mug of rice water … four, five o'clock, you start to think, Hey man, when am I going to get my mug of rice water?'[174]

The rice water punishment came to an end in 1973 when the wives of two prisoners, Kader Hashim and Terisa Vankatratnam, brought an urgent application to the Supreme Court to stop the use of spare diet and solitary confinement. As Ahmed Kathrada recalled: 'They got word that their husbands had been placed in the isolation cells for petitioning the authorities to improve food conditions. The two women won a major victory that ultimately benefited us all in that the

Rice Water

250g MEALIE RICE
1 *l* WATER

Boil the mealie rice for 2 hours until soft. Discard the
mealie rice and retain the water.

Phuzamandla

{the recipe below is for full-strength *phuzamandla* and will make
approximately one litre. Should you wish to taste Robben Island-style
phuzamandla, double the amount of water. The prison services bought
powdered pre-prepared *phuzamandla* in bulk. This pre-mix was fortified
with iron. The instant mixture is no longer available but the following
recipe approximates to the taste and ingredients once used}

4 CUPS WATER
½ CUP MEALIE MEAL
½ CUP IRON FORTIFIED SORGHUM
4 TABLESPOONS POWDERED YEAST

Bring the water to the boil. Add the mealie meal and sorghum,
reduce the heat and simmer gently until the mealie meal is cooked,
about 30 minutes. Leave to cool. Add the yeast and mix well.
If the mixture is too thick to drink dilute with a little extra
cold water. Strain and drink.

judge ruled that warders had no right to arbitrarily deprive prisoners of meals or to impose solitary confinement without a hearing.'[175]

SHARING BRAAIED MEALIES WITH NO TEETH

Food was a key site of struggle for political prisoners on Robben Island. As Madiba has argued: 'For us, such struggles … for equalised food were corollaries to the struggle waged outside prison. The campaign to improve conditions in prison was part of the apartheid struggle.'[176] From the passive resistance of food-sharing and the pragmatic meal supplementation of hunting and gardening to the active confrontation of hunger strikes, prisoners were not helpless recipients of their dietary fate.

At its most informal level, resistance to the racially based prison diets was made manifest by prisoners simply sharing their food allocations. Racism, by its very nature, seeks to minimise individual tastes and needs behind blanket colour-based classifications. Prisoners subverted this denial of individuality by sharing rations. Billy Nair recalled: 'I used to exchange my food with an old man from the Transkei who was doing a life sentence for attempting to assassinate Matanzima. He had hardly any teeth, so I used to exchange the samp or mealie rice for his mealies.'[177]

Such acts of kindness were not without risk. According to Michael Dingake, 'Prisoners were punished for sharing with other prisoners what they were not entitled to.'[178]

Even without the watchful eye of the guards, the efficacy of sharing food differed by prison section. Those, such as Madiba, in the relatively small B Section turned the reallocation of food into a well-organised catering system, but this was not possible in the communal cells. Laloo Chiba explained: 'In the general sections it wasn't really possible to share because the vast majority of the prisoners there were African prisoners. Let's come to the question of bread: we used to get a *katkop* every day, that's just four thin slices of brown bread. Now if you have about 20 or 30 Indian and coloured prisoners and a thousand African prisoners, it's just not possible to share equitably. But that's not the position in B Section. At one stage there were eight or nine Indian and coloured prisoners out of about 30 prisoners in total, so at the end of the day we could collect all that bread and it was possible to create a system to share. In the afternoons the African prisoners got boiled mealies and we used to get mealie rice, and when we went to work I looked forward to eating mealies – we managed to find some zinc, scrubbed it down, went to work and made a crude braai [barbecue], and we braaied the mealies, and that was actually lovely.'[179]

THE STRUGGLE FOR SEASONING

Passive resistance techniques were also applied by Madiba and Sisulu in an attempt to improve the bland monotony of the F diet. They attempted to make a sour porridge similar to the *inconco* which they had eaten in their childhoods, by keeping a little of their breakfast ration aside to make a culture. But their cells were raided, and when the warders found the soured mixture, they were both sent to the isolation section on spare rations in punishment.

There is only one known example of a seasoning ingredient being smuggled on to Robben Island by a visitor. According to Laloo Chiba: 'Govender the Hindu priest came to take care of our spiritual needs one Sunday and we were a small group of people: Madiba was there (because he used to go to all religious services), Kathy [Kathrada], myself, Mac [Maharaj], and others in the dining hall. Anyway, he took out a parcel and he dropped it on the floor and I immediately put my foot on it

Inconco

{*inconco* is a sour porridge common in Xhosa cuisine.
This is the flavour that Madiba and Sisulu were attempting
to recreate when they hid portions of their breakfast porridge
in order to sour them}

2 CUPS MEALIE MEAL
1 CUP SORGHUM
4 CUPS WATER

*Mix the mealie meal and sorghum in the water
and allow it to soak overnight. Cook the mixture over a low
heat in the soaking water for about 20 minutes.
Do not allow it to get too thick – the mixture should be runny.
If it gets too thick, add more water. Allow
the mixture to cool and rest for at least 4 hours in
order for the fermented flavour to mature.*

and concealed it under my foot because there were warders there and we didn't know what was in that parcel – maybe a message or something.

'And after the service he left, and as soon as the warders went away, I picked up the parcel. You know what we found in the parcel? We found chillies. So we said, "What are we going to do with these chillies?" It was about a dozen chillies or so. And we had never tasted chillies on the bloody island. So we said, "No, let's dry them and get the seed and plant the seeds," and that's what we did … And we used to go to the hospital and complain to the doctor, "Hey, this is wrong and that is wrong," and we requested olive oil and sometimes they gave it to us and we took that olive oil and we pickled the chillies in olive oil! And so, every time we had to eat our meal in the afternoon we took out one chilli and it really enhanced the taste of the food.'[180]

HUNGER STRIKES AND PERSECUTION BY SEAGULLS

Hunger strikes were the prisoners' most direct gastro-political weapon. Anthony Xaba said: 'The first ten years I stayed in Robben Island it was too tough, life was very bad and warders were very cruel but we were so brave and dedicated. We fought so many battles on Robben Island. If they did not listen to us we took hunger strikes. I remember sometimes we used to stay for three weeks without food, boycotting food, demanding our rights as prisoners according to the Boers' constitution. At one time we took 21 days. There's not a single year from 1963 to 1973, when I left Robben Island, that we didn't have a hunger strike. Sometimes twice a year. Every year there was a hunger strike, every year … because the situation was too tough.'[181]

According to Ahmed Kathrada: 'When it came to hunger strikes we, as the ANC, had decided that our leadership who were older or not well should be exempted, but Madiba and Walter [Sisulu] refused. They went through the hunger strikes with us.'[182]

The largest hunger strike was the six-day strike in July 1966 when about a thousand inmates from all sections of the prison took part. The strike started in the communal cells. Although communication between distinct sections of the prison was officially prohibited, secret prisoner networks ensured that Madiba and his comrades in B Section were informed by way of surreptitious communication with kitchen staff, and they joined in the strike action within 24 hours of its original onset.

Accounts of the exact causes of the 1966 hunger strike differ, but everyone agrees that it was gastro-political in origin. For Ahmed Kathrada the reason was gastro-architectural. 'I think that the cause of the hunger strike was that the prisoners had constructed a shelter, to eat in and so forth, at the lime quarry to protect them against the weather, and the warders had broken it down. We came to hear of it and joined in.' Anthony Xaba remembered that 'the 1966 hunger strike was taken up largely against the general treatment and the food – how it was prepared. We were given rotten food, vegetables and, you know, beetroot would simply be taken from the field into the pot still with soil about it and on to your dish of porridge. Before you can start to eat, you've got to remove the soil.'[183]

According to his cellmate Philemon Tefu: 'In 1966 the common law prisoners were working in the kitchen and they were smuggling with our food, particularly the meat. So we were getting less meat than the little that you know the prison was giving. So we went on a strike for that.' When the authorities attempted to break the strike by producing the most appetising rations ever seen on Robben Island, the prisoners held firm in solidarity.

The 1966 hunger strike had both positive and negative outcomes. For Michael Dingake, the most obvious positive outcome was the building of a dining room 'so that prisoners no longer had to squat in the dust being persecuted by seagulls who not only stole the food but augmented our cold meagre rations with their liberal droppings'.[184]

Laloo Chiba remembered the negative consequences in that 'one of the things about being a prisoner is that once you are sentenced, you become perceived as the property of the state. For instance, if you are working and you hurt yourself and it's thought that you were negligent, you are liable to punishment for the damaging of state property! So those who had negative health consequences stemming from the strike were liable for punishment. I recall that one or two prisoners were punished for that. We were under the jurisdiction of the prison services, who regarded us as their damn property.'[185]

By far the strangest outcome of the 1966 strike was that the junior and bachelor warders themselves embarked on a hunger strike. They felt that their own diet was inferior to that offered to the married warders and senior officers, and demanded an improvement.

SMUGGLING IN COOKING POTS

Prison warders and gangsters were not the only ones smuggling on Robben Island. Because the prison authorities went to great lengths to try to prevent contact between the Rivonia prisoners and the general prison population, the inmates took to smuggling messages in and out of their section in cooking pots. In the words of Laloo Chiba: 'We would prepare messages for the general section of the prison (about political decisions we had taken or news developments we had learnt about) and then we would use the plastic and Sellotape (that we had been able to get from our study privileges) to wrap the messages. We tied up the message in such a way that not even steam from the pots would let it get damaged, and we would put it at the bottom of the empty drums that we sent back to the kitchen. We would put all sorts of rubbish on top to hide the message – mugs, plates and all that – and then in the kitchen they could retrieve it. And then they would do the same on their side. We had to dish right to the bottom of the pot to see their messages. It was laborious but efficient as a method of communication with a section of the people who we were otherwise totally isolated from.'[186]

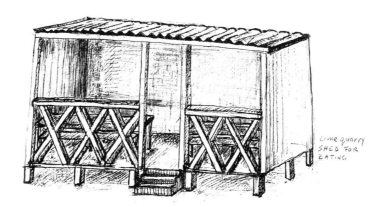

PRISONER'S SKETCH OF LIME QUARRY SHED
FOR EATING, AND BIRD BATH

While warders were skilled at smuggling food out of the kitchen and off the Island, culinary smuggling *on* to the island was almost unheard of. Farida Omar is one of the very few people who ever managed to smuggle food into the prison. 'My husband was Mr Mandela's lawyer for all those years. I always used to send *samoosas* and nice savouries with him when he went to the Island. But every time they would search Dullah's case and all the *samoosas* would come back and I was so, so disappointed. But one day my luck was in. In 1979 Dullah had a heart attack, so another lawyer, Ismail Ayob, came to Cape Town for a few days to conduct some business for Mr Mandela instead of Dullah. After his first meeting on the Island, Ismail came to see me at the Salt River Market (where I was working at the time) and he said to me, "Mr Mandela said I should come and see you and find out how is Dullah." He really is a real gem, all those worries of his own and he still wanted to know how Dullah was. So I gave him a packet of fruit, and the next day Ismail came flying in by the market and said, "Mandela said to say thank you for the nice fruit." He said that Mandela had said, "Ah, a banana! It's the first time I see a banana in 15 years.' For some reason they hadn't searched his case and when he told me that, I just cried and cried.'[187]

THE HUNTER-GATHERERS OF ROBBEN ISLAND

In addition to the gastro-political struggles to improve their diet, prisoners developed various methods of supplementing their official food intake. In 1978 prisoners of B Section were given permission to establish a garden 20m x 1.2m in the exercise courtyard. As Madiba explained: 'A garden was one of the few things in prison that one could control. To plant a seed, watch it grow, to tend it and then harvest it offered simple but enduring satisfaction. Being a custodian of this patch of earth offered a small taste of freedom.'[188]

Gardening was not easy on Robben Island. As Laloo Chiba recollected: 'The warders didn't allow us to use fresh water for the garden because there was a shortage of fresh water on the Island, so we had to find ways of saving water from bathing and so forth to put into the garden.' Soil enrichment was another problem. Laloo Chiba again: 'Madiba became very passionate about the garden – he was one of the main chaps in the garden – and whenever we went to work, he would collect dried ostrich dung because that was fertiliser, and as a result we produced very healthy vegetables in that small little patch.'[189]

There were set-backs, which Madiba took very hard. He wrote to his wife about a tomato plant he had tended from a seedling that had grown well and then withered and died despite all his attempts to nurture it back to health. One can perhaps read the account of how he eventually dug it up and buried the plant 'thinking of the life that might have been' as a metaphor for his powerlessness to nurture his own marriage.[190]

The garden was not only a source of emotional and nutritional support but also became a vital resource in the composition of the first draft of Madiba's autobiography, which was much later published

Mandela [had] said thank you ... 'its the first time I see a banana in 15 years'

WORK DETAIL (LEFT TO RIGHT) MADIBA, TOIVO JA TOIVO, JUSTICE MPANZA,
PRESUMED SPECIAL BRANCH POLICEMAN, 1977

as *Long Walk to Freedom*. Madiba's comrades decided that his memoirs should be written and smuggled off the Island to serve as a source of inspiration for younger generations of freedom fighters. Chronicling such a life was illegal, and the consequences of being caught engaging in such an action were extreme. The writing was undertaken at night, and every morning Madiba would secretly give Walter Sisulu the draft for comment. Thereafter it was given to Laloo Chiba and Mac Maharaj to transcribe in a tiny script. This last version was ultimately smuggled off the Island when Mac Maharaj was released from prison. All the same, the prisoners did not want to destroy the original draft until they knew that he had successfully deposited the manuscript with the ANC in Lusaka. Thus it was that the original

large-print version was retained, rolled up in empty Cadbury's Bournville Cocoa canisters (which the A Category prisoners could buy) and buried in the garden. Unfortunately the prison authorities decided that the isolation section was not sufficiently secluded and began work to construct a new wall. During the digging of the foundations for this wall, the buried cocoa tins were discovered. Not only was the manuscript lost but the study privileges of those whose handwriting was found on the document were withdrawn.

STOCKING JEFF MASEMOLA'S FRIDGE

Another way for prisoners to regain a degree of control over their gastronomic fate was by hunting. Christo Brand, who was a warder on Robben

'trapping birds and rabbits was the "in" thing on Robben Island'

Island from 1979 to 1982, recalled: 'Trapping birds and rabbits, that was the "in" thing on Robben Island ... Sometimes the warders will search the prisoners and they will find and take the pots and pans – I don't know where it comes from but always the prisoners have pots and pans with them. Even if it's a coffee tin or something, always they have something to cook with.'[191]

Interference from prison authorities could almost always be circumvented by cutting individual warders in on the catch. Laloo Chiba remembered: 'Let's say we caught, say, three or four guinea fowl. Well, that's quite a bit of meat for 20, 30 people, and then the warder says, "You give me one," and we would give him his share and he would have a braai there too.'[192] Despite the searches and the disappointment of losing a portion of the catch to the warders, certain prisoners pursued the Robben Island wildlife with skill and dedication. According to Ahmed Kathrada: 'At the lime quarry we hunted and trapped guinea fowl, partridges and rabbits. Skin them, braai them, prepare them, cut them up, de-feather the birds and so forth. And the person who did that best was Jeff Masemola from the PAC (he died a couple of years ago). He was very, very skilled, very innovative, very creative. He made magnificent traps.'[193] So skilled and dedicated a hunter was Masemola that he constructed a fridge of which Laloo Chiba told: 'There was a natural cave there; he converted that into a makeshift fridge. I don't quite know how it worked but it had to do with cold water. And the nights are cold on Robben Island, so if you left some meat, a rabbit

or a partridge or whatever the case may be, in that fridge it was still fresh the next day.'[194]

Not all hunting and gathering produced edible results. Said Laloo Chiba: 'There were eggs too. The partridge and guinea fowl had eggs worth eating, but the seagull – but we didn't eat those eggs – one or two people tried out the seagull eggs but they weren't nice. We also tried to trap seagulls for food but the seagull's meat was too scanty – it was more bone than flesh, so we didn't bother with them.' But taste is a very individual thing and Philemon Tefu remembered that 'the adult seagulls weren't good to eat but we used to search for the young birds – the chicks were soft and tasty meat.'[195]

In 1973 Madiba and his comrades were removed from the hard labour of the quarry and instructed to collect seaweed, which was subsequently dried and sold to Japan as fertiliser. The atmosphere on the shore was relatively relaxed, and for the first time since his herdboy days Mandela was able to augment his diet with the abundance of the seas. Of this time he wrote: 'We relished the seaside because we ate extremely well there. Each morning when we went to the shore, we would take along a large drum of fresh water ... and a second drum in which we would make a kind of Robben Island seafood stew. For our stew we would pick up clams and mussels. We also caught crayfish which hid in the crevices of rocks ... *perlemoen* were my favourite ... We would take our catch and pile it in the second drum. Wilton Mkwayi, the chef among

WILTON MKWAYI, 1957

SEA-LION – THE OTHER RED MEAT

On one occasion the seafood stews were augmented by a sea-lion barbecue. According to Laloo Chiba: 'We were on the seashore collecting seaweed and there was a sea-lion on the shore and of course the prisoners just didn't waste time. We killed that sea-lion with our spades, and after it died, we went to the person who was in charge, who was a sympathetic warder, and we said, "Look, man, this thing has died. We can't allow this to go to waste," so he said, "Alright, *gaan maar aan* [go on] but on condition you don't take nothing back into the cells"

us, would concoct the stew. When it was ready, the warders would join us and we would all sit down on the beach and have a kind of picnic lunch.'[196]

Ahmed Kathrada remembered the occasions as much less gourmet affairs. He said: 'It was more out of mischief than hunger. Whatever was not allowed we had to do. Wilton and Chiba were the cooks. But often we didn't have fresh water so we put the crayfish and abalone and limpets into boiling sea water and it was so salty that it was almost inedible … I have since had *perlemoen* once or twice as it should be eaten and so I know that what we made in prison, it was over cooked – just like rubber.'[197]

– because if you do he can lose his job, they are actually violating prison regulations. So the warder lent us his knife and we started skinning it and we broke the bottles that we found on the shore and used the glass to skin the sea-lion and after that we cut it into pieces and we braaied it – it was lovely healthy red meat, I must say that. Solid red meat, like a lamb.'[198]

Not all wildlife became lunch. Wilton Mkwayi remembered: 'I used to scrape food together and feed the birds in the afternoon. But it was not much liked by the comrades because the place where I fed the birds had been washed by the comrades earlier in the day. They were always complaining, going to Mandela, asking him to speak to me not to dirty the place. But instead he just used to take a broom and water and cleaned instead of coming to me.'[199]

STARVING ON A FULL STOMACH

There are many ways to starve. Even when the food on Robben Island was nutritionally adequate, prisoners were aware of the danger of dietary monotony destroying their sense of self. Food has a social as well as a nutritional purpose. All human beings use diet to define who they are. Madiba recognised this in a letter to his wife: 'A human being whatever his colour … ought never to be compelled toward the taking of meals simply as a duty. This is likely to be the case if the product is poor, monotonous, badly prepared and tasteless.' On Robben Island prisoners worked hard to ensure that they could express their humanity by way of food. In particular food was used as a method of nurturing younger prisoners and expressing religious belief and describing amorous sentiments.

BIRTHDAY BOYS AND KEEN CONGREGANTS

Ritual, whether it be a birthday party or a religious rite, is a core element in human social interaction. Fikile Bam recollected: 'I share a birthday with Nelson Mandela, something we discovered quite by accident in prison in 1964 … Our group was in single cells along one passage, the Rivonia people were along another. Both groups started singing birthday songs on the 18th of July. We could hear the singing and they could hear us. So my guys assumed that the Rivonia people knew my birthday and the Rivonia group in their turn were assuming that we knew it was Madiba's birthday. We then had to go out in the early morning to wash. We used to share the showers and it was discovered about our mutual birthday. Subsequent to that, every year on 18 July, Madiba would give me a birthday present … a packet of biscuits or chocolates. We were only allowed to buy these things over Christmas and he would keep it until 18 July. By that time, of course, I would have squandered all mine, so I never had anything to reciprocate with!'[200]

The monotony of the Robben Island diet was occasionally broken by the observance of religious ritual. Those priests who were brought in to minister to the prisoners were legitimately allowed to bring food items in honour of specific festivals. Many prisoners, Madiba included, developed fluid religious affiliations in order to take advantage of the temporary respite from prison food. As Laloo Chiba recalled: 'The authorities would come around and say, "How many people are observing Eid?" Or "How many are celebrating Diwali?" And hell, everybody was suddenly converted to Hinduism or Islam or whatever it was, including Madiba and Walter Sisulu! With Madiba you must remember he genuinely respected all religions and he did use to attend all types of service. So it was a show of respect for other people's religion, not just about the food. But we were all born again quite often! Muslims, Christians, Hindus: we were everything!'[201]

Hindu festivities were catered for by the prodigious culinary commitment of Pretoria's Mrs Thayanayagee Pillay. Sinda Naidoo remembered that her mother's Diwali parcels contained '*jalebis, barfi, morcu, chevron, vardee* and *bundi*'.[202] According to her niece Shanthie Naidoo: 'She always used to make food for the prisoners at Diwali time. You see, Diwali is a festival of light and it's a victory over evil. And you always get up as children and take sweetmeats to your relatives and your friends, so she did so for the prisoners … the priest was from Pretoria, his name was Mr Padayachee – he [has] died, I think – he was Ambla Padayachee but he used to go to Robben Island once a year on Diwali and Mrs Pillay used to make sweetmeats and cakes and all that and give them to him to take to the prisoners.'[203] In addition to the sweetmeats Diwali provided an opportunity to pass information to the prisoners. Sinda Naidoo said of the occasion: 'You were only allowed to speak English or Afrikaans not Tamil, but Padayachee always used to slip in bits of news in Tamil.'[204]

Islamic festival food reached the Island by a more circuitous route. In a speech that Madiba gave in 1988 at an intercultural Eid celebration, he acknowledged the role that Islam and Muslim clerics had played in enlivening the diet of prisoners on Robben Island. 'Eid Mubarak! I join you today filled with admiration for the communities who for the past month have fasted from sunrise to sunset … it begins to explain the make-up of people like Sheikh Mantura from whose *kramat* on Robben Island, we as prisoners drew deep inspiration and spiritual strength when our country was going through its darkest times.

THE KRAMAT *AS SEEN FROM THE PRISON*

That contact with Islam through the *kramat* and the regular visits by Imam Bassier also had its lighter moments. We noticed that the prisoners assigned to clean the *kramat* had grown very fat, while prisoners in general lost weight. It was only later that we discovered that they had in fact been eating the *biryani* and *samoosas* which visitors had left behind.'[205]

Besides specific religious festivals there were also religiously inspired foodie moments. Christianity had its culinary followers. Mac Maharaj recalled an occasion when 'Father Hughes announced that he would be taking those who were Anglicans for communion. Of course those of us who were not religious didn't go to that, but when the few who went came back and reported that they had communion bread and a thimbleful of wine, the queue began to increase for communion.'[206]

While most of the food for ecclesiastical eating came in from the outside, there are rare examples of prisoners making their own festive food. In 1978 Laloo Chiba took on the role of Christmas cake-maker. It was not a cake in the conventional sense of the word but all those who tasted it swear that it was delicious. The chef remarked: 'Let me start by saying that right from the early 1960s Wilton Mkwayi made representations to the prison authorities year after year after year that the prisoners should be allowed to buy with their own money one loaf of white bread at Christmas (because we only ever saw brown during the year). Ultimately they agreed. So the family would have to send the money (bread at that stage cost 10c a loaf) and every Christmas we bought a loaf of white bread – even then we had to share because

OPPOSITE: LALOO CHIBA, DECEMBER 2007

LALOO CHIBA'S

Christmas Cake

4 LOAVES WHITE BREAD
10 TABLESPOONS COCOA
10 TABLESPOONS WHITE SUGAR
200g CURRANTS
750ml *PHUZAMANDLA*

*Break the bread into pieces and put inside an old biscuit tin.
Sprinkle with cocoa, sugar and currants. Soak in phuzamandla for at
least 12 hours. After 6 hours place a food plate on top of the mixture
and put a stone on top of the plate in order to weigh down and compact
the cake. Allow the cake to solidify over night. Slice it and eat it.*

some prisoners didn't even have 10c. So that bread was the main ingredient of the Christmas cake. The other component of the cake was cocoa and sugar and currants, which we bought because some of us were A Group prisoners. And the key ingredient, the *phuzamandla*. We broke the bread into pieces and soaked it in the *phuzamandla* and then we added the other ingredients to make a thick, firm dough. And we left it overnight and then we were able to slice it and share it … I don't remember the exact ratio of liquid to bread but the consistency, you know when you bake bread, the dough that we made for the B Section Christmas cake was much harder than that. And we sliced it and ate it for a couple of days. Even if I say so myself, I really was impressed with the cake I made, and all the prisoners remarked that "this is a wonderful thing". So we had a bit of fun and it relieved the boredom of prison life.'[207]

PRIVATE PASSIONS EXPRESSED IN FOOD

Many of the most moving moments of the Robben Island story are to be found not in the actual meals but in food-related dreams and letters retelling memories of meals past. If the preparation of food is one of the ways in which couples express their love for each other, dreams of imagined meals can be a reflection of love and longing in the imprisoned. In a context where letters are not private but subject to the eyes of the prison censor, descriptions of meals are a way of expressing intimate emotions and anxieties in a public space. For Madiba, resistance to the psychological intrusion of the censor had a culinary component.

In a letter to his wife dated 31 August 1970, Madiba spoke of her cooking in a manner that so clearly demonstrates his perception of her strong personality. 'I long for the wonderful meals you prepare so carefully at home, putting your whole heart into it – fresh homemade bread, macaroni with mince meat, egg and cheese, ox tongue and tail, chops, liver and steak, porridge and honey with the high flavour that was always mixed with your dishes.' A decade later his ardour was no less intense when he wrote: 'I remembered your birthday with a real feast. I put 4 teaspoons of Nesquik in a mug, 3 teaspoons of Milo, 2 teaspoons of brown sugar, and buried the whole mixture in hot water. It was a magnificent brew fit for a monarch.'[208]

THE BISCUIT STEALERS OF ROBBEN ISLAND

The arrival of large numbers of new inmates as a result of the 1976 Soweto Uprising introduced a youthful dynamism to the prison population but it was not without dietary complications for Madiba. He and his Rivonia comrades, by virtue of the length of their incarceration, had gradually been upgraded to A Category prisoners and were consequently permitted to receive a small amount of money from relatives with which they could buy limited stocks of biscuits, cocoa, bread and dried fruit from the prison store. As Billy Nair said: 'When Tokyo Sexwale, now a multi-millionaire businessman, and Terror Lekota, our present Minister of Defence, came to Robben Island with the Black Consciousness Movement in the 1970s … these two rascals were not used to prison food and they used to go into Madiba's cell looking for biscuits. Madiba would go in there in the afternoon after work and all the stuff would have disappeared.'[209] When asked to confirm or deny the story, Sexwale laughed and conceded: 'Terror and I were like marauding lions.'[210]

MADIBA'S

Birthday Treat

4 TEASPOONS NESQUIK
3 TEASPOONS MILO
2 TEASPOONS BROWN SUGAR
150ml BOILING WATER

Mix well and serve.

Chapter Eight

NO MAN IS AN ISLAND

No man, not even one confined to an island, is an island. When a man is removed from his family, everyone suffers.

Madiba's powerlessness to protect his family from the pain of his absence and the persecution of the state was used as a form of psychological torture by his jailers. The well-being, even the nutritional circumstances, of his nearest and dearest were thus directly relevant to his gastro-political experience.

EVELYN AND THE BOASTING COW

As a Jehovah's Witness Evelyn Mandela was not involved in party politics and her suffering at the hands of the apartheid state was restricted to petty persecution. Even after Madiba's 1990 release from prison, the first Mrs Mandela felt strongly that her ex-husband had, unacceptably, put a political cause above the welfare of his family.

Whatever her resentments, Evelyn Mandela coped admirably under difficult circumstances. Her daughter Dr Makaziwe Mandela commented: 'My mother divorced in '58 and my dad was gone by '62. But we had

a lot of emotional support … She had the support from her family and also she had a lot of support from the Mandela family because the family was against the divorce. So … she was never alone, she was never isolated. And she had always had an income of her own. Even when they were married she was working – she was supporting a man who was not there … She was a strong woman. She got on with her life.'[211]

At the time of the Rivonia Trial, Evelyn Mandela was holding down two jobs: running her brother's butchery business in Orlando East all day and nursing in the Baragwanath Hospital labour ward at night. In 1968 the butcher's shop was sold and she returned to her home district of Cofimvaba in the Eastern Cape, where she supported her children and grandchildren by means of her formidable business acumen.

There were personal tragedies along the way, including the death of their eldest son, Thembi, in a

OPPOSITE: (from top left) ZONDI MANDELA (MAKGATHO'S SECOND WIFE), MAKGATHO MANDELA
Row two: EVELYN MANDELA, HER GRANDCHILDREN NDABA, THEMBELA; NDILEKA
AND AN UNKNOWN CHILD, CIRCA 1984
© Mayibuye Archives
ABOVE: WINNIE MANDELA WITH HER DAUGHTERS WHILE MADIBA WAS UNDERGROUND, 1961

© Alf Kumalo

© Reuters

MADIBA'S HOUSE IN QUNU, 2007

was running three shops: a supermarket, a café and a vegetable shop. The shop was called Mala and she became well known for her entrepreneurship – to the extent that we were known as "the kids of Mala" after the name of the shop. We weren't Mandela's children; we were the kids of Mala!'[213]

In addition to her talents as a shopkeeper she was a passionate farmer. As Nkosi Zwelilvelile said: 'She loved her cattle. There was one incident I remember that made me a great believer in cattle. I myself have my own herd today because of her. She had this beautiful Nguni cow which was called Maqhayisa, which means the "one that brags or shows off". As a child I herded her cattle, including Maqhayisa. I remember one incident when this special cow was heavily pregnant, and we had gone out to collect the cattle and it was raining so we had rushed, and by the time we got home she was standing there counting her cattle as they came in, and we were about to close the shed and rush into the house and she just called us in and she said, "Where's my cow, where's my cow. I want Maqhayisa!" and none of us recalled seeing Maqhayisa, and she sent us out in the rain to fetch Maqhayisa and we went out in that thick black rain looking for Maqhayisa. And it was raining and thundering and I was crying and the next thing I heard, it was just crying out and it had just given birth, so we came back with the calf. And since that day we learnt as the young kids in the family, me and my cousins, that cattle, especially to her, were the real treasure that she had. She was very fond of her cattle.'

NOSEKENI MANDELA AND THE HOUSE IN QUNU

Madiba's mother Nosekeni Mandela died in 1968 and the circumstances of her life and death were a constant source of self-recrimination to her son. In many ways he was still the young man who had

motor car accident in 1969. Father and son were estranged at the time of his death and Madiba had never met the young widow and her two small daughters, to whom he wrote from Robben Island: 'Ndindi and Nandi must be asking shall we never see our daddy again? Is he now together with Grandpa of Diepkloof. Will Tatamkulu never return from Robben Island? Who will now bring us dresses and chocolates?'[212] As Madiba was denied permission to attend Thembi's funeral, his ex-wife buried him and busied herself with the business of providing for his children in the manner that befits a strong, rural woman.

Throughout her life Evelyn Mandela pursued her interests with the fervent determination that had marked her behaviour in the years of her marriage. Nkosi Zwelivelile, who grew up in his grandmother's house, recalled: 'For 30 years she maintained the family. She worked very hard – she

vowed to use his education to restore his mother's social and economic status and in this respect he felt that he had failed her. And yet Mrs Mandela senior and her daughters were strong women, and their strength gave Madiba a home to return to.

In 1995, when Madiba built his home by the roadside in Qunu, many outsiders wondered why he had chosen this relatively unprepossessing spot. Though there are prettier views in the district and locations with more privacy, he built where he did because this was his ancestral land. Speaking from his grandfather's house in 2007, Nkosi Zwelivelile explained: 'What is untold is about the strength of the women within the Mandela household. My grandfather's mother and sister, when he had been imprisoned, in this patriarchal society of ours, they held on to this Mandela land in Qunu. Even when male relatives tried to take it from them and strip them from the land, they resisted and stayed. It is because they held firm that my grandfather could build his home here in Qunu. That was the achievement of the Mandela women who maintained rights to this land against great odds.'

The house in Qunu is no rich man's holiday home. Rather, it is a working farm with rows of cabbages, mealies and indigenous vegetables. Most of all, it is a family space with children and dogs and a life that would never have been possible without the tenacity of Madiba's mother and sisters. Similarly, the house in Orlando, through Winnie Mandela's numerous detentions, was retained by her sister Nobantu Mniki, whom Madiba instructed to 'cling to the house until Winnie returns'.[214]

WINNIE'S PEACHES AND PELLAGRA

Winnie Mandela's political stance attracted unrelenting state persecution. Even before Madiba's arrest, his underground commitments made holding down a paying job impossible and the second Mrs Mandela was supporting and feeding her children on her social worker's salary. In 1962 she was banned under the Suppression of Communism Act, which imposed a dawn-to-dusk curfew and prohibited her from taking part in any gatherings or communicating with any persons under a similar order. In 1965 her ability to work was completely destroyed when she was barred from moving outside Orlando township, and as a result she lost her job with the Child Welfare Society. Under her banning order she required special permission from the Chief Magistrate of Johannesburg to visit her husband on Robben Island. The conditions of the banning order made the practicalities of everyday life almost impossible. In 1968 her sister Nobantu Mniki, brother-in-law and their children came to fetch a shopping list from her, and she was charged with violating the conditions of her banning order, which 'prohibited her from receiving any visitors other than her doctor and her children'.

For several years the family survived thanks to an arrangement between Madiba, Desmond Tutu and Dr Nthato (Harrison) Motlana. According to Dr Motlana, 'It wasn't really a trust like the kind set up by businessmen or lawyers. It was more of an understanding, a community kind of thing. We never formally met, but Madiba called me up and he said, "One day when I go to jail, you must look after my family," and we did. I tried my best to look after the family and make life a little more comfortable. The children called me "Uncle Harry" and they knew they could call me if there was a problem. Being the family doctor, I have a joke that in all the years, I have never submitted a single bill. He's never paid me for looking after the family – it's a joke that we have.'[215]

It was in these moments of financial and political stress that Winnie Mandela found that she had untapped culinary strengths. The peach trees that

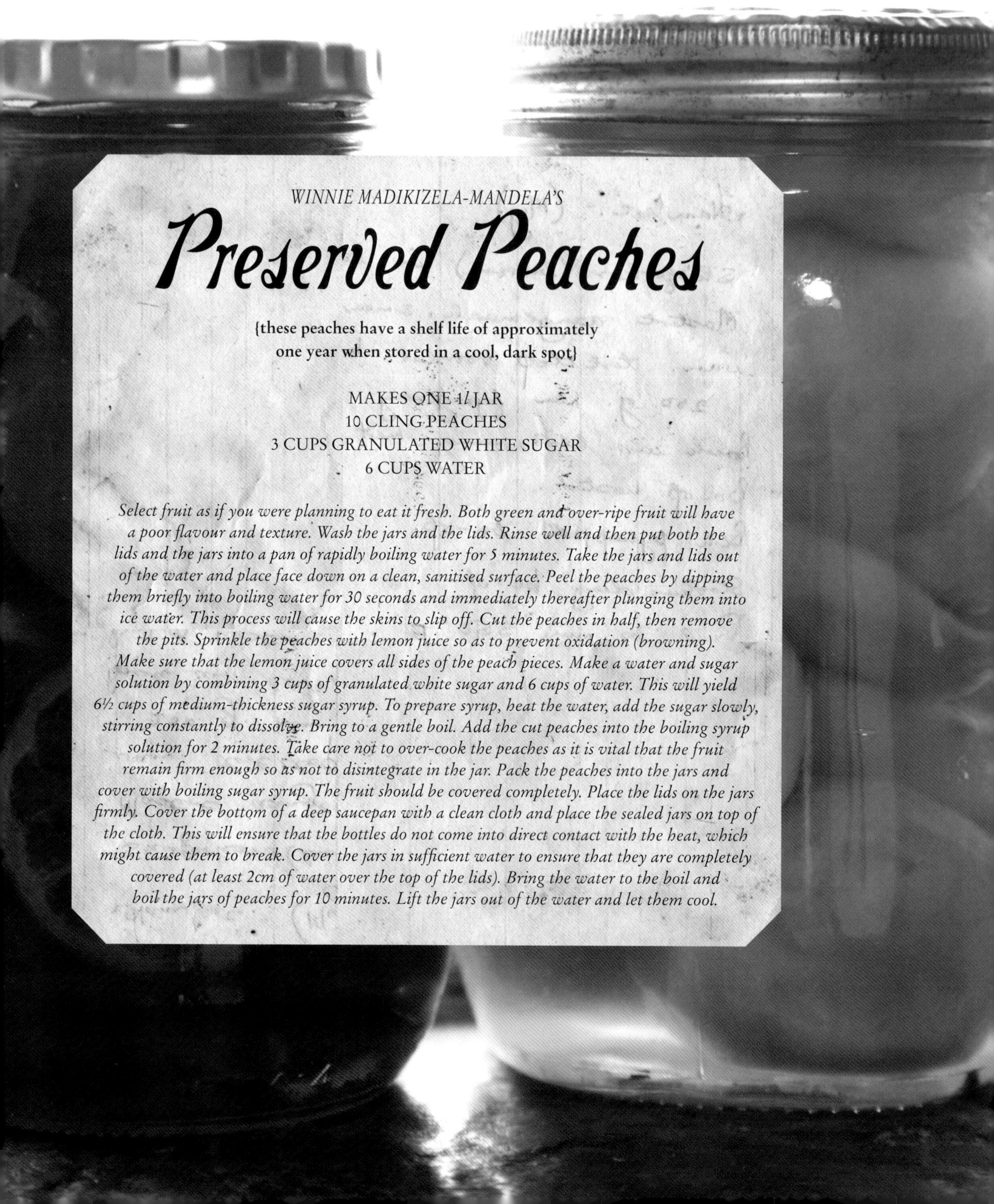

Preserved Peaches

{these peaches have a shelf life of approximately
one year when stored in a cool, dark spot}

MAKES ONE 1ℓ JAR
10 CLING PEACHES
3 CUPS GRANULATED WHITE SUGAR
6 CUPS WATER

Select fruit as if you were planning to eat it fresh. Both green and over-ripe fruit will have a poor flavour and texture. Wash the jars and the lids. Rinse well and then put both the lids and the jars into a pan of rapidly boiling water for 5 minutes. Take the jars and lids out of the water and place face down on a clean, sanitised surface. Peel the peaches by dipping them briefly into boiling water for 30 seconds and immediately thereafter plunging them into ice water. This process will cause the skins to slip off. Cut the peaches in half, then remove the pits. Sprinkle the peaches with lemon juice so as to prevent oxidation (browning). Make sure that the lemon juice covers all sides of the peach pieces. Make a water and sugar solution by combining 3 cups of granulated white sugar and 6 cups of water. This will yield 6½ cups of medium-thickness sugar syrup. To prepare syrup, heat the water, add the sugar slowly, stirring constantly to dissolve. Bring to a gentle boil. Add the cut peaches into the boiling syrup solution for 2 minutes. Take care not to over-cook the peaches as it is vital that the fruit remain firm enough so as not to disintegrate in the jar. Pack the peaches into the jars and cover with boiling sugar syrup. The fruit should be covered completely. Place the lids on the jars firmly. Cover the bottom of a deep saucepan with a clean cloth and place the sealed jars on top of the cloth. This will ensure that the bottles do not come into direct contact with the heat, which might cause them to break. Cover the jars in sufficient water to ensure that they are completely covered (at least 2cm of water over the top of the lids). Bring the water to the boil and boil the jars of peaches for 10 minutes. Lift the jars out of the water and let them cool.

WINNIE MADIKIZELA-MANDELA

Madiba had planted at the Orlando West home in the early years of his first marriage bore fruit. As she recalled: 'I used to can my own peaches – we had the trees in the garden. I would can them and then we would eat them in December. It was cheaper to do my own canned fruit. I made soap, I baked bread. I learnt to do those things because of the difficult times. It goes hand-in-hand with poverty. I was unemployed and unemployable most of the time, so I did these things for my children.'[216]

Throughout the 1960s and 1970s, Winnie Mandela was repeatedly detained by the apartheid security police under conditions of extreme emotional, physical and nutritional stress. By the mid-1960s police brutality with political detainees had increased by an order of magnitude relative to that of the late 1950s and early 1960s and she bore the full brunt of the new order. In May 1969 Winnie Mandela was arrested under Section 6 of the Terrorism Act – with the children 'grabbing at my skirts, screaming, "Mummy, don't leave us. Mummy where are you going?"'[217] – and spent

22 months in solitary confinement. As a result of this ordeal she fell victim to claustrophobia, depression and ultimately clinical malnutrition for which she had to be hospitalised.

During interrogation by the notorious torturer Swanepoel, threats of death were interspersed with 'gifts' of food in an attempt to confuse her. 'When we were arrested … we were held incommunicado. During the seven days and seven nights of interrogation I would be taken from Pretoria Central Prison and driven to the building called Compol that was the headquarters of the Security Branch. I would then be served with these bacon and egg sandwiches by the security police. I don't know whether they got them from the police canteen or what, but they were always the same – for those seven days and seven nights. Even just the smell of that sandwich reminds me of those days of torture, when they tortured us and you didn't know who else was being interrogated. They would make it a point that in the next room that prisoner screams, and then they would say, "Do you want us to do that to you?" Interrogated non-stop seven days and seven nights, no sleep, no rest, nothing, to the extent that the only time I got relief was when I fainted. I never knew that God provided such a way of getting the body to rest because when you fainted from the strain of torture it was a temporary release and then I would be woken up with buckets of water. You were completely detached from life, held incommunicado, the only people you saw were your interrogators … Back in the cells I would keep myself alive by conversing with my children. I found myself talking to them as if I was with them. I would actually pretend I was preparing food for them and call their names, and that's how I associate that bacon and egg with that kind of life.'[218]

After the initial interrogation Mrs Mandela was 'dumped in my cell' for almost two years. When she and her co-accused had spent two hundred days in solitary confinement, lawyer Joel Carlson was granted access to them and recalled their saying 'that the food was inedible and could only be eaten when they were driven to it by hunger'.[219]

Winnie Madikizela-Mandela said: 'When we were in jail, they served us food as if they were giving to dogs. They used food to insult us, to demean us, to insult in a manner that so demeaned you that you didn't feel human – in a manner that said, "I am giving you food that I give to pigs and dogs" … every day there were cooked mealies and porridge that had maggots. In the mealies, some of the worms weren't dead. We never saw another vegetable. On the day that they say it's meat, there is just lard and the fatty part of pork that you can't eat … I was hospitalised several times in that prison. I was diagnosed with pellagra. My lips were red. I developed skin blemishes which are very deep. Even today I use products to clear them. My experience of having to be hospitalised was not uncommon. When I was in the prison hospital, I was kept separate from the others but I could see that they had the same problems as I had.'[220]

In her medical records the fainting fits which she described as 'the best thing about my detention' were listed as a symptom of malnutrition.
In the view of Dr Nthato Motlana, 'It wasn't just pellagra. She had a lack of all vitamins. A lot of vitamin A deficiency. Pellagra is mainly vitamin D and she had a lack of all vitamins – she was very badly affected by the solitary confinement. What disturbed me the most when she came out was her mental state. She was very unhappy and it had done a lot of damage. I'm not a psychiatrist or a psychologist but I could see it had done a tremendous amount of damage.'[221]

Although prisoners on Robben Island were refused newspapers and were deliberately isolated from developments in the outside world, prison warders showed Madiba press clippings documenting his wife's difficulties. Emotionally tormented by his inability to protect his wife and children, he tried in small ways to ensure that his love was present at their table. In 1973 she was charged with illegal communication when her friend the photographer Peter Magubane drove her daughters to meet her. For the crime of eating fish and chips in Magubane's car with her children, Mrs Mandela was sentenced to six months in Kroonstad jail. When his wife was finally released, the ever-solicitous Madiba sent instructions to her sister Nobantu Mniki to 'prepare ox tongue and tail and dumplings and champagne to wash it down.'[222] This letter exists in the prison records archive but the family have no recollection of it arriving in Orlando and no tongue or champagne was served.

ZINDZI AND THE MAGISTRATE FOR DINNER

The problems of explaining a complex political struggle to very young children weighed heavy on Madiba's mind and conscience. Since prison regulations barred children under the age of 16 from visiting inmates, Zindzi and Zenani Mandela

and shaken

You and Zeni, and perhaps even Mummy, may be justified in thinking that the magistrate who seemingly treated us with such pettiness and lack of feeling, is a cruel man. He himself probably has a wife and children, just as I have, and would certainly be aware of the hardship created by keeping Mummy and Daddy in forced separation for so long, and of denying us the pleasure of seeing each other. Yet I know that, as a person, he is far from being cruel. On the contrary, and within the limits imposed by certain traditions which have become accepted in our country, he is kind and courteous and I consider him in all sincerity to be a gentleman. During the 9 years in which I practiced as attorney I frequently appeared before him, and I found it a pleasure to argue before a man I regarded fair and just.

MADIBA'S LETTER TO HIS DAUGHTER ZINDZI

lived through the darkest days of their mother's persecution as very little girls with nothing but written contact with their father. In December 1970, Madiba wrote to 9-year-old Zindzi attempting to explain why a magistrate had refused her mother permission to visit him after her release from jail.

'You and Zeni … may be justified in thinking that the magistrate who seemingly treated us with such pettiness and lack of feeling is a cruel man. He himself probably has a wife and children, just as I have, and he would certainly be aware of the hardship created by keeping Mummy and Daddy in forced separation for so long and of denying us the pleasure of seeing each other. Yet I know that as a person he is far from cruel. On the contrary and within the limits imposed by certain traditions which have become accepted in our country, he is kind and courteous and I believe him sincerely to be a gentleman … One day the old systems will be pushed aside and new ones will arise. The system

as a whole will change. Only then will good men have the opportunity to serve their countrymen fully and well. Then Mummy will not have to travel to Cape Town to see Daddy. I will be at home. Together we shall sit around the fire and chat warmly and gaily. We might even invite the magistrate for dinner.'[223]

STRAIGHTENED HAIR, RIBBONS AND UNCLE ISH'S EGGS

During Winnie Mandela's repeated detentions Zindzi and Zenani were cared for by a range of friends and relatives. Initially Peter Magubane and Winnie's sister Nonyaniso Madikizela looked after them, but both found themselves imprisoned for their trouble. As the girls grew older, the problem of finding schools that would accept the children often required that their mother billet them on people living outside Soweto. Zindzi Mandela recalled the situation thus: 'If there's anybody's lap and shoulder I remember most, it's Amma

Naidoo's. She made this thing that we loved with warm rice and butter and sugar. Thinking about it now, I'm sure it was because of her budget actually but, yow, we loved that thing. She used to make that for us all the time. I was in Grade 1 and Zeni was in Grade 2. They had to do a fiddle to get us into the school – because we never lasted in any of the schools in Soweto. The moment they learnt who we were, the principals were harassed and we were asked to leave. We went to Coronation, Kliptown, Doornfontein and so forth, and my mother would have to give us false surnames and straighten our hair and make us wear ribbons and all types of things, but it never worked for very long because the cops would catch on to us. I remember that's even how we left Amma's because we had been schooling somewhere around there and they caught on to us.'[224]

Shanthie Naidoo said of the Mandela girls' 18-month stay in her parents' home: 'First it was Zeni only who stayed with us, I think it was about 1965, '66 or so – she was just schoolgoing age. First Zeni came and then the next year it was Zindzi too. Winnie would drop the children on Sunday night and then pick them up again on Friday afternoon. So they were staying the week with us – you see, one of the relatives is Mtirara and the kids were registered as Mtirara in a Coloured school close to our home. And then the whole thing was disrupted by the police, but for the time

before they were found out, they were the children of the house, part of the family; whatever we ate, they ate. My mother had certain days she wouldn't cook meat or fish or eggs, just vegetarian: Friday, Tuesday, Monday. It was a religious thing. Like today, I am just cooking beans. Quite soon after that, in '69, I was detained and I refused to give evidence against Winnie.'[225]

Such arrangements ensured a degree of stability in otherwise chaotic childhoods, but eventually such police harassment became intolerable and the unlikely trio of Soweto shebeen tycoon Elija Msibi, English aristocrat Lady Birley and political stalwart Helen Joseph came together to provide the means to send the girls to boarding school in Swaziland, first at Our Lady of Sorrows and later at Waterford.

School holidays were often peak periods of police harassment. Zindzi Mandela remembered that 'we would come home from boarding school in Swaziland and they would lock my mother up that same day. So we would come home to an empty house. There was one unpleasant episode with relatives that because their home was not far, they would go and eat at their home so that they wouldn't have to buy groceries for me. I have never loved bread, salt and tomatoes so much as I did on that holiday.'[226] After the tomato and salt holiday, a plan was made whereby Dr Nthato Motlana,

© Vanessa Grobler

ZINDZI MANDELA

ISMAIL MEER'S

Fried Eggs

{recipe supplied by Zindzi Mandela}

2 TABLESPOONS SUNFLOWER OIL
1 ONION, GRATED
3 SMALL GREEN CHILLIES, FINELY CHOPPED
1 TEASPOON TURMERIC
2 TEASPOONS MASALA (CURRY SPICE)
4 EGGS

*Heat the oil and add the onion. Gently fry the
onion over a medium heat. When the onion is cooked through,
about 5 minutes, remove the pan from the heat and add the
chillies and spices. Mix well. Return the spice and onion mixture
to the heat, then crack the eggs into the pan. Cook until the eggs
are at the required level of softness. Serve with toast.*

Fatima and Ismail Meer, and Helen Joseph were on standby to provide emergency parenting.

Troubled times make for troubled children. Fatima Meer remembered that Zindzi and Zenani 'were rarely happy with the arrangements and often complained or became the targets of their benefactors' complaints'.[227] According to Ilse Wilson: 'Helen was very good to them but she had lived on her own for a very long time, she had never had children and it was difficult for her to cope with two teenagers. They would come with all their teenage clothes and live in a tiny room and there was nothing to do. They were probably safer than they would have been in the township but they were bored.'[228]

And yet with the relative serenity of hindsight, Zindzi Mandela is remarkably positive about her stand-in parents. 'We loved Aunt Fatima's curried eggs – well, they were actually Uncle Ish's eggs, Aunt Fatima doesn't cook. I now know they are great for a hangover too – they work wonders, especially on toast. But back then during school holidays, if mummy was sometimes locked up we would go to Aunt Fatima. Uncle Ish showed us how you fry an egg with grated onion, chopped up the chillies and masala. In recent years my kids have added a twist by putting grated cheese on top, but that's not in the original.'[229]

Similarly, Helen Joseph recollected that 'I was more than a little embattled' by the arrival of 'teenagers in my house and in my solitary life',[230] but mention of her elicited nothing but affection from Zindzi Mandela. 'I'm not saying we didn't get irritated with each other but she was always there for us when my mother was in prison or in Brandfort. We loved Aunt Helen – she was such an iron lady. I remember once she got cross with me because I used the word "pondering" instead of "pensive". But I loved Aunt Helen and she loved us, she was possessive about us. She was sad when we left. She

used to put potato chips – you know, crisps – in the oven with pork sausages, and when they came out she would put gravy. She had this lovely dog, a German Shepherd – what was its name? Yow, we loved that dog. And there was cake … every Wednesday sponge cake and Aunt Helen would treat us to these afternoon teas in her garden. It was nice there, it was different, because it wasn't the township, but it wasn't really safer because they also took pot shots at her house. But the point was that if mummy was locked up, she was there to look after us.'[231]

In Helen Joseph's words, 'cooking for us all on that little stove wasn't easy but friends rallied to our help with cooked chickens and tasty pies'. So it was that Ilse Wilson found herself driving *frikkadels* (meatballs) across town. The recipe was taken from her mother's much-annotated cookbook and was one that had fed Madiba at Molly Fischer's table in the 1950s. She recalled: 'We didn't have much money in the '70s. I would make my mother's *frikkadel* recipe and we would eke them out with bread and then race across town to Helen Joseph's house where the girls were staying in their school holidays from Waterford.'[232]

For Zenani and Zindzi Mandela, visits to their father on Robben Island began in 1973 and 1975 respectively. As Zindzi Mandela recalled: 'Even when we were older and we went to the Island, we use to depend on the generosity of others. Ayesha Ahmed and Ameen Arnold, they were both doctors and they were quite well off and they would spoil us rotten and then we would have to go back to our real lives. They looked after us so well. Anne Tomlinson in Bonteheuwel [Cape Town] and her mother's wonderful trotters – she would do a trotter-type curry with sugar beans that was never, ever sticky. These were all lovely families. We had good support structures – it made it so much easier dealing with whatever we were dealing with at the time because we had these

ILSE WILSON AND MOLLY FISCHER'S

Frikkadels

1 SLICE THICK CRUSTLESS BREAD
1 ONION, FINELY CHOPPED
500g BEEF MINCE
1 TEASPOON DRIED THYME
JUICE OF ½ LEMON
SALT, PEPPER
½ EGG
1 TEASPOON SUGAR
OIL FOR FRYING

*Heat a frying pan to a medium heat and sauté the
onion in 2 tablespoons of oil. Mix the fried onions
with all the other ingredients and form the mixture into
50g meatballs. Shallow-fry the meatballs until cooked
through, about 10 minutes.*

amazing families that were real family units looking out for us. Mum, dad, kids gave you a sense of security and stability, and it stayed with us for a long time after we left. And it was nice when you felt like you were part of that.'[233]

WINNIE'S OTHER CHILDREN

On 16 June 1976 Soweto school students took to the streets to protest against a ruling by the Minister of Bantu Education that certain subjects be taught in Afrikaans. This marked the start of the Soweto Uprising, which soon spread to other parts of the country. In the immediate aftermath of the shooting of 12-year-old Hector Pieterson, Winnie Mandela was detained for four months. When she was eventually released she found herself feeding the emotional, political and nutritional needs of a group of militant students who had emerged out of the school protests. While some student leaders lived permanently in her home – including Tokyo Sexwale, who stayed for two and a half years – others came to be fed under the cover of darkness. Zindzi Mandela recalled: 'I will never forget Majakathata [Mokoena] – he's an economist now – he was part of the June 16 group, and they used to sleep on the mountain to avoid being arrested and they would wait for everything to be dark when they were sure mummy wasn't being watched and so on, and under the cover of darkness they would come and consult with her, and they were living such desperate lives, and I will never forget, he went to the pot of chicken curry on our stove and put his hand in and scooped out a portion into his pocket to eat on the mountain. In his pocket!' According to her mother: 'They were underground cadres, but at the same time they were kids wearing school uniform, sleeping on the mountain, their shirts were so dirty, running away from the police with a pocket full of curry.'[234]

Dr Nthato Motlana recalled that era: 'If you called in on any evening Winnie would have four or five pots going and the house would be full of hungry people and she would be personally serving the food. Have you ever had her curry? One day you just have to taste her curry. She makes excellent curry.'[235] The logistics of feeding student activists required a hearty but economical cooking style. Out of this time have come several recipes that remain family favourites in the Mandela household. Winnie Madikizela-Mandela remembered 'pig's head … I was banned and under house arrest and I had all these kids to feed, so I needed food that would stretch a little, chicken and dumplings or a pig's head. The pig's head, I would cook it as it is and I enjoyed seeing them tackling it at table. It made me laugh. Cook it whole, like a smiley [a sheep's head]. Braise it and make it very nice, brown, and put it on the table and then they would tackle it. Some would go for ears. Tokyo [Sexwale] always went for the cheeks on the side of the jaw. It was a delicacy they had every weekend because we couldn't afford other meat.'[236]

BRANDFORT CUISINE

In the wake of the 1976 Uprising the state saw Mrs Mandela as an undesirable influence on the Soweto youth. On 16 May 1977 she was banished to Phathakahle township outside Brandfort. Zindzi (who was home for the school holidays), her mother and their household possessions were loaded on to a police truck and transported the 380km from Soweto to the heartland of the rural Free State.

They arrived to find a township community that had received warnings from the police to keep away, around-the-clock surveillance by the security police, a house that had no electricity and a pit latrine in the backyard. One communal tap served the needs of 80 households.

The dwelling, which George Bizos described as 'no more than a shack', was so small and the

WINNIE MADIKIZELA-MANDELA'S

Chicken Dumplings

1 LARGE FREE-RANGE CHICKEN
1 ONION, ROUGHLY CHOPPED
SALT AND WHITE PEPPER
1 GREEN PEPPER, GRATED
1½ CUPS SELF-RAISING FLOUR
1 TEASPOON BAKING POWDER
½ CUP MILK
1 TEASPOON AROMAT
3 SPRING ONIONS CUT IN HALF LENGTHWISE

Portion a large farm chicken (farm chickens are tougher but more flavoursome). Put the chicken pieces into a pot with the onion, salt and white pepper and sufficient water to cover the chicken (about 2l). Simmer the chicken until it is very soft, about 45 minutes (the exact time will depend on the age and size of the chicken). When the chicken is soft, add the grated green pepper and allow the mixture to simmer gently while you prepare the dumplings. Mix the self-raising flour, baking powder, Aromat and enough milk to make a soft dough. The exact amount of liquid will depend on the weather. Hot days need more liquid (about ½ cup of milk works on a temperate day). This is the standard amount of dumplings, but those with big families can make the meal stretch further by simply doubling the dumpling recipe and keeping the other ingredients the same. Divide the dough into whatever size dumplings you feel like. Mrs Madikizela-Mandela usually makes the dumplings the size of her fist but she says that little pingpong-sized balls are the tastiest. Put the dumplings into the simmering chicken stew mixture. Layer the dumplings with spring onions in a lattice pattern and put a lid on the pot (so that the dumplings can steam) and simmer the stew until the dumplings are cooked through and fluffy, about 30 minutes.

Milk Tart
Pastry

110g BUTTER
½ CUP WHITE SUGAR
1 EGG
2 CUPS CAKE FLOUR
1 PINCH SALT
2 TEASPOONS BAKING POWDER

Cream together the ½ cup of sugar and the butter. Add the egg slowly to the sugar and butter mixture, beating with each addition. Beat in the cake flour, salt and baking powder, and then roll out the dough and press it into a 20cm pie tin. Chill the pie pastry in the fridge for 30 minutes, then line with greaseproof paper and fill three-quarters of the cavity with baking beans. Blind bake the pie crust at 180°C until cooked through and golden, about 20 minutes.

Filling

3 EGGS
1 CUP OF SUGAR
4½ CUPS MILK
2½ TABLESPOONS CAKE FLOUR
2½ TABLESPOONS CORNFLOUR
1 TEASPOON SALT
1 TEASPOON VANILLA ESSENCE
20g BUTTER, MELTED
2 TABLESPOONS OF CINNAMON SUGAR

Beat together 3 eggs and 1 cup of sugar. Warm the milk until it is just about to boil, then remove from the heat and slowly add to the egg and sugar mixture, beating well with each addition to ensure that it does not curdle the egg. Add the flour, cornflour, salt, butter and vanilla essence to the egg, sugar and milk mixture, and beat well. Gently cook the mixture over a low heat until it comes together as a custard. You will need to stir the mixture constantly to ensure that the eggs do not scramble. The custard mixture is ready when it is thick enough to coat the back of the spoon. Allow the custard to cool to room temperature, then pour it into the cooked pastry cases and leave it to cool and set completely, at least 1 hour. Once the filling is set, sprinkle the top with cinnamon sugar.

doors were so narrow that most of the Mandelas' furniture, including the kitchen table, wouldn't fit through the front door. In transit the police had been extremely rough with their possessions and there had been numerous breakages. Mrs Mandela was distressed to discover that the delicate white

WINNIE MANDELA IN BRANDFORT, 1978

© Avusa Media

piping on the edges of her wedding cake, which she was saving in hopes of her husband's release, had been smashed and that the pettinice coating had cracked. On their first night, the exhausted mother and her daughter huddled together amid their scattered possessions and ate a packet of potato crisps.

The lack of electricity in the house meant that they couldn't use their Soweto refrigerator. In Zindzi Mandela's words: 'We had to have the fridge connected in the garage at the police station. So we had to walk to the police station to collect our things. We were in the township and we had to go into the town on the main road – well, everything in Brandfort is on the one main road. Eventually we got a gas fridge but it's not as good, so even then you couldn't have it, like, well stocked because things would quickly get spoilt. But we used it because we didn't look forward to going to the police station – they would really try to humiliate you – you had just gone there for chicken pieces and, my God, it would be like such a mission, you know. So mummy was having to marinate her meat in red wine to keep it fresh to avoid going there every day.'[237]

Tiresome as it was, the cooling of ingredients

was relatively low down on Winnie Madikizela-Mandela's list of complaints. So stringent were the conditions of her banning order that she was prohibited from having contact with more than one person at any time during the day and was allowed to meet with no one but immediate family at night. When a hawker tried to sell her a chicken while she was talking to her neighbour, Albertina Dyas, the three of them were charged with attending an illegal gathering. During the subsequent trial a *New York Times* reporter asked the prosecutor: 'Sir, I don't want to be impertinent but don't you feel silly asking so many questions about a chicken?' An exhausted and frustrated Mrs Mandela was quoted by the reporter as asking: 'In what other country would the price of chickens be entered as evidence? Did they think I was buying a Rhode Island Red?'[238]

Strenuous attempts were made to cut the family off from their Johannesburg friends and support structures. Initially, the Mandela women's only link with their former life was the public telephone box outside the Brandfort post office. Friends who visited were often subject to persecution. When Helen Joseph and Barbara Waite came to see Winnie Madikizela-Mandela on her birthday bringing with them a milk tart, they were arrested. Barbara Waite remembered: 'When Winnie was banished to Brandfort we used to make sure she got a visit at least once a month. At the time Helen was a listed person, although she was an Anglican and a Christian, she was banned as a Communist, and so she and Winnie weren't allowed to communicate,

Isonka Sombhako

{this bread is known colloquially as *umbhako*, which refers to the
fact that it is baked (usually in a cast iron pot) – makes 1 large loaf}

2 CUPS CAKE FLOUR
1 CUP WHOLEWHEAT FLOUR
5ml SALT
10g INSTANT YEAST
CORN KERNELS FROM ONE GREEN MEALIE CUT OFF THE COB
45ml BROWN SUGAR
2 LARGE EGGS
25ml OIL
250ml WARM WATER

*Combine the flours, salt, yeast and sugar. In a separate bowl, combine the
eggs, oil and warm water. Slowly add the wet ingredients to the dry
ingredients, mixing gently between each addition of liquid. Fold the corn
kernels into the batter and then pour the mixture into a well-oiled
cast-iron pot or a loaf tin. The mixture should fill three-quarters of the tin.
Set the tin aside in a warm place until the mixture has grown to
fill the tin: this will depend on the external temperature but is usually about
45 minutes. Bake in a preheated 180ºC oven for 1 hour or until
a skewer inserted comes out clean.*

but she used to make the trip every month and just sit in the car and perhaps wave at Winnie so that Winnie could know she was with her in spirit. We used to telephone before we went and Winnie would meet us in Brandfort town because we weren't allowed to go into the township … Usually we were very aware of police watching us, but this time there seemed to be no one about and so Helen got out of the car and embraced Winnie and they had a long chat. They had lots to discuss because it was shortly after Steve Biko's death. But then the policeman Swanepoel jumped out from where he was hiding behind a bush and he said that Helen and myself must come to the police station and make a statement because Winnie was transgressing her banning order by talking to Helen. And we refused to make a statement. We wouldn't be responsible for sending Winnie to jail. I was terribly anxious because I am very law-abiding and a bit *poep* scared but I couldn't give a statement. I wouldn't.' Helen Joseph, then 72, was jailed for two weeks and Barbara Waite for a year (subsequently reduced on appeal to two months). Of her time in the Klerksdorp prison, Barbara Waite said: 'I was the only white woman prisoner, so I was kept in total isolation. They took away my watch, so it felt like a desert of time stretching out. I was treated well, but the total isolation – I could so understand how that kind of situation might drive people mad. When I got out I felt such joy at being part of the human race. I remember I went to Checkers [supermarket] – just to feel the pleasure of bumping shoulders with people pushing trolleys was heaven.'[239]

Despite her jail sentence Barbara Waite, who was a formidable baker, continued to make and deliver comfort food to the beleaguered family. Zindzi Mandela remembered: 'Those lovely steak and kidney pies that she would bring all the way to Brandfort. Oh, they were so lovely. We met her through Aunt Helen. She was the wife of the cricketer [John Waite] and she came from a very conservative family. Her relationship with Aunt

Helen had been struck up at the Cathedral, through the church. They were fellow worshippers, and before she knew it she was in the middle of this *swartgevaar* [black peril]. She was so elegant, elegantly coiffed, and then these pies and that milk tart – these are people who kept us alive. We would never have survived without such people. She knew we couldn't live without her milk tart, so she kept sending them even when we were moved to Brandfort. Even when she got arrested, she continued to come with Aunt Helen. To take such a risk, to bake all these pies and take them all the way to the Free State: what a lovely woman.'[240]

SILVER LININGS TO RAINLESS FREE STATE CLOUDS

It was in the Free State that the second Mrs Mandela came to share her husband's passion for gardening. According to Zindzi Mandela: 'In Soweto we had those apricot, fig and peach trees that my dad had planted, but when we got to Brandfort that is when mummy really started gardening: onions, tomatoes, spinach she had, and maize. It's not easy to garden in the Free State – so cold and dry in the winter, but she did it. And she started teaching the other families and we started organising seeds for them. There was no running water – one tap per street – but she found a way of pulling the water in through channels – as only my mother would. In addition to the gardening, she started a soup kitchen and taught people how to make beautiful bread, *umbhako* – it's a typical Xhosa bread. People weren't ignorant, they just lacked resources, so Operation Hunger came into the picture and they helped her with seeds for her to distribute in the township, so by the time she left Phathakahle township it was quite green.'

WINNIE AND ADELE, THE FRIENDSHIP THAT 'SAW TOMORROW COMING'

It was around a Free State dinner table that a significant cross-cultural friendship was formed with far-reaching political consequences. The Mandela and the De Waal families came into contact when Mrs Mandela's Johannesburg lawyer, Ismail Ayob, suggested that she get a lawyer in the district to help her in situations which required immediate, local attention. Since the terms of her banning order prevented her from leaving Brandfort, she approached Piet de Waal, the only lawyer in town.

The initial meeting was not promising. According to Winnie Madikizela-Mandela: 'The first day I went to De Waal's office, there were three huge farmers, his clients, wearing safari suits and combs in their socks. You should have seen the horror in their faces when I arrived in the waiting room. One farmer stood up, turned red and walked out, and after that they all followed and I remained alone! They thought, Good God, what is this, what has happened? For me to walk into this office – it had two [entrances] – one entrance for blacks and one for whites. At the time there were two entrances everywhere in Brandfort. So I was ushered into Mr De Waal's office. He was drinking coffee – I remember he couldn't even handle the cup, he was trembling so much. I couldn't make it out why he was shaking. Was it out of fear or what? I just don't know what they had said about me, but he couldn't finish his coffee and he had a pen and he kept dropping it while he was taking a statement from me.'[241]

Unbeknown to Mrs Mandela or Ismail Ayob, Piet de Waal was a childhood friend of the Minister of Justice, Kobie Coetsee, whose family had a farm near Brandfort. Once a friendship had been struck up between the pair, 'Piet de Waal always told people we shared a common "friend" – in the sense that it was Kobie Coetsee who had sent me to Brandfort.' The significance of the 'common friend' only became apparent in the late 1980s and will be dealt with in subsequent chapters.

The transition from client to friend was initiated

by the lawyer's wife, Adele de Waal, who identified with Mrs Mandela's isolation and invited her to dinner. Adele de Waal's daughter Sonia Cabano described her mother as 'a very special person. I don't think I ever saw her angry with anyone, she never lost her temper. She just didn't have it in her. But she was often sad. Even as a child, I was aware of my mother's yearning for life, life and colour and joy, that she could never entirely have in a small town like Brandfort. She used to stand in front of the kitchen window that looked out on to the garden and the rest of the village lying in front of it and the desolate flatness beyond and sigh: *"Dis so plat hier, mens kan môre sien aankom"* [It's so flat here, you can see tomorrow coming] … She loved travelling and meeting new people. She had a sense of adventure about her. My dad, on the other hand, was just about the most unadventurous person you could ever meet. He was content to eat exactly the same food every day of his life. When he was a child he had to look after his family's cattle after school and his mother would keep his lunch warm until he had finished his duties, so his whole life he loved the taste of meat and three veg kept warm in a low [warming] oven. He once proudly asserted that he had not left Brandfort or its district for an entire year! His entire universe was Brandfort, it was his domain. He knew every person in that community intimately and he cared for them like a father.'[242]

Adele de Waal was a creative and innovative cook who liked to keep up with modern culinary trends and was always trying out new recipes. As Sonia Cabano recalled, she 'grew herbs when no one else even knew what herbs were. She read American food magazines and taught herself to cook classic French cuisine from Julia Child's step-by-step books. She subscribed to the Time/Life Food of the World series in 1970 and started growing basil and peppers. She was ahead of her times in so many ways. We grew up organic long before it was fashionable and she played loud opera and sang along with all the doors wide open while she

ADELE DE WAAL'S

Herb-roasted Chicken

{Adele de Waal did not write down the original recipe but this is her
daughter Sonia Cabano's recollection of the dish}

12 CLOVES OF GARLIC, CRUSHED
1 TABLESPOON FRESH SAGE, CHOPPED
1 TABLESPOON FRESH ROSEMARY, CHOPPED
1 TABLESPOON FRESH THYME, CHOPPED
1 LARGE FREE-RANGE CHICKEN
½ TEASPOON COARSE SALT
¼ TEASPOON BLACK PEPPER, GROUND
2 TABLESPOONS OLIVE OIL

*Combine the garlic and herbs. Rub the salt and pepper over the chicken.
Rub the inside cavity of the chicken with one third of the garlic and herb mixture.
Loosen the skin of the chicken and rub the flesh with the remaining herb and garlic
mixture between the breast meat and the skin. Allow the herbs to marinate into the
chicken in the refrigerator for at least 2 hours (ideally 24 hours). Place the
chicken breast side down on a rack in a shallow roasting pan, and brush the outside
with oil. Roast the chicken for 15 minutes at 200°C, then turn the chicken
breast side up and reduce the temperature to 180°C. Continue roasting until the
chicken is cooked through, approximately 50 minutes. Remove the chicken
from the oven and cover it with foil and let it stand for 10 minutes.*

cooked ratatouille and chicken Kiev with hot garlic butter spurting when you stabbed it with a fork. She even managed to find soy sauce and sesame oil and cooked us Chinese food, which she served in bowls with chopsticks.' Her son Meyer de Waal said: 'My father was a very conservative eater, and once after my mother presented us with a meal from a new recipe book, he told her she must bring out a recipe book "A Thousand and One Ways to Fuck Up a Chicken". Everyone else loved the recipe.'[243]

 So began an unlikely friendship. Winnie Madikizela-Mandela said: 'It was the first Afrikaans-speaking family I interacted with at that level in the Free State. People were dead scared – our people, let alone whites, were dead scared, and yet Adele extended such a wonderful hand of friendship. She went out of her way to make us feel welcome in Brandfort when we were like leprosy … she had us for so many meals. Bobotie, lovely soup with beans, very nice roasts, very, very nice. She did her chicken so nicely with all the herbs. We had so many meals with her. We used to share so much. I was devastated when she died. I still can't take it.'[244]

While Piet de Waal began his relationship with his new client in a state of anxiety, he was soon struck by her charisma, charm and her extreme vulnerability to state persecution. His daughter Sonia Cabano recalled that 'before long he saw that she was a wonderful woman, lonely and in need of protection. I remember they used to sit together at our home eating biltong and talking late into the night. He would carve off little slices and she would laugh at him and say, "I'm an African, I've got strong teeth. Give me bigger slices."'

Friendship with the Mandelas was not without consequences. Zindzi Mandela remembered that her mother and Adele de Waal became 'like sisters. She would make mummy some jams and also bake for her. And then the cops started harassing her – I don't know how many times poor Adele de Waal was stopped over a traffic fine – and we would then come in our ANC colours over this traffic-fine thing and be sitting there staring the magistrate down.'[245]

In June 1984, when Zindzi Mandela (who had not been banned and had returned to Soweto to continue her education) was assaulted, her mother violated the conditions of her banning order and returned to Johannesburg, where she remained – effectively unbanning herself.

THE IMPOSSIBILITY OF RETURNING TO SPAGHETTI AND MINCE

Throughout his time in prison, Madiba idealised his wife as a romantic icon and as such she was a significant source of strength for him. While his political commitment to country, comrades and party never wavered, his vision of an egalitarian future always included his wife with spaghetti and mince on the table and children playing in the peach trees of the Orlando West garden. As with all fantasies, the reality was rather different. By the time he came home, the young woman and tiny children he had left in 1962 had lived through banishment, bombings and solitary confinement. After her return to Orlando West in the mid-1980s, Winnie Mandela's sometimes controversial profile introduced strains into the relationship. After her husband's release from prison in 1990, these tensions became acute. In April 1992 Madiba announced his separation from his second wife: 'I shall personally never regret the life Comrade Nomzamo and I tried to share … I part from my wife with no recriminations. I embrace her with all the love and affection I have nursed for her inside and outside prison from the moment I first met her.'[246] The life that the Mandelas tried to share is undoubtedly one of Africa's great thwarted love stories. The couple deserved a great deal more spaghetti and mince than they were granted.

Brandfort-style Biltong

12½kg VENISON OR BEEF (FILLET OR RUMP)
550g FINE SALT
125ml BROWN SUGAR
30ml BICARBONATE OF SODA
10ml BLACK PEPPER, GROUND
125ml CORIANDER SEED, COARSELY GROUND
250ml VINEGAR
2½ l WATER

Cut the meat along the muscle lines into long strips about 7–10cm thick. Ensure that there is some fat on each strip. Mix the salt, sugar, bicarbonate of soda, pepper and coriander, and then rub this combination into the meat pieces. Place the meat strips in layers and sprinkle one third of the vinegar over each layer. Set the meat aside in a cool place for two days. Mix the remaining two-thirds of the vinegar with the water and dip the biltong into it, then remove the strips of meat from the vinegar mixture and hang them on S-shaped butcher's hooks in a cool, dry, well-ventilated place. Do not hang the meat too close together as air must be able to circulate around it. Leave the meat strips to dry for 2 weeks.

Chapter Nine

POLLSMOOR AND THE BUZZING BEES

ON 31 MARCH 1982 Madiba, Walter Sisulu, Raymond Mhlaba and Andrew Mlangeni were transferred from Robben Island to Pollsmoor Prison in Cape Town.

While no reason was given for the move, it seems likely that it was made in response to the increasing pressure of local and international anti-apartheid forces centred on the recently formed Free Mandela Campaign.

Soon after Madiba arrived at Pollsmoor, a broad alliance of mass-based civil society groups (including trade unions, civic structures, religious and youth organisations with the unstated but ever-present collaboration of the ANC in exile and underground ANC cadres) formed themselves into the United Democratic Front (UDF), which immediately began calling for 'the release of our leaders'. Unbeknown to the anti-apartheid forces there were rumblings of uncertainty in the belly of the government beast. Those who had previously provided unequivocal support to the South African regime were beginning to reconsider their attitude towards Madiba's continued incarceration. And their wavering stance was being expressed at the highest levels of state. François Ferreira was a chef in then President P.W. Botha's kitchen. 'I remember a dinner for Henry Kissinger. It was 1982 or '83. And of course everyone in the kitchen knows everything that happens at the table. One of the conversations went about Mr Mandela, which I picked up on because those who were serving at the table were talking about what they had overheard.

They were talking about Kissinger and mimicking the way he spoke, and apparently Mr Botha was not very courteous when he tried to raise the subject of Mandela. Every time he tried to raise it Mr Botha just said "Mm, mm, mm" and wouldn't talk … I made very traditional food that night because Mrs Botha liked to entertain in a manner very like an Afrikaans family inviting people for dinner – that type of meal. So there were roasts, sweet pumpkin and malva pudding: traditional, with a bit of a twist but not too much of a twist.'[247]

SPAGHETTI AND DREAMS

In superficial terms the conditions at Pollsmoor were much improved when compared with Robben Island. Certainly the quality of the food was better. In place of *pap* and *phuzamandla*, there were hearty plates of nourishing, if institutional-style, stews with vegetables. Although Madiba had been an A Category prisoner since the mid-1970s, the move off the Island enabled him to purchase a much broader selection of food and toiletries. Living conditions were more spacious and there was easier access to newspapers. All the same he complained that his new cell felt more confining and that he missed the open spaces and wildness of the Island.

OPPOSITE: ZINDZI MANDELA ADDRESSES A RALLY ON BEHALF OF HER FATHER, JABULANI STADIUM, 1985
© Morris Zwi

ELIZE BOTHA'S

Malva Pudding

{as supplied by François Ferreira}

Cake

1 EGG
250ml SUGAR
15ml SMOOTH APRICOT JAM
250ml CAKE FLOUR
5ml BICARBONATE OF SODA
GENEROUS PINCH OF SALT
15ml BUTTER
5ml VINEGAR
125ml MILK
125ml CREAM

Preheat the oven to 180°C. Beat the egg, sugar and jam together to a creamy consistency (about 15 minutes). Sift the flour, bicarbonate of soda and salt into a bowl. Melt the butter and add vinegar. Add the milk and cream to the egg mixture and beat well. Add the flour and then slowly add vinegar and butter beating well after each addition. Pour the batter into a dish about 20cm in diameter, cover with foil and bake for 45 minutes to 1 hour. The pudding is cooked when it is a consistent, rich brown colour. If it is still pale in the centre on top, it will need a little longer.

Sauce

250ml MILK
250ml CREAM
180g BUTTER
250ml SUGAR
125ml HOT WATER

Melt all the sauce ingredients together and pour over the pudding as it comes out of the oven. If you re-heat the pudding and it is slightly dry, pour over a little boiling water.

In retrospect it seems likely that the sense of claustrophobia derived, at least in part, from an awareness that the seeds planted at Rivonia were finally beginning to bear fruit. From 1982, Madiba was frustrated by the sense that he was trapped in the cocoon of Pollsmoor while the rest of South Africa was undergoing a period of rapid change and turmoil. Whatever the cause of the unease, his love letters to his wife, always passionate and full of concern, increasingly focused not on memories of past meals and happier times, but rather on fantasies about a possible home-coming. The letters of this time are filled with very specific requests for what should be on the table for his welcome-home feast. Once again, his love of domesticity is apparent and food metaphors are everywhere. In a letter written to his wife in 1986 he dreamt about release in the following way: 'If I don't get your spaghetti and mince when I return some day I will dissolve the marriage on the spot.'[248]

Writing to his old student friend Ismail Meer in 1985, Madiba seemed full of optimism that their struggle, though hard fought, would be ultimately successful. 'As I watch the world ageing, scenes from my younger days … come back so vividly, as if they occurred only the other day. Prodding endlessly on text books, travelling to and from Milner Park [Wits University], indulging in a bit of agitation, now on opposite sides and now together, some thoughts, some fruitless polemics, kept me going throughout those lean years by a litany of dreams and expectations. Some of which have been realized, while the fulfillment of others still elude us to this day. Nevertheless, few people will deny that the harvest has merely been delayed, but far from destroyed. It is out there, our rich and well-watered fields,

even though the actual task of gathering it has proved far more testing than we ever thought.'[249]

Amid the dreams of a ripening harvest that would culminate in a spaghetti-laden home-coming, there were clearly anxieties about the problems of readjustment that might accompany such a return. Throughout the 1970s and 1980s Madiba was issued with a desk diary such as one might use to record appointments in the outside world. Prisoners have few appointments and Madiba began to use his calendar to record his dreams – dreams which give clues to the inner turmoil and anxieties of a man cut off from his family. On 2 October 1982 he had what appears to be an anxiety dream about the state of his marriage: 'dreamt Zami [Winnie] and I were eating from one dish. After only a few spoons I left to attend to some urgent business, hoping to return soon and continue eating. Alas, I was delayed for several hours and became acutely worried as to Zami's reaction.'[250]

WORMS IN THE BRINJALS

In order to counteract the claustrophobic atmosphere of Pollsmoor, Madiba requested that he be given space to plant a roof garden. Ahmed Kathrada, who joined the other four prisoners seven months after their arrival at Pollsmoor, recalled: 'It was tough to persuade them to give us a garden. Only Madiba could do that. It was three floors up and only concrete. So Madiba got them to cut metal oil drums horizontally and the poor common-law prisoners had to cart soil up three floors.'[251]

In 1982 Christo Brand, a warder who had worked in B Section on Robben Island, got married and applied for a transfer to

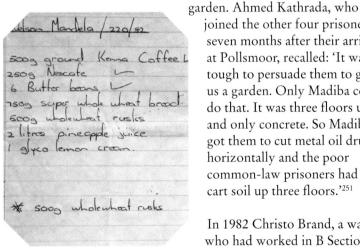

MADIBA'S FOOD REQUESTS, POLLSMOOR PRISON

the mainland so that his new wife Estelle could continue to work in Cape Town. Thus it was that the young warder arrived at Pollsmoor in the same week as the Rivonia trialists. Of the roof garden's beginning he remembered: 'The roof garden was thirty 44-gallon drums that were cut in half and placed next to each other with bricks underneath so water can drain and they don't rock around. Mr Mandela and Mr Sisulu mixed the soil with such gentle care.'[252]

As on Robben Island, not all the gardening was a success. According to Christo Brand: 'At first some of the plants got damaged by the south-easter, so later we put a net on the side to protect the seedlings. In the evenings when they went to the cell I used to hang up the net. Mealies weren't a hundred per cent successful – because the drums were too small. Tomatoes, onions worked well. But he loved his spinach and that purple spinach. Once he tried beans but there was a worm that cut off the beans as they came out. I took him strawberry plants and we made holes in the side so they could hang out. Then one year lice attacked the garden – especially, what do you call those purple fruit? Brinjals [aubergines]. The plant lice attacked them.'

Even when the agricultural endeavours were unsuccessful, the vegetable garden was of huge psychological significance to Madiba. 'When he got out of the cell in the morning, always he first goes to the garden – even if he just looks around here and touch there. Then he has breakfast. Always to the garden, first thing. And in the afternoons he was always busy in the garden and he talks to those

plants, and one day I laughed at him and teased him for that, but he told me, "You must talk to your plants so that they will grow and give you fruit."'

Despite the set-backs, there were moments that culminated in culinary triumph. As Christo Brand recalled: 'Other years the brinjals were very nice – he grew them and when he harvested them, we sent them to the kitchen. And when he harvested things he would send word to this prisoner who worked in the kitchen, Louw. When he got these messages, Louw would keep their meat back that day and then the next night he would put all that extra meat into their stew, big pot of stew, and put it with the vegetables Mandela had sent. And that lovely stew would be sent up full of vegetables – so much that Mandela said Warrant Officer Terreblanche and I, we must also taste. So we shared.'

HOT PLATES AND RUGBY

Inflexible prison routines remained an irritation. Evening meals would be delivered in the late afternoon and were consequently cold by the time that Madiba and his comrades came to eat them. Though the prisoners developed creative ways of warming their food, these were not without problems.

Christo Brand became desperate for a solution. 'I was in charge of the section, and what troubled me a lot was that every month you must get a new urn – because the food would arrive in the afternoon, and in the evenings Mr Mandela and the others would lift up the lid of the urn and put their plates in – so as to use it like a hot plate to warm the food. And it's not a hot plate, it's an urn, so the element must then constantly heat up to boiling, and because of that it was constantly burning out. Every month I had to apply for a new element. So I said to them, "You must get a hot plate." And Mandela said, "What's a hot plate?" so I explained to him what is a hot plate. And he said he had never heard of such a thing in his life but it sounded like a good idea. So Mandela sent in an official request for a hot plate but it was not approved, and all his attempts to appeal to Brigadier Munro and then General Willemse were also refused. But now Mandela was determined. When Mr Mandela visited Kobie Coetsee, he also requested a hot plate there. But even then, this was also not approved. And anyway the hot plate can't come to light, no one wants to approve it. Everyone says, "It's against prison regulations for prisoners to have a hot plate." Then one day I said to Mandela, "Major Van Sittert, he's back from leave and he don't know about the hot plate stories and how it has been refused. Approach him and ask again." But I explained to Mandela, "Van Sittert, he's a rugby fan. All what Van Sittert can speak is rugby." Then Van Sittert comes for an inspection of the section and when he comes to Mandela, Mandela says, "I am wanting to discuss Saturday's rugby game," and Van Sittert said, "So are you also liking rugby?" and Mandela said, "Of course, especially Saturday's game." And Mandela had read

CHRISTO BRAND

the papers and done some research, I'm sure of that. And Van Sittert was so mad about rugby that he sat down, and while they are talking about rugby Mandela says, "Man, I've got one problem. While I am watching my rugby I want hot food and my food is cold. I need a hot plate." And Van Sittert said, "Of course. Brand, why didn't you buy the man a hot plate?" and I said, "I need it approved in writing," so he wrote a written approval. That same day, I go to reception, get the money and buy the hot plate and put it in Mandela's cell. And immediately Kathrada and all the others put in requests and they were also approved. And then the hot plates were there.'

ORDERING IN POLLSMOOR STYLE

While Farida Omar had managed to smuggle a single banana on to Robben Island in 1979, it was at Pollsmoor in the 1980s that the smuggling of food into the prison came of age thanks to the combined ingenuity of Enver Matthews and the Omars. Ahmed Kathrada began the process. 'Enver Matthews was a friend of mine from school days. He lived in Cape Town – he was not allowed to see me when we were on the Island, but at Pollsmoor he could and he began smuggling food to us very successfully. Anything we liked. And Dullah, he was smuggling Farida Omar's *samoosas*, *rotis* and curries to us – by the end he would come in with a big bag of food, not books, in that briefcase. When

I came out of prison, people said, "What do you want to eat? You can have anything you like," and I said, "I've had everything at Pollsmoor."'[253]

MRS BRAND AND THE CAKES

Despite his many years of prison food austerity Madiba retained a fondness for sweet tastes. So it was that Christo Brand's wife's Christmas cakes were very enthusiastically received.

Estelle Brand recalled that the cake-giving began by accident. 'In 1984 I bought a microwave oven and with the oven I received five free lessons on how to make food in the microwave … So I started to make the fruit-cake and fudge and all these things in the microwave and so I see that this cake is lovely, and I still have that same microwave.'[254]

Her husband was so proud of his wife's new-found culinary talents that 'in 1985 in the cells Mandela gave me some fruit-cake that he had bought with his money but I said, "Mandela, your fruit-cake is not nice. It's too dry. My wife makes nicer fruit-cake. I will bring you some." And when I did he loved it, they all did, even Mr Kathrada, and then they all wanted her to make that fruit-cake for them. And I said, "I will make a plan that you can buy the cakes from her," because nothing was allowed in without a receipt. Now remember, only 500g was allowed into Pollsmoor and this cake is about 2kg. So I booked it in at 500g. And I remember I charged it as R18 for a fruit-cake. And all of them were buying and wanting this fruit-cake.'

The Christmas cake giving has withstood the political transition and is still a favourite of the former Pollsmoor inmates. The affection in Ahmed Kathrada's voice shone through as he recalled: 'When we were in jail Mrs Brand used to make me that cake every Christmas – a cake that she starts in October – I don't know what is the process – but since the mid-'80s, every year there has been cake. And then even when we got to Parliament she still baked it for me – but now it's twice a year. On my birthday too! And biscuits. She doesn't fail.' For the record, Mrs Brand said the biscuits she makes are Hertzog cookies.

CHILDREN, CHIPS AND CHOCOLATES

By 1983 Madiba was permitted five visits a month (which was considerably more than the two visits a year that he had been entitled to in 1964). As a result of a hunger strike that took place on Robben Island after he left, the rules pertaining to visits by children under 16 had been relaxed across the prison system and visits from his grandchildren became frequent.

As Christo Brand noted: 'After 1983 he was allowed to receive his grandchildren, and then with his monthly groceries he always bought some sweets and always he had them in his pockets when children came. But they were not allowed to take away the sweets; they must eat them there. But he had always chocolates and sweets.'[255]

Certain young members of the Mandela family were bursting with sweets even before they got to the prison. Mandlesizwe Mandela (now Nkosi Zwelivelile) said of his first visit to Pollsmoor in 1983: 'I was 9 when I went with my step-grandmother, Winnie. I had met her for the first time in Brandfort the night before – you see, she was still banned to Brandfort, and up until then I had known only Evelyn and my mother's mother as my grandmothers. It was a Friday night and I had driven from Soweto with Aunt Zindzi, and when I first met her I was thinking, "Who are these people?" and she gave me a lot of chocolates – I think she picked that habit up from my grandfather. And the following day at about

ESTELLE BRAND'S

Christmas Cake

500g MIXED FRUIT
250g DATES FINELY CHOPPED
100g GLACE FRUIT
1 CUP DARK BROWN SUGAR
130g BUTTER OR MARGARINE, CHOPPED INTO SMALL SLIVERS
1 CUP COFFEE (250ml HOT WATER AND 2 TEASPOONS NESCAFÉ)
1 TEASPOON BICARBONATE OF SODA
2 CUPS CAKE FLOUR
½ TEASPOON BAKING POWDER
½ TEASPOON MIXED SPICE
½ TEASPOON GINGER
½ TEASPOON CINNAMON
1 PINCH OF SALT
2 EGGS
8 GLACÉ CHERRIES, HALVED
3 TABLESPOONS BRANDY

Put the butter, sugar, mixed fruit, dates, glacé fruit and coffee into a bowl and microwave for 5 minutes on full power. When it comes out of microwave, add the bicarbonate of soda and let the mixture stand for 5 minutes. In a separate bowl, sift the flour, baking powder, all the spices and salt, and then fold this into the dried fruit, coffee, bicarbonate of soda and butter mixture. Beat in the 2 eggs and fold in 8 glacé cherries and mix well. Line the base of a microwavable bowl with baking paper and grease the sides with butter. Tip the cake batter into the prepared bowl. The bowl must be approximately three-quarters full because the cake will rise about a quarter. Bake at medium to low power for 32 minutes. (Mrs Brand said: 'Because ours is an old microwave and the power is weak at night – the original recipe says 30.') When it comes out of the microwave, put the brandy over the top immediately, then leave it to cool for a few minutes. Once you can touch the sides of the dish, turn it out on to a rack. Once the cake is cold, wrap it in foil and every second week add a further 3 tablespoons of brandy. Mrs Brand said that it is important to make the cake on the first of October so that it can have long enough to get moist and brandy-laden by the Christmas season.

four am we woke up and drove to Bloemfontein and we caught a flight to Cape Town, and when we got to Pollsmoor Prison, we met with my grandfather, but he was then too caught up in seeing Winnie and he didn't notice I was there, and they started chatting for a while, and then he said, "So where is he?" and I was sitting in the corner and with these two strangers, and they were trying to convince me that they were my grandparents. My grandfather was inquisitive about me. He wanted to know, "Are you a boxer?" But I said I was a soccer player and so it came about that he sent me soccer boots, Patrick's. My first pair of soccer boots, Patrick's, was bought from Pollsmoor.'[256]

Farida Omar recollected an occasion when 'Mandla Mandela was coming to see his grandfather. And Mandla was a little, little boy. Dullah was away but he phoned me to say, "Mandla is coming tonight – fetch him from the airport." So I went to fetch him and I knew immediately as he came off the plane that this must be a Mandela child. So I went up to him and I said, "I'm Aunty Farida, I'm coming to fetch you." And Mandla said "okay". But as we were waiting for his luggage a security policeman came up to me and said, "Are you fetching Mandla?" and I thought, Oh my God, it's the Security Branch and I'm only one and I'm alone with this child. And I could see they were following the car all the way home. But we got home and I gave him some nice things to eat and I said to him, "Tomorrow when you go to your grandfather, you must take this parcel of *samoosas*, *roti* and chicken curry and some fruit." Next morning, Sunday morning, I took Mandla through to the prison and we went into the waiting room. It was a very hot day in February, and then the policeman said, "You can both go in now," because the policeman didn't know that I didn't have a visit – only Mandla was supposed to go in. And we walked there (with me praying the whole way

that they wouldn't throw me out). I remember that when we arrived at the visiting room, there was Mr Mandela and he had a chocolate and packet of chips for his grandson. And he was holding them out for the child. And I brazenly followed Mandla in and he said, "Farida, how lovely to see you." He recognised me from the photos because I was in the papers with the Detainees Parents' Support Committee. And then the police realised their mistake and took me out, but before I left I made sure the policeman gave him his parcel of *samoosas* and curry. And then Mandla had his visit and I sat in the waiting room and I was so scared because what had happened was a breach of security and I was so worried about what would happen next – and there was nothing to read in the waiting room and I only had a comb and lipstick in my bag – so I combed my hair and put on lots of lipstick and eventually Mandla came out and there were no repercussions and Mr Mandela got his *samoosas*.'[257]

THE POWER OF PEANUTS

In March 1985 Madiba was diagnosed with an enlarged prostate and he was immediately scheduled for surgery. He left Ahmed Kathrada in charge of the Pollsmoor roof garden with 'two pages of detailed written instructions'.[258] Under Kathrada's care, a bumper beetroot and leek crop was marred by what the agricultural understudy acknowledged as 'shamefully poor tomatoes and cucumbers'.

At Volks Hospital, in Cape Town, the fruits of freedom were faring better than those of the tomato plants. The day before Madiba was scheduled for surgery, Winnie Mandela flew to Cape Town and found herself on the same plane as the Minister of Justice, Kobie Coetsee. Despite the fact that he had signed her banishment order, he was relatively well disposed towards her because of her dinners with his Brandfort friend Piet de Waal. Though he had a business class seat and she

FARIDA OMAR IN HER CAPE TOWN KITCHEN, 2007

an economy ticket, Winnie Mandela insisted on sitting next to him. Over airplane peanuts she so charmed the Minister that he undertook to visit her husband in hospital. Though the ensuing bedside meeting produced no concrete results, it was a clear indication to Madiba that there were elements in the National Party that were not opposed to the possibility of negotiations with the ANC.

What followed suggests that the Minister of Justice also understood that their bedside cup of tea was of enormous significance. Upon recovery Madiba was not returned to the roof-top cell but rather moved to a set of separate cells, away from the other political prisoners. While his new ground-floor rooms granted him the first real privacy he had known in nearly three decades, they were also isolating as he had to apply for permission to see his comrades, who now lived three floors

above him, and he couldn't get to the roof garden which he had so carefully nurtured. No official explanation has ever been offered for Madiba's move, but since prisons were the responsibility of Minister Coetsee, it seems likely that he separated the Pollsmoor five in order to cultivate a relationship with Madiba.

From the isolation of his new cell Madiba began to brood on the danger that the escalating violence across South Africa posed to his dream of a post-apartheid future. In July 1985 the government declared a state of emergency which gave the security forces unprecedented powers. The townships came under virtual police occupation and a series of military raids by the South African army on ANC safe houses in Lusaka, Harare and Gaborone resulted in considerable loss of life. After an intransigent speech by President P.W. Botha,

FARIDA OMAR'S

Chicken Curry

3 CARDAMOM PODS
1 PIECE CINNAMON
4 CLOVES
2 ONIONS SLICED THIN
3 TABLESPOONS SUNFLOWER OIL
1 TABLESPOON BUTTER
2 BIG TOMATOES GRATED
1 TABLESPOON TOMATO PASTE
2 TEASPOONS CRUSHED GARLIC
1 WHOLE CHICKEN, PORTIONED
AND SKINNED
1 CHUNK OF GRATED GINGER 2cm
3 TEASPOONS *DHANIA* POWDER
2 TEASPOONS CUMIN POWDER
1–2 TEASPOONS CHILLI POWDER
½ TEASPOON TURMERIC POWDER ON
THE CHICKEN
8–10 SMALL POTATOES, PEELED
AND QUARTERED

Heat the oil. Fry the cardamom, cinnamon and cloves in the oil until they release their aroma. Add the butter and the onions, and fry until translucent. Add the grated tomato, tomato paste and garlic, and cook over a low heat to form a thick sauce. When you see the oil coming to the top of the sauce, add the chicken pieces, ginger, dhania, cumin, chilli and turmeric. Braise the chicken curry with 1½ cups of boiling water until the chicken is cooked through, approximately 20 minutes. When the chicken is cooked, add the potatoes and continue to cook the stew until the potatoes are very soft, about 20 minutes. Serve with roti.

the economy went into significant decline when overseas banks refused to renew loans, and the increasingly intense application of cultural, sporting, political and economic sanctions began to sap the morale of the government and its supporters.

It was in this context that Madiba wrote to Coetsee with a view to establishing exploratory talks. Christo Brand remembered that in 1985, after several unanswered letters, 'when Mandela was in his own cell away from the others, I was told that I had to go straight away and give him a message that Kobie Coetsee was coming to see him. I was at home when the message came and my wife was out, so I took my young son Riaan with me. He was a baby really, not yet a boy, and when my son came into the cell Mr Mandela moved towards him because he always likes to be with children and there had never been one in his cell before – only in the visiting room. But Riaan was afraid of him and he hid behind me, so Mandela went to his cabinet and took out some sweets – liquorice I think – and he wanted those sweets, so he came forward, and after that he wasn't afraid to go there. He wanted to go there.'[259]

FOOD TOURISM AROUND THE FAIREST CAPE

In January 1985 P.W. Botha told Parliament that he would release Madiba from prison provided he 'unconditionally rejected violence as a political instrument'. The offer was rejected by Madiba who, in a speech read on his behalf by his daughter Zindzi Mandela at Jabulani Stadium in Soweto, reasserted his commitment to the existing policies of the ANC and insisted that it was Botha who must renounce violence by dismantling the apartheid state. Before a crowd of twenty thousand she announced: 'My father says: "Prisoners do not make contracts with their jailers. I cannot and will not give any undertaking at a time when I and you

the people are not free. Your freedom and mine cannot be separated. I will return."'[260]

While an impasse appeared to exist in the public domain, behind the scenes the negotiation table was being laid. From September 1985 there were a series of extraordinary walk-abouts when prison warders took Madiba out of jail. Each of these outings was accompanied by food. From grapes in a vineyard to beach-front fish and chips, the significance of these occasions has been long underestimated. When Christo Brand was questioned about them, he said that they were part of standard prison procedure aimed at re-assimilating long-serving prisoners prior to their release. Yet in 1985 there was no public indication that Madiba's release was imminent.

At that time, there seems to have been a struggle for hegemony within the National Party. There was a significant conservative faction that would not countenance release and yet the prison warders who supervised these extraordinary day trips were not acting on an individual whim. The trips into the outside world were authorised by the prison authorities, who, in turn, reported to the Ministry of Justice. The lack of a clear direction is evident in the fact that in the same month that Madiba went on his first secret day trip out of Pollsmoor in 1985, the UDF organised a protest march to the prison demanding his release, and 31 protesters were injured. In his 1996 statement to the Truth and Reconciliation Commission, Sheikh Abdul Hamied Gabier testified that 'nobody was spared from the violence of the police; children, women and old people were all beaten and those who were part of the march had to run for their lives'.[261] This act of extreme state violence against unarmed protesters resulted in a currency crash and the destruction of what little was left of international investor confidence.

With every fizzy drink that Madiba consumed and every visit to a beach-front restaurant where he ate with prison warders, the changing power balance among the various factions of the National Party became more apparent. Of these trips Christo Brand recollected: 'The first day we just went outside Pollsmoor's gate and then you turn right and then right again and you are in a vineyard; the golf course is built there today. So we stopped the car there and let him walk through the vineyard alone and he picked some grapes and he even took a few bunches back to the prison. The second trip, me and Brigadier Booysen, we took him to Pollsmoor dam and let him walk there on the dam. There were children there catching fish, so Mandela walked to them, he greeted them, and at the end of the time Mandela was standing there with a fishing rod, talking to the children. And we just stood at a distance and then he came back on his own after a while. And he said, "Those lovely kids are enjoying themselves," but he was very worried for them all alone by this dam. But we said he mustn't worry, they can swim.'[262]

On 24 December 1985, Madiba was taken by Colonel Gawie Marx on a drive around the Cape Peninsula. On the way back to Pollsmoor they stopped at a café to buy Coca-Colas and Madiba was left in the unlocked car. He later recalled that the temptation to run was extreme, modified only by the suspicion that this could be a set-up and that to attempt an escape would play into the enemy's hands.

In June 1986 there was a visit with warder James Gregory and his son Brent to the Hex River mountains in which the car was delayed by a traffic jam caused by a mudslide. The boredom of the traffic jam caused Brent to volunteer to walk to a nearby shop to buy fish and chips which everyone, Madiba included, ate from the newspaper wrapping.

And still the confusion in the government's policy was apparent. Even while Officer James Gregory was sharing chips with Madiba the June 1986 state of emergency, with harsh and wide-ranging powers, was declared. In the first week of its operation there were so many arrests in Port Elizabeth that the police ran out of prison cell space and resorted to using warehouse facilities, designed for storing beer, as a detention centre.[263]

Later, there were other outings, after Madiba had been transferred to Victor Verster Prison in Paarl. Warder Jack Swart said: 'We were given orders that whenever he goes to the doctor, we can take him wherever he wants to go in the Western Cape after the doctor. He asked once to go to Hout Bay, and when we got there he asked for crayfish, so we drove to the Harbour Café and he bought crayfish for himself and for me and Gregory too – with his money – because he said he had last eaten crayfish on Robben Island.'[264]

Some trips were less successful social events. 'We went to Saldanha and we passed land that was full of a plant that in Afrikaans is called *kafferwaatlemoen* [watermelon with green flesh]. And he said, "What are those?" so I told him and immediately he got upset. You never see Mandela angry, he just sort of makes irritated little snorty sounds like *mmph*, *mmph*, *mmph*. So I said to Gregory who was driving, "What are they called in English because he's cross for the word *kaffer*," but Gregory said there is no English word for a *kafferwaatlemoen*. I know now it's called a *makatane*, but I don't think that's an English word either.'

The warders were undoubtedly performing their duty in reacclimatising their prisoner to the outside world. The question that needs to be answered is: who was considering his release?

even while officer Gregory was sharing
chips with Madiba, a state of emergency
was declared

SANDWICHES AND NATIONAL INTELLIGENCE

In 1987, after several private meetings, Coetsee suggested to Madiba that they widen their discussions to include the National Intelligence Service's Niël Barnard and the Commissioner of Prisons, General Willemse. Such a meeting upped the stakes considerably because Niël Barnard was a close ally of P.W. Botha. Madiba insisted therefore on meeting with his Pollsmoor colleagues, and after some robust discussions it was decided that he should continue to participate in such exploratory talks.

Despite the banning of the UDF in February 1988, weekly meetings were held at the Officers' Club in the Pollsmoor complex from May of that year. Niël Barnard later claimed that he 'was moved to see Mandela relishing the sandwiches. I felt deep down a sense of sympathy for this man in prison overalls and boots. And he was thin.'[265] Barnard described the meetings as an attempt to establish 'how Mandela's head worked' on a diverse spectrum of issues, ranging from economic policy through to definitions of war criminals.

Barnard initiated a series of meetings with the ANC in exile. One of the better-known is that which took place in Dakar, Senegal, in 1987 between about 50 Afrikaner intellectuals and representatives of the ANC. But already in the previous year Barnard had facilitated a meeting between Thabo Mbeki and the chairman of the Broederbond, Professor Pieter De

Lange, at a Fifth Avenue hotel in New York. After several hours of political discussion, the pair was joined by De Lange's wife Christine for dinner. Mrs De Lange chided the ANC leader for ordering fish and chips when there were several healthier options on the menu. During the course of the meal, Mbeki told her that she was the first Afrikaner woman he had ever had dinner with. Though this may not have been true, it seems to have made the De Langes feel the significance of their role in history. Over coffee De Lange declared that he would henceforth dedicate his life to racial reconciliation. He went home to South Africa, resigned from his job as the Rector of the Rand Afrikaans University, urged President P.W. Botha to release Nelson Mandela and told his Broederbond colleagues that 'the greatest risk for us as Afrikaners is to take no risk at all'.[266]

For all the progress, the National Party still insisted on three conditions that were impossible for Madiba and the broader ANC to accept: that the ANC must renounce the armed struggle, break its alliance with the Communist Party and abandon its commitment to majority rule. A letter from Ahmed Kathrada from this time reveals how very far the prison authorities still had to go and the minuscule nature of the concessions that were being made. Kathrada wrote of a visit to Madiba's cell on New Year's Day 1987: 'We were served tasty snacks in the mess and even had tea in tea cups! When one is used to metal utensils for almost 23 years it was not without nervousness that I handled a cup and saucer.'[267]

CONSTANTIABERG AND THE
ACTIVE HIVE

In July 1988, Madiba was diagnosed with tuberculosis and was taken to Tygerberg Hospital in Bellville. After six weeks he was transferred to the Constantiaberg Medi-Clinic in the southern suburbs of Cape Town, becoming the first black patient ever to be admitted to the hospital. On his first morning there, he was visited by Kobie Coetsee and Pollsmoor's Deputy Commander, Major Marais.

Fiona Reed (née Duncan) was a 20-year-old nurse at the time. 'He was with us at Constantiaberg for nearly four months. We weren't told who was coming – they just asked four of us to look after this mystery person. I had no idea he would be a prisoner. I was expecting maybe a president. I think they chose the four of us because we were the most apolitical girls they could find in the whole hospital. The security called us in beforehand and told us that the security police had everything on us and our families. So we weren't to try anything funny. I asked them a couple of questions just to test how much they knew, but they really did know everything and it was quite scary.'

While the nurses came to love their patient, their initial reaction was one of fright. Reed recalled: 'At school I had only been taught that he was a terrorist and a man to be feared and of course no one knew what he looked like at that time. But on my first meeting with him I walked into his room and I just froze because, even though there had been no pictures for so long, I instantly knew exactly who he was and I had no idea what to do. But he

FIONA REED (NÉE DUNCAN), 2007

just approached me and took both my hands and he said, "I know you and I are going to be good friends," and I just stood stock still, I didn't know what to do or say. But he was right, we did become the best of friends. And often during that time friends would say to me, "How can you care for a man like that? Don't you know what he's done?" and I just wouldn't talk about it because I knew they couldn't understand. I became very protective of him.'

While Fiona Reed and her colleagues saw Kobie Coetsee and Niël Barnard come and go from their patient's room several times, they had no idea that they were witnessing the beginnings of a significant political transition. They were aware, however, that their patient had been cut off from the outside world for many years and that he was desperate to find out about modern social mores. 'He would ask us about our lives in great detail and he was like a sponge because I think he needed to learn about all the things he had missed out on and learn how it was today. He was like a grandfather with us so he would chat about everything with us: food, fashion, make-up, everything. He loved to learn about what happened when you went out at night, how etiquette worked – basic youth etiquette left him dumbfounded. He didn't understand why men didn't open doors for women … When we went on dates, the next day he would always say, "Where did you go, what did you eat, why did you want to go there?" So he knew all about my friends and so forth. He's a great listener and he was just learning, gleaning information about what was happening outside.'

Madiba's curiosity about the world outside prison was most

CONSTANTIABERG

Chocolate Mousse

{in 1988 Fedics Food Services ran the Constantiaberg kitchen and Sue Glanville was the catering manager. The Fedics chocolate mousse recipe in 1988 is as follows}

MAKES 8 SERVINGS
500ml FRESH CREAM
4 LARGE EGG YOLKS
3 TABLESPOONS CASTOR SUGAR
1 TEASPOON VANILLA ESSENCE
200g DARK CHOCOLATE

Whisk together the egg yolks and the sugar until they are light and fluffy. Add the warm cream to the egg yolk mixture, and whisk. Place the egg, sugar and cream mixture on a low heat and stir constantly to make a custard. Add the vanilla essence. Melt the chocolate. Whisk the custard mixture into the melted chocolate and then let the chocolate and custard cool. Whisk the remaining cream to soft peaks and fold it into the chocolate mixture. Portion the mousse into your serving containers and let cool and set.

acute in matters culinary. 'We used to talk to him about food and what we had eaten on dates and he was so curious about it all. We managed to sneak in chocolate mousse and a couple of pizzas, which he had never had before. He wanted to try them because we were all raving about them. The rules around food were quite strict and all of his food was tested and tasted by the guards, but eventually as time went on we used to sneak in all sorts of things – because he hadn't experimented with food at all – he had only known prison food for the last 25 years. So we used to give him all sorts of exotic stuff.'

Madiba's experiments in the culinary habits of the youth were not terribly successful. 'He wasn't wild about the pizza. He likes his food to be really good quality but he doesn't like it to be too rich. And when we offered him a hamburger, he was intrigued to learn that you could have avocado on it, so he tried that – but again he wasn't wild about it – I don't think he would have ordered it again. We used to give him all these forbidden things because he really wanted to get back into the groove and see what the modern world was eating.'

In addition to the food that they brought up from the canteen there were gourmet gifts that the nurses brought. Madiba's desk diary of 11 September 1988 reads: 'Sister Marlene Vorster brings chocolate cake.'

The young nurses became so comfortable with their patient that they tried to take him to the staff Christmas party. Fiona Reed recalled: 'At the beginning of December we always had a big Christmas party that the matron organised and there would be a bar and music and all the staff were allowed to take our partners. And we thought we would spice it up by taking him along. We

didn't think about the implications of it; we just asked him and he loves a party, he really does, so he was very keen to go. He's so social and he really wanted to go. The party was to be held in the canteen. And we were so innocent that we genuinely thought they would let us take him along. He'd been there three and a half months – what was the big deal? But then James Gregory said no. And after that Mr Mandela went on and on and on and on and on at James Gregory because he really wanted to go to the party. He's a huge socialite, so friendly, and he really wanted something Christmassy. And eventually we said: "We won't go down there to the party if he can't come, so let's have our own party up here." So we had turkey and ham and a Christmas pudding and we ate all together round the table and we had some crackers (which of course were checked and put back together again). We had a lovely time.'

Even in the hospital ward there were listening devices. Said Fiona Reed: 'He used to talk in metaphors because there were quite a few bugs in all the rooms. And he seemed to know when they were on. He would indicate to us by pointing to the roof that they were on. And one afternoon, after he had been there for about four months, he asked me if I was going to be back tomorrow and I said, "Definitely, I am working a seven to one shift," and he said to me, "The bees are buzzing, the activity in the hive is high," and I didn't get what he meant and it worried me. And the next morning he was gone – they took him at two in the morning out the back emergency exit and I didn't get to say goodbye to him. And after that I understood what he meant about the bees. He knew they were planning to take him away. And that's when he went to the prison in Paarl [Victor Verster].'[268]

1335/88: NELSON MANDELA   23·12·88

Dear Fiona,

I was really disappointed to leave the Instantiatery Medical Clinic without saying goodbye to you. I missed you even before I left the ward. I was, however, happy to see in a newspaper your photograph as you prepared that bed the morning after my departure.

It will probably inspire you to know that your colleagues at the Clinic and others, who came into contact with you during the last three months, believe that there is a lot of talent in you, and that you are easily one of those young ladies who can have the world at her feet. So give yourself the chance to live up to these expectations. For my own part I will always think of you as one of those inmates of your clinic who spared no effort to make me happy and comfortable. Fondest regards and best wishes.

Sincerely
N Mandela.

Sister Verslie Aiken,
Aurelie Bay X 6003,
PAARL SOUTH. 7620

THANK YOU LETTER TO NURSE FIONA REED (NÉE DUNCAN)

Chapter Ten

VICTOR VERSTER AND RIP VAN WINKLE IN THE KITCHEN

ON 9 DECEMBER 1988, MADIBA WAS REMOVED FROM CONSTANTIABERG MEDI-CLINIC and informed that, rather than going back to Pollsmoor, he was to be transferred to Paarl's Victor Verster Prison in the Cape winelands.

He arrived at his new 'home' to find that it was not a cell but a four-bedroomed, whitewashed warder's house in the prison grounds. The house was equipped with a stove, microwave, fridge, deep freeze, toaster and a personal chef in the form of Warrant Officer Jack Swart. Charming as the new set-up was, prison is prison – Warrant Officer James Gregory stood guard over a house that, like its garden, was riddled with listening devices.

Jack Swart and Madiba's paths had crossed before under less salubrious circumstances. When they were reintroduced at Victor Verster, Swart reminded Madiba that in 1968 he had driven the truck that transported prisoners from the cells on Robben Island to the lime quarry. By his own admission, the experience had not been a happy one for the prisoners. 'I was 21 years old and I was a hell of a driver. I didn't think about what I was doing really. We had orders, from the head of the prison I think, to deliberately make it a little uncomfortable: to go fast over bumps and stop quick and swerve. I remember one day when I unloaded them, Mandela came to the window and he knocked on it and I wound it down and he asked me, "What the hell do you think we are

– bags of mealies?" but I didn't pay any attention then, I just rolled up the window of the truck and continued driving the same way. I thought to myself, Oh shut up, don't complain, don't tell me how to do my job. You see, we didn't know what political prisoners were. We just thought if you were a prisoner you had done something bad. Years later when I arrived at the house at Victor Verster to work, I told him this story and he said, "Oh, were you that driver? I hope you are a better cook than you were a driver!"'[269]

Since his days as a driver on Robben Island, Jack Swart had retrained within the prison catering division. By the time that he reconnected with Madiba he was 'running the Victor Verster officers' mess; the Coloured officers' mess and the white officers' mess and the shop and the two bars (one black bar and one white)'. Initially he was reluctant to take the position of Madiba's personal chef because 'it was horrible cooking they wanted me to do – he was on a special diet – high-protein, low-cholesterol diet. He came with that from Constantiaberg. So it was all sorts of things like haddock and fillet steak and things which were not usual for a prisoner. It was all measuring out 15g of

OPPOSITE: MANDLESIZWE MANDELA IN THE OMAR'S LOUNGE, 1988
© Rashid Lombard

this and 20g of that and you must put it in these big prison pots. And I was used to cooking for large numbers, so I had to learn how to cook for one person with a special diet.'

Despite his inexperience with the cooking style required, Swart showed himself to be considerably more conscientious and talented a cook than he had ever been a driver. Madiba's first breakfast in the new house was a slap-up meal of oatmeal, two fishcakes, a poached egg, homemade wholewheat toast and a pot of tea. The wholemeal bread was a huge hit with the prisoner. 'It's what we call in Afrikaans a *roer* bread, a stir bread. I took a basic recipe that my wife makes, but a friend of mine has a farm and I put wheat into the bread – not from the shops; wheat straight from that farm. The more wheat you put into it the more he likes it.' After this feast Madiba received his first visitor, Minister Kobie Coetsee, who brought him a house-warming present of a case of local wines. The incongruity of bringing house-warming presents to an imprisoned man seems to have been lost on the Minister.

MICROWAVABLE FUN IN RIP VAN WINKLE'S KITCHEN

Jack Swart discovered how very long two and a half decades is when he showed Madiba around his new kitchen. 'Everything in the kitchen, even the microwave oven, was something new to him. When he first came I showed him how to use it by taking a plastic cup with water in it and I put it in the microwave for one minute and then I asked him to touch it and he felt that it was very hot, and after that, when Walter Sisulu and Kathrada came, it was always the first trick he would show them, and he would laugh and enjoy that very much when they were surprised by the heat.'

The Victor Verster microwave took up where the Pollsmoor hot plate had left off: it meant that Madiba could be in control of the timing of his evening meal. According to Swart: 'I made him *umngqusho* – you know, samp and beans. I would make it in huge pots and then put it in the fridge in 400g portions, so at supper time he could just take one out. That was all he wanted at night – sometimes if he had had visitors he would add some leftovers but mainly just *umngqusho* … Anyway, he'd take out a packet in the evening and put it in the microwave oven and warm it, and I taught him that it's two minutes, and when the bell rings then he could take it out and eat it. This worked well except on a few occasions the power went out and the microwave had to be reset before you could use the thing. Then he'd phone me and he'd say that the oven has broken down. Then I would have to come down from home and reset the time on the microwave oven.'

While the microwave may have got the better of him, there were many other successful culinary encounters. Jack Swart's home-brewed *koringbier* (wheat beer) was a favourite recipe and the prisoner liked to to participate in its production. 'It was that same wheat as I got from my friend's farm for the bread and we made our own home brew. He helped me – with stirring and pouring off the liquid. You see, to make it you have to soak things and then pour off the liquid several times before you bottle it (you make a sort of a plant that causes it to ferment). You put the wheat and the water and sugar and raisins and stir and then you throw off the water and add more sugar and yeast and water and so on. He would pour off the water and put it through a sieve if I was busy making breakfast or something. He liked to call it "our home brew" because it was his job to throw off the water.'

FROM THE SOPRANOS TO SWEET WINE

Walter Sisulu worried about Madiba in his new prison home. When he visited the Victor Verster

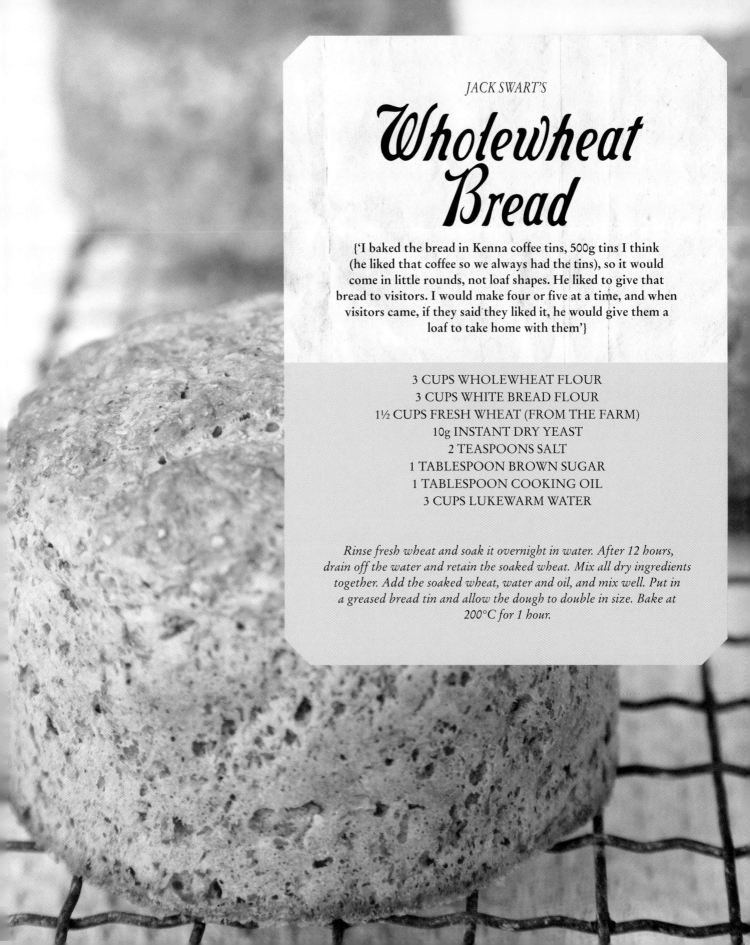

Wholewheat Bread

{'I baked the bread in Kenna coffee tins, 500g tins I think (he liked that coffee so we always had the tins), so it would come in little rounds, not loaf shapes. He liked to give that bread to visitors. I would make four or five at a time, and when visitors came, if they said they liked it, he would give them a loaf to take home with them'}

3 CUPS WHOLEWHEAT FLOUR
3 CUPS WHITE BREAD FLOUR
1½ CUPS FRESH WHEAT (FROM THE FARM)
10g INSTANT DRY YEAST
2 TEASPOONS SALT
1 TABLESPOON BROWN SUGAR
1 TABLESPOON COOKING OIL
3 CUPS LUKEWARM WATER

Rinse fresh wheat and soak it overnight in water. After 12 hours, drain off the water and retain the soaked wheat. Mix all dry ingredients together. Add the soaked wheat, water and oil, and mix well. Put in a greased bread tin and allow the dough to double in size. Bake at 200°C for 1 hour.

JACK SWART'S

Koringbier

(Wheat Beer)

1 CUP WHEAT
1 CUP BROWN SUGAR
6 CRUSHED RAISINS
¼ CUBE FRESH YEAST
½ *l* LUKEWARM WATER

*Soak the wheat in water for 24 hours, then strain the
wheat and discard the liquid. Combine the brown sugar, raisins,
and yeast with the lukewarm water and stir well until the
sugar dissolves. Cover the mixture with a lid and leave
for a further 24 hours. Sieve the contents and discard the
liquid. Set aside the 'plant' that you have created. The
plant is the fermenting agent for the beer. Add another cup
of brown sugar and another ½ litre of warm water to
the plant and stir well. Bottle the mixture and allow it to
rest for 24 hours. Pour off the liquid, retaining both the
liquid and the plant. The liquid can now be rebottled
and served as ice-cold koringbier. The plant can be re-used
at least another 5 times by adding more sugar and
warm water. Serve ice cold.*

house, he teased his friend about his 'five-star accommodation complete with room service'. At the same time he wrote to Connie Njongwe that 'we found him well though obviously lonely. How can it be otherwise when he talks only to prison warders? If we could be allowed to visit him more regularly it would make a bit of a difference.'[270]

Pleasant as the home brew and bread-baking was, the key question is, Why had the apartheid state moved the man who was by this time the world's most famous political prisoner into the house at Victor Verster? Zindzi Mandela offered the most plausible explanation. 'Victor Verster was very strange. It was almost like they were trying to create a new reality for the family, but we were very conscious that it was still a prison. I remember my father showing me around and saying this is so-and-so's room and this is so-and-so's room and me thinking, "No, it's absolutely not." For him he was so desperate for it to be a family environment, and for us it was not our reality. So it was very strange in that sense that for a few hours we could humour him and try and fit into his picture of this home environment, but the reality would be that as we left we would be going through the prison gates without him. I think the strategy at the time was that they were hoping the family would be able to move in with him there and then, and they would be able to start to compromise the legend that was Madiba. They were trying to reduce that martyr status, because if you think, he's – like – chilled behind bars, more like one of the Sopranos, you know, in prison running their own show, pampered whilst in prison. Also they were trying to create that separation between him and his comrades, but luckily because their relationship and loyalty was so strong, nothing could compromise their loyalty, dedication and commitment to the movement. Nothing could take that away.'[271]

Over time, a curious reversal took place in which the prison warders came to play butler to their prisoner's gracious host. George Bizos recalled an occasion on which he went to the house to consult with his client and 'three bottles of wine were brought out for me to choose from, and when I chose one he said, "George, you had better watch it – they know too much about you – I told them to buy a stein wine that I like because you were coming for lunch and they said, 'You know, Mr Mandela, Mr Bizos won't want the wine you are drinking.' And so I said, 'There's money in my account. You go and choose some bottles that you think Mr Bizos will like,' and you know, they even know what wine you drink, so you'd better be careful." Little did we know that when we took walks in the gardens in the hope of confidentiality that the flowerbeds were bugged.'[272]

Though the state failed to break the bonds between Madiba and his comrades, the house at Victor Verster clearly became extremely important to him. According to Zindzi Mandela: 'Swart was such a nice man, to the extent that if we wanted to sit in the house with my dad and the kids wanted to swim, he would go and watch them for us. His relationship with my dad was something else, and he made the stay at Victor Verster very special for my dad, to the extent that the house in Qunu is a duplication of that house and we all thought this was quite bizarre, but it was his first connection with an almost normal environment and that's why it was special to him.'[273]

TOO MUCH WASHING UP – EVEN FOR MADIBA

Jack Swart and Madiba had a companionable relationship. Madiba would leave notes on the stove as to what he would like to eat the following day. Their only point of contention was who would do the washing up. While Madiba insisted that this should be his domestic contribution, Swart attempted to keep his erstwhile boss from the sink.

It was Swart's sense of propriety that ultimately won out owing to the sheer number of visitors who came to visit the prisoner. Madiba enjoyed the relative freedom of his new environment and entertained a wide range of friends. His long-time physician Dr Nthato Motlana remarked that he 'held court like Peter the Great of Russia'. His visitors were diverse in scope and included his first employer Lazar Sidelsky, academic Dr Mamphela Ramphele, businessman Richard Maponya, Robben Island comrade Eddie Daniels and Defiance Campaign colleagues Amina and Yusuf Cachalia. Eventually Madiba was forced to concede that he could no longer insist on doing all the washing up himself.

In addition to the social visits there were a large number of political meetings. As George Bizos remarked, the house at Victor Verster 'was not so much a prison as an office'. Many of Madiba's visitors came to receive report-backs on the progress of his discussions with the South African government. Madiba was aware that he was entering a very delicate phase of opening talks about talks and his intentions could be misrepresented by both sides. The government might try to lever him away from his comrades while his contacts with the National Party could give rise to rumours of his selling out the ANC. These anxieties were partly allayed by Madiba's dispatching George Bizos to Lusaka to reassure ANC President Oliver Tambo that he would not enter into any agreement without ANC approval and by his holding a series of report-back sessions at the Victor Verster house.

Tokyo Sexwale recalled such an occasion when Madiba called key members of the ANC on Robben Island and the UDF leadership together. 'There were a group of ten of us, including

Terror [Lekota], and on arrival there was a kind of banquet table in prison – never seen food like that in prison – like a banquet of the bandits. He wanted to brief us on his negotiations. He said to Swart and Gregory, if Tokyo and Terror are coming, they must prepare the best, and lots of it. But I think we surprised even him with our appetites. Not only did we eat everything but we cleared out the cupboards too. We have had many meals since then, but that was the first formal sit-down of prisoners and leaders, and it was the best.'[274]

For all the sandwiches, fears and accusations, Madiba had yet to achieve his goal of a direct meeting with the State President. Such an encounter was further delayed when in January 1989 P.W. Botha suffered a stroke, which temporarily incapacitated him. For several months, the National Party was preoccupied with internal political wrangling and jockeying for power, and Botha was replaced as leader of the party (but not yet as State President) by F.W. de Klerk. The competition for power was no bad thing for Madiba since both sides were seeking to best their opponents in finding a solution to the 'Mandela problem'. Eventually a meeting between Madiba and P.W. Botha took place on 4 July 1989 at Tuynhuys, the Cape Town office of the President of South Africa. Here finally was evidence that even conservatives within the National Party were beginning to accept that there could be no solution in South Africa without Madiba and, by extension, the ANC.

Though Madiba expected the worst at Tuynhuys, P.W. Botha poured them both a cup of tea and struck up a relatively amicable conversation about Afrikaner history. Adroitly, Madiba attempted to draw parallels between the 1914 Afrikaner Rebellion and his own struggle for freedom. But when Madiba requested the release of all political prisoners, the pleasantries and tea stopped short. Of the tea itself, Amelia Grobelaar recalled: 'I worked in the kitchen, baking and the like. I was based at Westbrook on the Groote Schuur land [estate] but we did most of the preparation for Tuynhuys – cabinet meetings and such. We made the food but we often didn't know for what we were making it. But the food at such meetings was never biscuits. It was small salty savouries – little *frikkadels*, small chicken pieces, small sandwiches, tiny sausages, little savoury tartlets topped with cheese, tuna and sometimes small pieces of sausages and the like, so I imagine that was what we sent that day.'[275]

In September 1989, a protracted struggle within the NP hierarchy culminated in the displacement of the ailing P.W. Botha and his replacement by F.W. de Klerk as State President. In his inaugural speech on 20 September, De Klerk declared he would talk to any group committed to peace. On his first day in office Madiba wrote to him requesting a meeting and urging him to show his commitment to reform by releasing all political prisoners. On 10 October Walter Sisulu, Ahmed Kathrada, Andrew Mlangeni and Raymond Mhlaba visited Victor Verster where Madiba informed them about their imminent release. They were released on 15 October 1989, five days later. They sat under the trees drinking tea and eating sandwiches made from Jack Swart's wholemeal bread. The sadness of parting was mitigated by the knowledge that theirs would be only a temporary separation and that Madiba's release could not be far behind.

On 2 February 1990, De Klerk announced in Parliament that his government was unbanning the ANC, the PAC and the Communist Party and would release Nelson Mandela unconditionally. A week later Madiba was taken to Tuynhuys, where De Klerk informed him that he was to be released that weekend in Johannesburg. There was a dispute as to where and when the release should occur. Madiba argued that such a rapid, unplanned step would result in chaos, and asked to be released at a later date and from the prison gates of Victor Verster. Though the date of the release was not moved, Madiba's view about where it should take place prevailed.

Jack Swart brought a uniquely domestic view to the dispute. 'They told me that he would visit the President, and that I must pack food for them, for about seven people. As I heard afterwards, it would have been the people who were to be on the aeroplane [to Johannesburg]. I packed the sandwiches and fried sausage and boiled eggs. So the Friday when he left … they told me he didn't know that he would be released. They would tell him there, and this is how I went home the Friday afternoon after they had left. Saturday morning they came to pick me up again and told me that I had to go and clean the house. When I walked into the kitchen, the box in which I'd packed the breakfast … was standing on the kitchen table. So I was already a little confused, because why was the box standing there? And then he came down the passage, and said to me, "Are you surprised to see me?" I said to him, "Yes. Did you then not leave?" He says, "No, I did not leave. They are going to release me the way I want to be released, not the way they want me to."'[276]

'they are going to release me
the way I want to be released'

OVERLEAF: MADIBA'S RELEASED COMRADES AT PRESS CONFERENCE IN SOWETO, OCTOBER 1989
© Graeme Williams

Chapter Eleven

FIRST MEAL OF FREEDOM

IN ANTICIPATION OF MADIBA'S FREEDOM, the UDF and the newly unbanned ANC had formed a National Reception Committee but no one had anticipated such a rapid release. With less than 48 hours to prepare, Cape Town was frenetic with activity.

From security concerns to speech writing, resources were stretched. As Farida Omar recalled: 'Our house was full of people. And everyone from the youngest child to the top, top comrades had a job to do to help prepare for the release. Dullah and senior UDF comrades (Trevor Manuel, Ebrahim Rasool, Cheryl Carolus and some others) were all here in meetings. I was busy making sandwiches with my neighbours and lots of young comrades so that the marshals for the rally the next day wouldn't go hungry – thousands of sandwiches: polony, cheese, eggs and rolls, lots of rolls – thousands and thousands, darling. And because all the grown-ups were working, we told my young daughter, she was about 8, to answer the phone. And suddenly she shouted, "Papa, there's a phone call for you. It's a man who says he's George Bush but I don't know him." And it was George Bush (the father) who wanted to speak to Dullah about the imminent release. And then Dullah and them went to the prison to meet Mr Mandela one last time as a prisoner and they came back and said to me, "Farida, tomorrow you must go and fetch Winnie from the airport and take her to her husband." So then I was so happy and I said,

"Now I have had enough of sandwiches and I must go and sleep so I can drive her nicely on this special day."'[277]

At the Victor Verster Prison house, life continued as usual. According to Jack Swart: 'I came to make him breakfast on the Sunday morning, and by mid-morning quite a number of people had come to visit him. So I made snacks for the people, and for the last time made that beer that he likes. The house was full of people, they ate everything – by the time they left there was no food left, no cold drinks, nothing. And the problem was that Mrs Mandela was late arriving. Trevor Manuel – he was sort of in command – he telephoned to find out where she was, and all the time helicopters flew over the house so that there was dust everywhere and you couldn't hear anything.'[278]

CHICKEN IS THE SAFEST THING

And so it was that on the afternoon of Sunday 11 February at 4 pm Madiba took his wife's hand and walked through the gates of Victor Verster Prison. Of this moment Madiba himself wrote: 'As I finally

OPPOSITE: MADIBA, WITH WINNIE MANDELA, WALKING OUT OF JAIL, 11 FEBRUARY 1990
© Graeme Williams

walked through those gates … I felt, even at the age of 71, that my life was beginning anew. My ten thousand days of imprisonment were at last over.'[279]

Several hours later, standing on the balcony at the Cape Town City Hall at dusk, Madiba spoke directly to the South African people for the first time in 27 years. From there, he was driven to the official residence of Archbishop Desmond Tutu, where he was to spend his first night of freedom. The timing of Madiba's liberation had caught the staff at Bishopscourt off guard. In the words of Lavinia Crawford-Browne, the Archbishop's personal assistant: 'We all knew that the release was imminent but no one knew when it would come exactly. The Archbishop and Mrs Tutu were in Johannesburg, and at about 11 am on the Sunday I got an anxious phone call from Lillian Ngoboza, the housekeeper at Bishopscourt, saying that Nelson Mandela would be coming for the night. Lillian was alone in the house and understandably quite nervous at the prospect. The Archbishop couldn't get on a scheduled flight at such short notice, so he hitched a ride with the media crews from Johannesburg and Mrs Tutu was left behind. We had no idea what [Madiba] liked to eat, so we thought, well, chicken is the safest thing, and I rushed to the nearest 7-Eleven [convenience store] because it was a Sunday and the big supermarkets weren't open on Sundays in those days. I bought up every chicken piece I could find and a crate of Coke – which turned out not to be enough and I had to go back. Then I went home, and my husband and I went to the Grand Parade and listened to Mr Mandela address the crowd. This was before cellphones. We got home at about six, and we had barely walked in the door when Lillian called again and said I should come back to the Archbishop's house. So I dashed back to Bishopscourt. I walked into the kitchen and as I did so I saw a host of lights from the cavalcade coming up the driveway. Lillian was busy with the food and the Archbishop was in the car behind the Mandelas. Everyone else was busy and so I went to the door and opened it to find Winnie and Mr Mandela on the other side!'[280]

Lillian Ngoboza remembered that day well. 'When I got the message that Madiba was coming, I ran downstairs to tell the lady I was working with, Mrs Nakani, and I said, "Listen here, Daddy (we all called the Archbishop 'Daddy') is coming on a jet from Jo'burg fast, fast because Nelson Mandela is going to be released." And we were so excited that we couldn't believe it ourselves and we said, "What are we going to do now? Which room shall we prepare for him to sleep in and what are we going to cook? First meal of freedom! It must be so nice and tasty." And Lavinia, she said: "Lillian, I am coming now, now, now, now," and she dropped the phone; she came to Bishopscourt. And finally Daddy arrived and he said, "Lillian, over to you. I don't know how

LILLIAN NGOBOZA WITH LUNGA CUTHALELE

LILLIAN NOSIPHO NGOBOZA'S

Chicken Curry

1 CHICKEN
4 TABLESPOONS OLIVE OIL
2 ONIONS, FINELY CHOPPED
1 GREEN PEPPER, ROUGHLY CHOPPED
1 TABLESPOON HOT CURRY POWDER
1 TEASPOON TURMERIC
½ CUP CAKE FLOUR
1 RED CHILLI FINELY CHOPPED
SUFFICIENT WATER TO COVER THE CHICKEN
(AT LEAST 3 CUPS)
1 TABLESPOON PAPRIKA
SALT AND PEPPER TO TASTE

Wash the chicken, portion it and set aside. Combine the flour and spices and mix this combination with the chicken pieces, then put the chicken covered in seasoned flour into the fridge for at least 1 hour. Dust the excess flour off the chicken pieces. Put 2 tablespoons of oil into your pot and brown the chicken over a medium heat, taking care that the flour does not burn. When the chicken is browned on all sides, remove from the pan. Add the remaining oil to the pan and sauté the onions and the peppers over a medium heat until they are soft, about 5 minutes. Return the browned chicken to the pan and add sufficient water to cover the mixture. If the stew looks as if it might boil dry, add more water and reduce the heat. Simmer until the chicken is tender and cooked through, at least 30 minutes. Serve with rice and a green salad, yoghurt and chutney.

many people are going to be here. But please just decide what to cook and don't disappoint." And so I chose a recipe that Aunty Leah [Mrs Tutu] liked to make and she had taught me – she was like a mother to me. So even though she couldn't be there, I felt like she was helping me and calming me for this special day. So we were working very nicely together – we were so excited we didn't even know we were busy. And we were so careful with the spices and we made sure to coat the chicken well – when you make this curry you must make sure all the chicken is coated with spiced flour. And we did it so nicely, one piece, one piece, one piece, and then we left it to simmer and to get so lovely. And there were so, so many people, but we laid a little table for the family upstairs and Daddy joined them and they had supper like that. It was late at night because all the people wanted to greet him, so it had taken a very long, long time to get to the house. And they had their dinner with rice and a green salad and I put out chutney and plain yoghurt – so in case they maybe thought it was too hot. But later, even though he was tired, he seemed so, so strong and, even late as it was, he came to the kitchen to greet us and he said that they had loved the curry a lot. And then you know the Archbishop always likes to have rum and raisin ice-cream, so they had rum and raisin with lots of custard.'[281]

WELCOME TO JOHANNESBURG BY STORMS AND A ROW OF SMALL CHILDREN

Although the plan had been to return to Soweto the next day, all attempts to reach the Mandelas' Orlando house were thwarted by security concerns about the huge numbers of people who had flocked to the home. So it was that Sally Rowney, a Parkhurst Primary School teacher, received a telephone call 'at about four in the afternoon of 12 February. It was my friend Jean de la Harpe, who was working at the time for the National Reception Committee for the release of the leaders. She said:

"Sally, can you and your five children vacate your house tonight? We need to accommodate a family of seven," and then she asked if I wouldn't mind cooking dinner for them. I think they chose us because we were near the airport. I knew exactly who she meant was coming, so I anticipated that more people might come too. No one knew exactly how many might come but Jean did warn me that there were what she called "a few small planes" arriving from Cape Town.'[282]

As time was not on Sally's side, she 'rushed to change the sheets and there was no time to shop, so I looked in the deep freeze and took food out. Thank goodness later someone from the Reception Committee was delegated to go to Checkers [supermarket] and get more food because we would never have had enough. And about two hours later press helicopters started circling (even before the gate intercom had rung, the press seemed to know where they were going). And, of course, just as the first car got into our garage there was suddenly lightning and all the electricity went out! A real Jo'burg storm came crashing in: rain, thunder, the works. And so it was that Madiba was welcomed into my house in semi-darkness by a row of my five small, excited children. My 6-year-old son (who was already so pleased by the helicopters) said, "Are you Mr. Mandela? I saw you on the television!" And Madiba just hugged him. And then suddenly the kitchen was packed with people. Everyone from Winnie with daughters and grandchildren to Frank Chikane, Cyril Ramaphosa, Jay Naidoo, Valli Moosa and so many others. And the garden was full of ANC youth who weren't really trained in security but who had been deployed to guard the property.

'We put out candles and luckily there were gas cookers. And eventually the electricity did come back. The counters of the kitchen were packed with food and my deep freeze was empty and still we cooked and cooked and cooked – we needed to

SALLY ROWNEY'S

Mushrooms

3 BIG HANDFULS OF MUSHROOMS,
CLEANED AND THINLY SLICED
SEVERAL SPRIGS OF FRESH THYME,
LEAVES PICKED AND STALKS DISCARDED
2 BIG BALLS OF MOZZARELLA CHEESE,
PULLED INTO ROUGH PIECES
SALT AND PEPPER TO TASTE
OLIVE OIL
BALSAMIC VINEGAR

Spread the mushrooms on an ovenproof dish.
Sprinkle the thyme, salt, pepper, vinegar and olive oil over
the mushrooms and throw the pieces of cheese over the top.
Place the whole dish under a hot grill until the cheese starts to bubble,
about 5 minutes. Check often because the cheese can burn.

feed everyone – the youth in the garden, Madiba, everyone. Supper was an informal affair. I put it out on warmers and people helped themselves and ate on their laps, and the discussion was mainly about the preparations for the speech for the rally the next day.

'My housekeeper Elizabeth Mathebula and I served what we had and what we could buy locally, so there were steak sandwiches in crusty bread rolls, chicken legs that we roasted in the oven, and an awful lot of mushrooms.'

The next morning Madiba rose several hours before any of the other members of the household. Much to Sally Rowney and Elizabeth Mathebula's chagrin, he not only made his own bed but also found his own way to the breakfast cereal.

RETURN TO THE CENTRE OF THE WORLD

The next day Madiba spoke to a hundred thousand people at a packed Soccer City stadium in Soweto. Finally, on his third night of freedom, he slept in his own bed at No. 8115 Ngakane Street, Orlando West. Of his return he wrote: 'It was only then that I knew in my heart that I had left prison. For me, No. 8115 was the centre point of my world, the place marked with an X in my mental geography.'[283]

The return to Ngakane Street was not without problems. The Mandelas found that almost 30 years of trauma and deprivation made it difficult to reconnect emotionally, especially when they were constantly interrupted by an endless stream of visitors. Of the early days after her father's release, Zindzi Mandela recollected: 'No matter how much you are prepared, you're not prepared. It takes time to adjust and it wasn't just a question of adjusting to each other. It was more about adjusting to each

other with 40 other people around all the time. We were never alone – we would have these crazy meals with CNN and so-and-so watching us. It took such a long time for us to be just family. And the house was very small, so we were all cramped together. In fact it was only when he moved to the bigger house, the one they call "Parliament" in Diepkloof, that we got to have any privacy.'[284] If Winnie Madikizela-Mandela was criticised for the 'vulgar excesses of her house'[285] in Diepkloof, her daughter's words give a new perspective on her reasons for wanting to live there.

On the domestic problems associated with his release, Madiba commented: 'Happy as I was to be home, I had a sense that what I most wanted and longed for was going to be denied me. I yearned to resume a normal and ordinary life, to pick up some of the old threads from my life as a young man, to be able to go to my office in the morning and return to my family in the evening, to be able to pop out and buy some toothpaste at the pharmacy, to visit old friends in the evening. These ordinary things are what one misses most in prison, and dreams about doing when one is free. But I quickly realized that such things were not going to be possible. That night, and every night for the next weeks and months, the house was surrounded by hundreds of well-wishers. People sang and danced and called out and their joy was infectious. These were my people and I had no right and no desire to deny myself to them. But in giving myself to my people, I could see that I was once again taking myself away from my family.'[286] According to George Bizos, 'Winnie complained that the house was no longer her own and that despite her objections, the UDF leaders had taken over. She had put her foot down about Sunday lunch, which would be a traditional affair for family only.'[287] But there is only so much that a solitary Sunday lunch can do when so much pain has been endured.

As Madiba himself said at his daughter Zindzi's wedding in 1992: 'When I came out of prison my children said, "We thought we had a father and one day he'd come back. But to our dismay, our father came back and he left us alone because he has now become the father of the nation." To be the father of a nation is a great honour, but to be the father of a family is a greater joy. But it was a joy I had far too little of.'[288]

MRS PILLAY AND MRS NAIDOO HUGGING MADIBA IN ORLANDO, 1991

© Pillay family collection

REUNIONS AND FISH CURRY

Friendships were easier to re-establish than familial bonds. Within a week of his release Madiba telephoned Mrs Thayanayagee Pillay. Mrs Pillay, who had made so many meals for him during the Treason Trial, and later for Diwali celebrations on Robben Island, immediately put on the green, gold and black sari that he had given her as a present in 1961 and rushed over to his Orlando home. Her daughter Vasugee Moodley recalled that she took with her a Tupperware filled with fish curry.

Similarly, a few weeks after Madiba's release, Nat Bregman, his colleague from the law firm he was once articled to, was 'sitting in my office and I was told that he was on the phone. And he

phoned, not once, he tried to get hold of me three times personally, and he eventually got through to me and he said we must have a firm reunion dinner of all those who were involved when we were articled together at Sidelsky. I called Sidelsky and I managed to get hold of one of the typists, Anita Feinstein (Anita Goodman she became), and she was thrilled to come and several others, and we had a reunion dinner at the Carlton, not at the actual hotel; across the road they had a restaurant in the annexe to the Carlton. And the most interesting thing was, he had just come out of jail, he wasn't the President or anything yet, but as he entered the room, everybody in that room stood up. And he hugged me.'[289]

In late February 1990 Madiba returned to his favourite restaurant, Kapitan's, with Cyril Ramaphosa. Of this visit restaurateur Madanjit Ranchod recalled: 'Mandela had his old favourite – mince meat curry and rice. Ramaphosa had my ginger pickle, he swears by it and says no one can make it like me.'

PEACH COBBLER AND THE INTERREGNUM

In addition to the complexities of returning to his family and the simpler pleasures of returning to

© Bregman personal collection

MADIBA AND SIDELSKY AT THE FIRM REUNION DINNER

MRS PILLAY'S

Green Mango and Fish Curry

{as provided by her niece Shanthie Naidoo}

2 TABLESPOONS OIL
1 TEASPOON FENUGREEK
1 ONION, FINELY CHOPPED
4 CLOVES WHOLE GARLIC
1 TABLESPOON DURBS SPECIAL (SOUTH INDIAN MASALA)
½ TEASPOON TURMERIC
3 WHOLE GREEN CHILLIES
5 TOMATOES, GRATED
2 AUBERGINES CHOPPED INTO CUBES
2 GREEN APPLES CUBED OR 3 GREEN MANGOES CUBED
1 TEASPOON TAMARIND GEL MIXED INTO ½ CUP OF WATER
1kg KINGKLIP (CUT INTO THICK 2-FINGER-WIDTH SLICES
ON THE BONE)

Heat oil, add fenugreek (take care not to let the spice burn). Sautée the onion until golden then add the garlic, masala, turmeric, and mix well. Add the tomatoes and chillies, aubergine and the fruit to the onion and spice mixture and, when it is soft, add the tamarind liquid and cook down. Add the kingklip and cook for a further 10–15 minutes, then serve with rice.

his friends, Madiba was thrust into an extremely difficult political context. He was well aware that he was a key actor and the symbolic figurehead in a process that, it was hoped, would lead the country into a negotiated settlement. And yet a democratic future was far from certain. There were very real fears that South Africa could be heading for civil war, and attempts to keep the negotiations on course were repeatedly stalled by violence.

Despite the political and domestic stresses in his life, Madiba embarked on a series of international trips. Within weeks of his release he had attended an ANC National Executive Committee meeting in Lusaka, visited Oliver Tambo (who was recuperating from a stroke in Sweden) and travelled to Zimbabwe, Tanzania and Egypt. Within the first six months of his freedom he had circumnavigated the globe in a world tour aimed at rallying support and funds for the ANC. His journey took him from toasting Namibian independence celebrations in Windhoek to cocktail parties with the Commonwealth Secretary-General Sonny Ramphal and the Archbishop of Canterbury in London. A triumphant visit to India saw him drink holy water from the Ganges and savour a six-course state banquet in Delhi, India. His trip to New York began with peach cobbler at Sylvia's restaurant in Harlem, moved on to a fund-raising dinner hosted by Eddie Murphy, Spike Lee and Robert De Niro at the Tribeca Grill, and culminated in the city's

NAT BREGMAN, 2007

first black mayor, David Dinkins, throwing a celebratory banquet at City Hall. He addressed the United Nations General Assembly before moving on to Washington, where he spent the night as the guest of President George Bush at the White House.

In the three months between Madiba's release from prison and the beginning of the preliminary talks, a cloud of uncertainty hung over South Africa. In the broad sense Madiba and his comrades knew that what must follow his liberation was a broader liberation of the country in which the apartheid edifice had to be dismantled. But the details of how this was to be achieved and the specifics of reconstruction after apartheid were still uncertain. It was in this period that Madiba was finally free to visit his childhood home in the Eastern Cape. In Qunu he realised the full extent of the challenge that faced him. The social and economic destruction that had taken place since his imprisonment three decades earlier became starkly apparent to him. The local community 'seemed as poor if not poorer than they had been then … when I was young the village was tidy, the water was pure and the grass was green and unsullied as far as the eye could see. Kraals were swept, topsoil was conserved, fields were neatly divided. But now the village was unswept, the water polluted and the countryside littered with plastic bags and wrappers …' Pride in the community seemed to have vanished.'[290]

Chapter Twelve

ALL SIDES TO THE TABLE

NEGOTIATING AN END TO APARTHEID required considerably more than the release of Madiba and his Rivonia comrades.

Every aspect of South African life had been racialised under apartheid and developing a framework for dismantling such an edifice proved to be an extremely complex undertaking. At the outset the adversaries were united by little besides a commitment to talks borne out of a stalemate in the long history of conflict, a state of 'violent equilibrium between a government that cannot be overthrown and a spirit of mass resistance that cannot be crushed'.[291] When the first ANC delegation arrived in May 1990 at President De Klerk's official Cape Town residence, Groote Schuur, for initial talks about talks, very few, if any, of the participants could imagine the intricacy of the recipe that was ultimately required to create a post-apartheid South Africa.

WEEPING SUGAR CAGES AND THE WINDS OF CHANGE

Initial progress was slow and to many it seemed that South Africa's white elite was carrying on much as before. But change was in the air of even the most reluctant sectors of society. In the household of President De Klerk, Chef François

Ferreira recalled: 'In 1991 Marike de Klerk said to me, "What are we going to do for the state banquet this year?" So I said to her, "Let's serve fish as a main course," and she said, "You know, it's never been done but let's be adventurous and change with the times." So we did Cape Salmon and the diplomatic corps were all in seventh heaven that we were serving fish at a state banquet but the *boere* [staunch Afrikaners] were quite upset. For them this was one step too far with the winds of change.'[292] In order to understand how radical a departure this was, one need only look at the menu for the previous year, at which were served liver terrine, cream of mussel soup, rosettes of lamb, sweet and sour tongue, cherry pudding, coffee and port.

If the changing of meat for fish was not enough to show the carnivorous parliamentarians that the times were changing, the dessert course left them in no doubt that they were living through the end of an era. According to François Ferreira: 'The dessert was called "Cape in a cage" and we made caramelised sugar cages, you know the ones you make over a ladle, and we put them on a biscuit

OPPOSITE: MADIBA AND GRANDSON BAMBATHA, 1995
© Louise Gubb

175

and inside was grapes and things – everything of the Cape. But I must say, the day before the state banquet it was a very, very moist wet day, so all the sugar cages started to collapse – we literally had to work right through the night to redo all the cages because the humidity caused all the sugar to weep – weeping sugar and collapsing cages, which was quite upsetting … The sugar was literally weeping – 300 people, 300 cages, and more like 800 by the time we had finished doing them all again.'

FRANÇOIS FERREIRA

THE TRUST OF A TROUT

By late 1991 the negotiation process, which ultimately ushered in the new democracy, was under way. At the World Trade Centre in Kempton Park, delegates from 19 political parties as well as the leaders of the nominally independent Bantustans met in the Convention for a Democratic South Africa (Codesa). Notably absent were the white right-wing and Inkatha. Even among those participating there was an atmosphere of distrust engendered by the long and bitter history of conflict. If they were ever to reach a mutually agreeable solution, there was an urgent need to establish relationships of personal trust.

It was a relationship formed at the very highest level – over whisky and fish – that set the tone for the whole negotiating process. In late 1991 the National Party's chief negotiator, Roelf Meyer, and his opposite number, ANC Secretary-General Cyril Ramaphosa, were invited by a mutual acquaintance, the businessman Sidney Frankel, to Havelock Trout Farm in the Lowveld. What was intended to be a three-man fishing trip became a two-man détente when Frankel had to leave after his daughter broke her arm, and consequently left the two men alone. The story that follows is so saccharine that it almost defies belief, but all those involved swear that it did take place. Meyer got a fishing hook embedded in his finger and Ramaphosa, having first given his patient a glass of single malt, fetched a pair of pliers, and uttered the words, 'If you've never trusted an ANC person before, you'd better get ready to do so now,' and wrenched the hook from Meyer's finger. Amidst the blood and the whisky Meyer is said to have observed, 'Well, Cyril, don't ever say I didn't trust you.'

With such a significant meeting of minds it is no wonder that by the end of 1993 the Codesa participants had committed themselves to the concept of a five-year power-sharing agreement under a Government of National Unity. Trust, fish and whisky had prevailed.

CHICKEN SOUP IN THE CHAOS

While sugar cages wept at the state banquet, outside the walls of Parliament it was the bloody feud between supporters of Chief Mangosuthu Buthelezi's Inkatha (with covert state security force complicity) and those of the ANC and UDF that induced real tears. Despite the parties' agreement to 'the resolution of the existing climate of violence and intimidation from whatever quarter, as well as a commitment to stability and to a peaceful process of negotiations', conflict escalated across South Africa. In June 1992 Inkatha-supporting hostel residents went on a rampage through the township of Boipatong near Vereeniging, killing 46 people. Suspecting security force involvement, the ANC suspended negotiations and accused the National Party of collusion in the attacks.

Sugar Cages

2½ CUPS GRANULATED WHITE SUGAR
¼ CUP LIQUID GLUCOSE
½ CUP WATER
COOKING SPRAY

Place the sugar, glucose and water in a heavy-bottomed saucepan and cook over a medium heat. Do not stir the mixture as this is likely to create sugar crystals. Insert a sugar thermometer and cook the mixture until it reaches hard-crack stage (155ºC), then remove the sugar from the heat. Because of the liquid glucose, the sugar will remain clear rather than turning a caramel colour. If you want your cages to be coloured, you need to add food colouring as soon as it reaches 155ºC. Wash, dry and lightly but thoroughly coat with cooking spray a ladle or small bowl. Use a clean, dry ladle that matches the diameter of whatever you are placing the sugar cage over. Dip the tines of a fork into the hot sugar and then wave the fork over the inside of the ladle, allowing the sugar to drip off the fork in long, thin strands. Using a sharp chef's knife, slice the edge of the cage clean by scraping the blade of the knife along the rim of the bowl. Set aside to cool completely, about 5 minutes. Gently pull the cage loose. Once the cage has released from the bowl, carefully lift it out and place it over the dessert. If the weather is dry, the cages can be stored, right side up, in an airtight container in a cool, dry place for 1 to 2 days. Silica will help to exclude moisture, but on a really humid or wet day nothing will prevent the sugar from weeping!

many in the ANC camp were outraged that the award appeared to give moral equivalency to the jailed and his jailer

And yet, even when formal negotiations were suspended, contact between the parties was retained behind the scenes. Chef François Ferreira remembered a working luncheon at the Presidential offices in the Union Buildings during the winter of 1992. 'Because it was in the winter, we served soup. I received instructions that Mr Mandela did not like heavily spiced food and ate quite lightly. This chicken broth was filling and tasty – at least I hope so.'[293]

SEATING PLANS AND THE NOBEL DINNER TABLE

In 1993 F.W. de Klerk and Madiba were jointly awarded the Nobel Prize for Peace for their roles in bringing an end to apartheid. But as the award ceremony in Oslo revealed, emotions on both sides were far from peaceable. Many in the ANC camp were outraged that the award appeared to give moral equivalency to the jailed and his jailer. Events of the past three years had taken their toll on relations between the two Nobel laureates. Since the Boipatong Massacre, Madiba had become increasingly distrustful of De Klerk's protestations that he knew nothing of 'third force' activities. Madiba was angered when De Klerk failed to acknowledge the National Party's responsibility for the evils of apartheid in his acceptance speech.

For its part, De Klerk's entourage felt that Madiba was deliberately appropriating the prestige which surrounded the award and was monopolising the attentions of the Norwegian public and press to the detriment of his negotiating partner. When the assembled guests at the Grand Hotel in Oslo tucked into seafood nordique and Chateaubriand of elk with morel sauce[294] at the post-award dinner, Marike de Klerk was incensed by the seating arrangements. These, she felt, favoured Madiba by placing him next to the Norwegian Prime Minister while her husband was seated next to a lesser dignitary.[295]

THE SWEETNESS OF SWEET CHICKEN

Significant progress may have been made in negotiating a new future for South Africa, but on the home front Madiba's personal life was in tatters. In the almost three decades of his incarceration everyone in the Mandela family had built emotional barriers to protect themselves from pain. For all those years, his wife and children had largely subsumed their resentments and feelings of abandonment in antagonism towards an unjust regime, but with his release from jail his nominal freedom made his frequent absences all the more painful.

FRANÇOIS FERREIRA'S

Chicken Broth

1 WHOLE CHICKEN
1 MEDIUM ONION
3 LARGE CARROTS, PEELED AND ROUGHLY CHOPPED
A FEW SPRIGS PARSLEY
4 WHOLE CLOVES
I STICK CELERY, SLICED
1 CUP HARICOT BEANS
SALT AND BLACK PEPPER TO TASTE

Pour boiling water over the haricot beans and let soak overnight. Strain the beans and put into a large saucepan – about 5 l capacity. Wash the chicken and place the whole onion and parsley inside the cavity of the chicken. Rub the chicken with the salt and pepper and place in the saucepan. Add the carrots, cloves and celery. Cover the chicken with water and bring to the boil. Simmer for about 1½ to 2 hours. Remove the chicken and strain the liquid through a sieve. Return the liquid to the pot, bring to the boil again and simmer until reduced by a third. Meanwhile, remove the whole cloves from the vegetable mixture and liquidise the vegetables. Remove the skin from the chicken, take the meat off the bones and chop finely. Once the stock has reduced by a third, add the liquidised vegetables to the stock. Add the chopped chicken flesh, bring to the boil and serve. This is ideal with freshly baked bread and garnished with chopped chives.

In 1992, Madiba and his wife separated and he moved out of Soweto into a home in the suburb of Houghton which his long-time comrade Barbara Masekela had decorated in a well-meaning but ultimately unsuccessful attempt to 'hide his pain'.[296] Here chef Xoliswa Ndoyiya and housekeeper Gloria Nocanda were employed as household support staff. These women made it possible for Madiba to begin to rebuild his home life. As Zindzi Mandela remarked: 'They have an amazing rapport. He's vested a lot of trust in Sis' Xoli and he gets anxious if she's not there.'[297] Xoliswa Ndoyiya remembered: 'We were two ladies, my colleague Gloria Nocanda (who later worked for Deputy President Phumzile Mlambo-Ngcuka), and I. We stayed in the house to look after him and then he asked us if we could please also take care of his grandchildren. He said he knows that the ANC employed us just to look after him but he would like to stay with the grandchildren. For that I respect him – he asked us first before he brought the children to the house. He asked us if we were happy with it. So we said we were happy to give him this chance because we knew he hadn't had the chance to bring up his own children. So that's how Mandla, Ndaba, Mbuso, Rochelle and Andile came to stay. So we cooked, washed, cleaned. We took care of the kids making sure they went to school. Andile and Mbuso were very little babies in nappies and they slept with us in the cottage in the back until they were old enough to say, "Grandpa, can I go to wee?" and then they would go to the main house. They were enjoying each other's company … he didn't have much time to be with them but he really enjoyed coming back to that noisy house with children.'[298]

Of this time in his life, Mandlesizwe Mandela (later, Nkosi Zwelivelile) recollected: 'We moved in with him in '93. I was 19. My grandfather, having been denied the opportunity to raise his own children,

being in prison, and he put a lot of pressure on my father to go studying, and so he went back into studying in his later years and my grandfather assured my father that he would look after his children. So my father was studying and my grandfather, he took myself and my three brothers in, and we stayed with him in Houghton, and Sis' Xoli and Sis' Gloria were the two ladies who practically brought us up. For me, I came in I was already 19 so they saw me through circumcision. Andile was about 10 months old, so he was really a baby when he came. Mbuso was 2 years old and Ndaba must have been about 9, so they really saw us grow over the years.'[299]

Any household catering for five children has complicated culinary arrangements. Xoliswa Ndoyiya's menu planning had to take into account that 'Madiba is always happiest with traditional food. If you don't give it to him for a few days, he will call you and ask, "What's wrong? Why are you not feeding me well?" So there would always be homemade sour milk, very dry and sour, and *umphoqoko* because grandpa enjoys that but Ndaba used to hate sour milk – the others would join the grandpa, but even now Ndaba doesn't like sour milk. Mandla was easy, he ate whatever you put on the table.'

In a household where there are diverse tastes, it is good to have a family favourite that everyone will eat. For the Mandelas this dish is what they call 'Sis' Xoli's sweet chicken', of which she says: 'They all love the sweet chicken. That's the dish that they like to eat together as a family. Tata [Madiba] loves it too – all of them love it.'[300] After eating this dish President Bill Clinton offered Xoliswa Ndoyiya a job, to which Madiba retorted: 'In your dreams, Bill, in your dreams.' Oprah Winfrey also enjoyed the sweet chicken on several occasions.

XOLISWA NDOYIYA'S
Sweet Chicken

1 CHICKEN PORTIONED
1½ CUPS SWEET FRUIT CHUTNEY
1 CUP MAYONNAISE
2½ TABLESPOONS MILD CURRY POWDER
1 CUP WATER
1 TEASPOON PAPRIKA
2 TEASPOONS CHICKEN SPICE

Preheat oven to 200°C. Sprinkle the chicken with chicken spice and place it in an ovenproof dish. Roast in the oven for 15 minutes. Mix all the other ingredients together to form a sauce. Remove the chicken from the oven and cover it with the sauce. Turn oven to 170°C and return to oven. Cook until it is golden brown and tender, about 20 minutes. Serve with rice and your choice of vegetables.

ELECTIONS AND THE WORLD'S LONGEST COCKTAIL PARTY

By the middle of 1993 an election date had been agreed upon by the negotiating parties for 27 April the following year. Cyril Ramaphosa and Roelf Meyer, the chief negotiators, set to work developing an interim constitution, which was finally adopted in the early hours of 18 November 1993 (which, by chance, happened to be Ramaphosa's birthday). As the *New York Times* reported: 'After the vote, delegates adjourned to the bar of the World Trade Center where Roelf Meyer presented Cyril Ramaphosa with a vanilla cake with lemon icing to celebrate both his 41st birthday and the country's new non-racist constitution.' Roelf Meyer announced: 'This is not only Cyril's birthday, but South Africa's birthday as well.' And then the two men twirled giddily on to the dance floor and bopped to 'In the Mood'.[301]

The dream of a democratic South Africa became a reality on 27 April 1994 when millions of South Africans, Madiba included, voted for the first time in their lives. The elderly as well as pregnant women and people in hospital were allowed to vote on 26 April, and voting was extended for two days after the 27th to accommodate glitches that had occurred in various parts of the country. The ANC leaders and their supporters then headed in their droves for the Carlton Hotel in Johannesburg, where a victory party feast of finger snacks had been set out in the ballroom. Kevin Gibbs was the Executive Chef of the Carlton Hotel at the time and remembered that 'it was the world's longest cocktail party, that victory party; because the IEC [Independent Electoral Commission] kept promising to release the results and then they would be postponed and postponed and postponed. So everyone would arrive and they would eat and then they would have to go away again because there were still no results

to celebrate. Stop and start, with lots of people milling around, which is not great for other guests in the hotel or for the kitchen staff. We just had to keep redoing and refreshing. And we just kept the ballroom open indefinitely until the results were finally announced. We had three days of that.'[302]

The ANC ultimately obtained 62.5 per cent of the vote and F.W. de Klerk conceded defeat. From the Carlton Hotel's ballroom bash Madiba congratulated his rival for being 'the kind of man that after harsh words you can shake hands with and sit down to drink coffee'.[303]

On 10 May Madiba was inaugurated as President of South Africa with F.W. de Klerk and Thabo Mbeki as Deputy Presidents. The inauguration dinner was a joyous event, and dignitaries as diverse as Prince Philip and Fidel Castro tasted the confusion of the hour. In the menu it was possible to see how far the country had come and how far it still had to go.

A presidential inaugural dinner has far more to do with symbolism than it does with taste buds. Whatever the menu, it is alimentary nationalism that is served. Internationally, such events are cooked up to demonstrate rank and power and to showcase national agricultural, viticultural and culinary finesse to the assembled dignitaries and world leaders. In 1994 Madiba's inaugural meal was planned by the outgoing administration and so it was that the 24 heads of state who gathered to witness the final act in the eradication of apartheid were offered such curiously unpatriotic dishes as Mexican chicken and Spanish rice. There was considerable use of the culinary traditions of *boerekos* and Cape Malay cuisine (*potjies* and *bobotie* were both presented) but only one reference to indigenous African food in the form of *umngqusho*. While the whole world was celebrating the arrival of democracy, the kitchen had neglected to decolonise the menu.

OPPOSITE: MADIBA AND AHMED KATHRADA, 2001
© Mark Skinner

Chapter Thirteen

PRESIDENTIAL POWER LUNCH

As the guests at his inauguration dinner swallowed the last of the fanned avocado slices topped with peeled prawns, Madiba made his own transition from freedom fighter to President.

Without any previous parliamentary experience and bound to a civil service inherited from the old order, Madiba's administration worked at a prodigious pace to consolidate democracy, construct national unity and overcome the heritage of apartheid.

Between May 1994 and June 1999 the first administration achieved, amongst other things, a democratic constitution, a comprehensive bill of rights and the establishment of the Truth and Reconciliation Commission to investigate politically motivated human rights abuses committed during the apartheid era. A battery of progressive legislation was introduced under the auspices of the Reconstruction and Development Programme, which aimed to address poverty, restore the dignity of citizens and allow for the creation of a unified national identity through a focus on meeting basic needs, building the economy and democratising the state.

It rapidly became apparent that dismantling apartheid social relations and dealing with poverty was more complex than the ANC had anticipated. And yet, even amid the labours of the task, the joy of the first democratic administration was

deliciously apparent. On Saturday 20 July 1994 the Presidential Guest House in Pretoria thronged with over a thousand veterans representing the ANC, the PAC, the Communist Party, the Congress of Democrats, the Black Consciousness Movement, the Black Sash and the Liberal Party. Sitting down to a slap-up lunch of pot roasted beef, cinnamon pumpkin, *pap* and gravy, the veterans enabled Madiba 'to celebrate my birthday with my peers … it is wonderful to meet with so many old friends, comrades and combatants who stood firm in their fight for peace and justice. We should not forget those who never returned to enjoy with us the fruits of victory.' While a dessert of crème caramel and ice-cream would be considered an indecent amount of dairy within classical menu planning parameters, the participants at the lunch had earned their excess.

KOEKSISTERS FOR CABINET

South Africa's interim constitution provided for any party holding 20 or more seats in the National Assembly to claim one or more cabinet portfolios and enter the Government of National Unity (GNU). And so Inkatha's Chief Mangosuthu Buthelezi (Minister of Home Affairs) and National

OPPOSITE: MADIBA AND GRAÇA CELEBRATE WITH ZANELE MBEKI, 1998
Herbert Mabuza © Avusa Media

20 July 1996
President's Message to Veterans of the Struggle for Freedom.

Dear Friends and Comrades,

In greeting you to-day, I want to acknowledge South Africa's debt to all those who made such enormous sacrifices during the apartheid years.

I am very happy that this year, it has been possible for me to celebrate my birthday with my peers throughout the country. This is the last of five parties to be held representing all the provinces. It is wonderful to meet with so many old friends, comrades and combatants who stood firm in their fight for peace and justice. We should not forget those who never returned to enjoy with us the fruits of victory but they shall always be remembered as heroes who gave their lives in a great cause. Their deaths were not in vain.

Together we still have to consolidate our gains. You, who played such a major role in bringing South Africa to where it is to-day, must ensure that we continue along the path of freedom and equality for all and for future generations.

Thank you for joining me to-day.

NELSON MANDELA
President

Special Lunch Menu

Fresh Vegetable Soup
Curried Chicken, White Rice and Fried Onion
Potroast of Beef
Roast Potatoes
Cinnamon Pumpkin
Cabbage Casserole
Pap & Gravy
French Salad
Beetroot Salad
Carrot, Pineapple & Raisin Salad
Breadrolls & Butter

Homemade Cream Caramel with
Fresh Fruit & Ice Cream

Halaal Meat.

MADIBA'S MESSAGE AND MENU AT THE 1996 VETERANS' REUNION

Party stalwarts such as Pik Botha (Minister of Mineral and Energy Affairs) sat cheek by jowl with ANC Robben Island veterans like Mac Maharaj (Minister of Transport) and UDF activists like Trevor Manuel (Minister of Trade and Industry).

Cabinet meetings are secret in terms of parliament and national intelligence procedures and remain so for 20 years in terms of the National Archives Act, so it is impossible for us to be vicarious spectators. However, interaction between the ANC politicians and the old order public servants (whose jobs had been assured by way of sunset clauses negotiated at Codesa) provides an indication of the initial tensions and difficulties experienced by such broad coalitions. Joe Matthews, then Deputy Minister of Safety and Security, recalled: 'We had a huge problem because we were in government surrounded by a whole lot of Afrikaner officials, so what you got in our ministries, which we desperately tried to get changed, were all these little dainties – *koeksisters* and the things that Afrikaners like – little sweet things. And then there were the problems of food in Parliament itself – the meals provided by the restaurant were totally wrong, so we had to campaign to have the restaurant reflect the different food of the different cultures. And we would say, "Can't you bring some meat or chicken? All these are pretty but can't we have something real?" Even *boerewors* [sausage] would have been better. You never saw *boerewors* there. So we had to get them to understand. In fact in many cases they knew what we were talking about, from the farm etc. But because it was government they thought we wanted these dainties. But I must say that one thing they did really well, that was very nice and which we still insist on, you can't beat the Afrikaner women when it comes to flowers – flower arrangements. We don't know where they got those flowers. Some of us only knew one protea and they would make arrangements with all sorts of proteas. And they really know the indigenous plants. But that food was terrible. So dainty. Little bits of salmon. Ugh.'[304]

The civil servants' initial failure to understand what the new ministers and parliamentarians wanted to eat reflected a lack of cross-cultural understanding, which Madiba sought to alleviate in the most practical manner. It was not just a change in the menu that was required but also the manner in which people at different levels of government interacted with each other. Madiba used food and meals to win over those who were wary of the new ways.

As Ahmed Kathrada, who was Madiba's Parliamentary Counsellor in his administration, recalled: 'Entering government was a new ball game for all of us. When Mandela arrived in office he had nothing. To get a notebook or a pen he had to ask the civil servants. He was told every item of stationery had to be ordered from Pretoria. The same went for tea or coffee. It took time to get used to this. It is not that they were uncooperative. They just had their own style of doing things, and he had to adjust. But Mandela adjusted easily. He is a supremely confident person. Most people landing in a new situation are taken aback and take time to adjust. Not him. He settles in as if he is trained for everything. He has a commanding presence. When he gets into the office and meets new people, he immediately establishes a rapport with them. For instance, some of the staff in Pretoria – especially the black staff but some whites too – had never shaken the hand of a Minister, a Prime Minister or a President. Some had been working there for 20 years. Of the white staff, only the most senior had ever set foot in the official residence. Mandela put them at ease immediately by shaking hands with them, enquiring after their family circumstances. And very soon he started inviting these people to his home for meals. Unmarried ones were invited to bring their parents along.'[305]

Koeksisters

Syrup

1kg GRANULATED WHITE SUGAR
800ml WATER
30ml GOLDEN SYRUP
15ml LEMON JUICE

Dissolve the sugar in the water and boil for 1 minute. Add the golden syrup and boil for a further 10 minutes. Add the lemon juice. Take off the heat and cool overnight in the freezer. The outer crunch is entirely dependent on the syrup being ice-cold.

Dough

600g CAKE FLOUR
30ml BAKING POWDER
2ml SALT
50g BUTTER
375ml MILK

Sift together the flour, baking powder and salt. Rub in the butter until it looks like biscuit crumbs. Cut in the milk. Kneed dough lightly and wrap in cling wrap and rest for 2 hours. Roll the dough to 5mm. Keep dough covered with a damp cloth. Cut into 5cm x 1cm strips. Wind the left strip around the right. Pinch ends together and cover with a damp cloth. Allow to prove for 15 minutes. Deep-fry, drain and plunge into ice-cold syrup. Note: In order to keep the syrup ice-cold, work with the syrup sitting in an ice bath or have two bowls of syrup and keep one in the freezer so you can alternate as the syrup gets warm.

and he got so friendly that when the bread man got married, Madiba went to his wedding

Household Comptroller Ella Govender recalled: 'The lady who was the telephonist, typist cum receptionist, he invited her to come with her husband and children, and she even brought her mother. I think it did make people feel more comfortable but he also just did it because he is just very gregarious. He likes being with people and finding out about them. Like for instance, he always used to take his morning walk and he would meet the bread delivery man on his route. He would be walking up out of the estate up towards UCT [University of Cape Town] way and he would always bring back two loaves of bread, one white, one brown. And he got so friendly that when the bread man got married, Madiba went to his wedding.'[306]

In addition to changes in menu content, there was a significant increase in the number of state functions undertaken. According to John Reinders, Comptroller of the Household under P.W. Botha and Chief of Protocol for F.W. de Klerk, Madiba and later for Thabo Mbeki: 'The major change was in the number of official functions. In P.W.'s time, we were in the isolation times, there was basically one state banquet for the opening of Parliament and that was it. There was basically nothing going on in isolation times. It would be Pik and P.W.

and those people on their own with a bottle of red wine. Then Mandela came and everyone wanted to get to Madiba. The whole world wanted to come, and it just escalated enormously.'[307]

RECONCILIATION AIDED BY SHERRY

Having delegated a significant portion of the day-to-day running of government to Thabo Mbeki, Madiba focused his attentions on the promotion of nation-building and national reconciliation. He recognised that in a divided society nation-building is a prerequisite for all other endeavours in that social, economic and political investment in a society requires trust among individuals and broader social cohesion.

As reconciliation with and reassurance of white South Africans, who still held much of the economic power in the country, was vital to the success of the new nation, Madiba embarked on a series of symbolic dinner dates aimed at wooing them. These highly publicised occasions were criticised by some who argued that the policy of reconciliation spent too much time accommodating white fears and consequently allowed the beneficiaries of apartheid to remain insensitive to the poverty and deprivation it had produced. Madiba, on the other hand, believed such a policy came from a position of strength in that 'courageous people do not fear forgiving for the sake of peace'.[308] Indeed, so successful were his dinner dates that by the time that F.W. de Klerk took the National Party out of the GNU in May 1996, there was no longer any credible threat of a right-wing Afrikaner revolt.

According to Ahmed Kathrada, whether it was *koeksisters* in Orania with H.F. Verwoerd's widow Betsie, tea in the Wilderness with P.W. Botha or even an official luncheon with Percy Yutar, the prosecutor who had secured his Rivonia Trial conviction, 'Mandela brought the policy and philosophy of the ANC on reconciliation and nation-building down to ground level. Everyone talks of reconciliation. He gave it content.'

The table for gastro-political reconciliation was never so carefully laid as when Madiba hosted what his support team described as his 'the widows' tea party', although all those involved drank considerably more sherry than tea in order to calm their nerves. Rica Hodgson and Amina Cachalia were called upon to act as hostesses for a luncheon where Tienie Vorster was placed next to Urbania Mothopeng from the PAC and Elize Botha insisted on being seated next to Madiba. As Hodgson recalled:

MRS VORSTER AND MRS DIEDERICHS WITH MADIBA AT
A LUNCH FOR EX-PRESIDENTS' WIVES, 1995

© *Phyllis Green*

'My initial reaction to the idea was a bit of horror, but then I thought, Well, it's reconciliation. This is it. Mandela wants to placate the old Presidents' wives, widows … and we must play our part … Amina and I were greeting the people as they came in. And I have to say, they came in separately, but they all walked in looking as if they were about to get a slap in the face. They didn't look a bit comfortable and they all kind of huddled together in the lounge, in one corner. When the press people asked me what I thought about it, I said, "My husband would be turning in his grave. He was a hard-liner; he would not have approved of this at all. But if they're prepared to stand up for Mandela, I'm prepared to sit down at the table with them." I mean, that was it, and somehow we got through … One thing that struck me very much though, Walter [Sisulu] was not, of course, invited with the ladies, but he was determined to just come and have a look. He brought his wife in, you see. When he walked into the room, Mrs [Marga] Diederichs, I think, was sitting with Mrs. [Tienie] Vorster. And I think Mrs Vorster started to stand up when Walter Sisulu walked in the room. And Mrs Diederichs kind of did that, like "Don't stand for him," you see. But when Mandela walked in, they all very happily stood up to greet him, that's for sure. I mean, they were really very funny. They all put their

'*… everyone talks of reconciliation.
He gave it content*'

feet in it. I mean, one said, "I have never sat down with Africans before." They didn't know what to do. They were at a total loss. [Then there were] some of our women … there was Adelaide Tambo in this wonderful long, flowing plum velvet gown, with a hat on, and Duma Nokwe's old mother, nearly blind, in a little black dress with slippers and a little white woolly cap with a pom-pom on top, you know … for them it must have seemed really, really strange. They were funny. I mean, when we had the press conference outside, the photo call, Mrs Vorster was sitting in front of Nelson and he called Mrs [Ntsiki] Biko to come over to be in the picture. And Mrs Vorster started to stand up to give Mrs Biko, a much younger woman, her chair. Nelson said, "Sit down, you are so undisciplined, just like your late husband was." It was very funny …'

The encounter wasn't comfortable but it was done. As Amina Cachalia said: 'Most of our women didn't have too much to say to the other women. There was really very little rapport between them, you know. I mean, a woman like Mrs Adelaide Tambo, who was a giant in her days, going to jail over and over again for passive resistance, and the Defiance Campaign … I said to her, "Go and talk to one of these aunties," and she says, "Amina, what must I say to them?" I think they were a bit intimidated too. They probably felt we might take out our wrath and insult them or whatever. Nobody did that, but I think they felt a little bit intimidated. But by the time it was over, the ice had melted a little bit. And the sherry helped … the women were quite at ease towards the end, and said their goodbyes, and Nelson came to me and said, "You must invite them for coffee one of

© Henner Frankenfeld

MADIBA WITH BETSIE VERWOERD IN ORANIA

these days." And I said to one of them, "Would you like to come for coffee to my home?" and they said, "Oh, we'd love to." Haven't done it till this day, I must admit. One day I will, if they're still alive.'[309]

Of this event Jacques Human, who was chef at the official residence from 1995, recalled: 'It was a lovely to see all the previous first ladies, they really enjoyed being in a space that they knew so well. It was very emotional for some of them. Mrs Botha said it looked exactly the same as it had been in her time in the house. Mimi Coertse [the opera singer] was a special guest that day and I remember I opened the door to her and she said, "Ooh, what a déjà vu," because she had often been a guest in the house in previous years. I remember we cooked Ella [Govender]'s *biryani* with all the accompaniments and then we had fresh fruit and berries in sugar baskets.'[310]

An even more bizarre gastro-political tête-à-tête followed on from the widows' tea party. Ninety-four-year-old Betsie Verwoerd declined the invitation saying that she was too frail to travel but wrote that Madiba should 'drop in for tea when you're ever in the area'. Madiba responded by making a trip to her home in Orania, a remote whites-only community in the rural Northern Cape which had been explicitly built on the Verwoerdian principle of white self-determination. Madiba was accompanied by Amina Cachalia. 'I think he really and truly comes up with these ideas because he feels it is so important for the country and for people to reconcile, and it sort of blends the little bit of showmanship, but basically that's what he wants. I mean, even going to Betsie Verwoerd, all the way out to Orania, I thought

Biryani

Marinade

{preferably prepared 3–4 hours before so as to allow the spices
to blend into meat or chicken}

1 CUP PLAIN YOGHURT	1 GRATED TOMATO	2 CINNAMON STICKS
1 TEASPOON CRUSHED	2 BAY LEAVES	2 CARDAMOM PODS
GARLIC AND GINGER	2 TABLESPOONS CURRY POWDER (HOT)	1 SPRIG FRESH CURRY LEAVES
2 TEASPOONS GROUND *GARAM*	1 TEASPOON CRUSHED GREEN OR RED	2–3 MINT LEAVES
MASALA (CURRY SPICE)	CHILLIES	2 TEASPOONS OLIVE OIL
2 TEASPOONS GROUND CUMIN	2 STAR ANISE	SALT TO TASTE

Combine all of the above ingredients in a pot that is large enough to hold all the meat.

Meat

{lamb or beef or chicken}

1–1.5kg MEAT

Cut the meat into small pieces, add to the marinade mixture, then refrigerate this mixture for at least 3 hours.
Cook the marinated meat (with all the marinade) over moderate heat, stirring occasionally. After about 10 minutes a thick
gravy will form from the marinade. When the thick gravy forms, remove the meat from the heat.

Starch

2 CUPS BASMATI RICE	1 SPRIG CURRY LEAVES	2 HARD-BOILED EGGS,
2 TABLESPOONS OLIVE OIL	1 TABLESPOON FRESH THYME,	QUARTERED (FOR GARNISH)
1 CUP LENTILS, COOKED	FINELY CHOPPED	FRESH CORIANDER LEAVES
2 ONIONS, CHOPPED FINE	3 POTATOES PEELED, HALVED	SAFFRON (SOAKED IN 3
2 BAY LEAVES	SALT TO TASTE	TABLESPOONS HOT WATER)
2 STAR ANISE	OIL FOR DEEP-FRYING	
1 CINNAMON STICK		
1 CARDAMOM POD		

Cook the rice until al dente. Drain and set it aside. Cook the lentils until al dente. Drain and set it aside. Fry the
onions until golden brown in 2 tablespoons of olive oil, the thyme, the curry leaves, bay leaves, cardamom pod,
cinnamon, star anise. Deep-fry the potatoes until golden.

{layering the biryani}

Preheat the oven to 180°C. In an oven-proof pot, large enough for all ingredients, start by putting half the cooked meat
and thickened gravy in the bottom of the pot. Next add half the fried potatoes on top of the meat. Cover the potatoes with half
the rice. Next top the rice with half the cooked lentils. Repeat the process with the remaining cooked ingredients. Finally top with
fried onions and whole spices. Sprinkle in the saffron with water. Cover the pot, place in the preheated oven for ½ hour.
Remove from oven and garnish with the boiled eggs and coriander leaves.

even after he stepped down I was still sending biryanis from Cape Town to the Houghton house

was so ridiculous … I was so appalled at going there, but having gone and having been there, and seen the reaction of these people, and then getting them to listen to what this man Nelson Mandela is talking about, and telling them, made me feel that it was worth it in the end, to go there … *Ja*, I thought that was really crazy, going all the way to Orania, to visit this old girl who couldn't come and see him in Pretoria because her doctors advised her that she couldn't travel. But she was hale and hearty when we got there. I said to him, "Why are we going to Orania?" He says, "To reconcile with Mrs Verwoerd." I mean, it was just the craziest place one could think of going. We were the first blacks to go there in any case. I don't think any other people had ever been there … we had a lovely tea with them … and Mrs Verwoerd sat there, quite comfortably, and there was lots of communication. He was informing her what South Africa is going to be like and what he is going to do, and what the country is going to do, and she was listening very intently.' Afterwards Betsie Verwoerd remarked that she had served *koeksisters* and that Madiba had been 'a real gentleman'.[311]

CHOCOLATES AND SNIFFER DOGS

Behind the scenes Madiba's passion for Indian food, first developed in the 1940s, remained as intense and enduring as ever. When Jakes Gerwel, the Director-General in Madiba's Presidency, was

seeking to appoint a Household Comptroller for the presidential residences, he was explicitly told to look for someone who 'could cook *biryani*'. Ella Govender was appointed. She recollected that 'even after he stepped down I was still sending *biryanis* from Cape Town to the Houghton house. Sometimes I even got special requests for crayfish curry.'

Despite the busy social whirl of dining with former foes, Madiba was lonely. His executive personal assistant and spokesperson, Zelda la Grange, said of this time: 'It would break my heart to see him sitting alone at night. There he would be, in his favourite armchair in Qunu with a blanket over his legs, all alone. It was upsetting to see him sitting all by himself on overseas visits or in Qunu, at his huge dining-room table eating breakfast, lunch and dinner.'[312]

The arrival of Mrs Graça Machel in Madiba's life completed the post-prison emotional recovery that had been initiated by his grandchildren. Madiba first met the Frelimo liberation struggle stalwart, child rights activist and widow of President Samora Machel when he visited her homeland of Mozambique after his release from prison in 1990. The pair became better acquainted in 1994 when he officiated at a University of Cape Town ceremony at which she received an honorary doctorate, and later that year he agreed to take over the late Oliver

ELLA GOVENDER'S

Crayfish Curry

4–6 CRAYFISH TAILS
3 TABLESPOONS OLIVE OIL
1 ONION THINLY SLICED
SPRIG OF CURRY LEAVES
2–3 FRESH CHILLIES HALVED (RED OR GREEN)
6 CLOVES GARLIC, FINELY CHOPPED
2 TABLESPOONS CURRY POWDER
½ TEASPOON CUMIN
½ TEASPOON TURMERIC
400g TIN PEELED CHOPPED TOMATOES
1 TEASPOON WHITE SUGAR
CORIANDER LEAVES
SALT TO TASTE

*Remove meat from crayfish tails and slice each tail into
4 generous pieces, cover and refrigerate. Heat the oil in saucepan,
then add the onions, chillies and curry leaves, and sauté
the mixture until onions turn golden. Add the garlic, curry
powder and spices, and stir well. Add tomatoes and the
sugar, and cook the mixture over a medium heat, stirring
occasionally. Cook the mixture until it has turned
into a thick sauce, about 10 minutes. About halfway through
the sauce-making process, add the crayfish meat. Once
the seafood is cooked, remove from heat. Add the coriander
and serve immediately.*

CHOCOLATES FOR MRS MACHEL

He was the suitor and would not have thought to leave so important a task to anyone else. So the bodyguards had to sweep through the plush shopping centre with sniffer dogs, clear the area of any potential danger and then keep the crowds at bay.'[313]

The couple spent Christmas 1996 together in Qunu where Mrs Machel not only charmed her host but also educated his family in matters of Mozambican cuisine. Initially the culinary lessons were treated with some suspicion by certain members of the family. Mandlesizwe Mandela recollected: 'Aunty Graça went to a lot of trouble to make us a meal from her homeland. The table was just full of prawns and crabs and all various seafood, and my grandfather's sister Mabel says to me, "My grandson, what is this thing that looks like a crab from the river sands?" and I look and I say, "But it is, Grandma, it is a crab from the river." And she says, "Nonsense, man, we cannot eat such nonsense. We want meat on the table." And my grandfather had to explain to Aunty Graça, who was now very keen to hear what his sister had just said, because she could pick up that it was about the food. And my grandfather said, "Oh, she just commented on how nice the food looks, but they are not used to these things. Let's bring more meat." But Aunty Graça could tell that that was not what she said. When she later learnt that the Mandelas didn't want seafood, she was

Tambo's role of godfather to her children.

Though there was media speculation about early dates during the Bastille Day celebrations in Paris in 1996 and reports of kisses at President Mugabe's wedding banquet, the first tangible proof of his love was a shopping excursion for edible tokens of affection in Johannesburg. In the words of one of Madiba's bodyguards, Rory Steyn: 'I recall us having to go to Sandton City to buy chocolates for Graça at the end of 1996. Such a simple act, a simple exercise, turned into pandemonium because he insisted on personally choosing and buying the chocolates himself. Anyone on his huge staff would have been more than willing to perform this most basic of acts, but he would have none of that.

that is one thing Aunty Graça will always hold her flag very high on: 'I taught the Mandelas seafood'

GRAÇA MACHEL'S

Caranguejo Recheado
(Stuffed Crab)

{recipe provided by her chef, Esmenia Rafael Gemo}[314]

2kg SMALL CRABS (CLEANED AND STEAMED)
4 SLICES OF WHITE BREAD
ENOUGH MILK TO SOAK THE BREAD
2 MEDIUM ONIONS, FINELY CHOPPED
2 TABLESPOONS OLIVE OIL
2 GARLIC CLOVES, CRUSHED
2 BIG RED CHILLIES (*MELUGUETA*),
FINELY CHOPPED
1 BAY LEAF
1 TABLESPOON LEMON JUICE
2 TABLESPOONS PARMESAN CHEESE, GRATED
1 EGG WHITE
1 TABLESPOON PARSLEY,
FINELY CHOPPED
1 EGG YOLK

Take the crab meat from inside the shell and cut it into small pieces. Retain the crab shells, as you are going to stuff them. Soak the bread in the milk. Sauté the onions over a low heat in the olive oil until soft, and then add the garlic, chillies and the bay leaves. Increase the heat and add the crab meat, garlic and the lemon juice to the onion mixture and mix well. Remove the bread from the milk and add it to the crab mixture. Once everything is well combined, add the grated cheese and remove the mixture from the heat. Take the mixture from the pot and let it cool. When the mixture is cool, add the egg white and the chopped parsley. Set the oven to 140°C. Ten minutes before serving, put the crab mixture back into the crab shells and brush with egg yolk. Place the stuffed crabs back in the oven for 15 minutes. Serve hot.

disappointed because she had spent a lot of time in the kitchen. But over time we have learnt. Today, put seafood on the table, some prawns, some crabs, and they are the first things to disappear. The Mandelas will attack that food. That is one thing Aunty Graça will always hold her flag very high on: "I taught the Mandelas seafood."'[315]

WINNIE MADIKIZELA-MANDELA AND MADIBA AT THEIR
DAUGHTER ZENANI'S BIRTHDAY PARTY, 2008

Kevin Joseph © Mandela family collection

Madiba and Graça were married in a private wedding ceremony conducted on his 80th birthday on 18 July 1998. Though the service is always described as having been a secret to all but the couple themselves, there is evidence to suggest that those in the kitchen must have known what was happening. How do you order a wedding cake complete with peach-coloured icing roses if you don't know there is to be a wedding?

Whether or not the kitchen staff knew what they were preparing for, they were certainly informed that they were to prepare a special meal. According to Xoliswa Ndoyiya: 'The wedding meal was a lunch with both Mozambican food and South African food. We started with a mix of kingflip fish nuggets, prawns and tuna. I made the tartar sauce myself. Then there was a butternut soup, which they all loved. Then we had oxtail, grilled chicken, prawns, tripe, dumplings, curry rice, samp. And then for dessert there was fruit platter and trifle and a mountain of ice-cream – mix of chocolate and double toffee. The cake was a fruit cake – not a very fancy cake. It was just one tier, nicely iced, cream with peach roses to match with their attire.'[316]

The next day the couple held a joint birthday party and wedding banquet at Gallagher Estate in Johannesburg, and then went off to spend their honeymoon in Qunu. When asked two weeks after his wedding whether marriage would change his life, Madiba sipped his tea and said: 'I have only two priorities in my life right now. Number one, Graça, and number two, eating prawns in Mozambique.'[317]

CHRISTMAS IN QUNU

With the changing priorities has come an easing of family tensions. In this Graça Machel's prior experience as a stepmother helped. 'I'm the kind of woman who never knew what it is to start a family. I got married and I was a mother of six immediately.' She understood the Mandela children's sense of abandonment and resentment at having to share her husband with the nation, and she encouraged and assisted him to make himself more available to their needs. In the mid-1990s Winnie Madikizela-Mandela had lamented: 'My children still wait for the return of their father. He has never returned, even emotionally. He can no longer relate to the family as family. He relates to the struggle which has been his lifetime.'[318] But in the ensuing decade bridges have been built and mended to such an extent that the entire family, including Winnie Madikizela-Mandela, spent Christmas 2007 together in Qunu. The children's father had finally returned. It was not the way that they might have imagined their lives together, but everyone was at the dinner table.

GRAÇA MACHEL'S

Caril de Caranguejo com Camarão

(Crab and Prawn Curry)

{recipe supplied by her chef,
Esmenia Rafael Gemo}

2 GRATED COCONUTS
2 CUPS OF BOILING WATER
2 TABLESPOONS OLIVE OIL
2 CINNAMON STICKS
2 STAR ANISE
2 BAY LEAVES
4 GARLIC CLOVES, CRUSHED
2 TOMATOES ROUGHLY CHOPPED
2 TEASPOONS HOT CURRY POWDER
1 TEASPOON GROUND CUMIN
1 BIG RED CHILLI (*MELUGUETA*), FINELY CHOPPED
2kg CRAB, SHELLED AND CLEANED
½kg PRAWNS, SHELLED AND CLEANED
1 TABLESPOON FRESH CHOPPED CORIANDER

Make coconut milk by adding the boiling water to the grated coconut and allowing it to steep for at least 10 minutes. Set it aside. Fry the olive oil, spices, the bay leaves, the garlic, chilli and the tomato until a rich gravy is formed. Add the crab and prawns to the gravy and stir in order to combine the ingredients. Add the coconut milk and let it simmer, stirring occasionally until all the flavours merge, about 5 minutes. Add the coriander and serve with white rice.

Chapter Fourteen

HAPPY ENDINGS AND JUST DESSERTS

ON 16 JUNE 1999, MADIBA STEPPED DOWN as South Africa's first democratically elected President after one term in office.

The following day the menu for Thabo Mbeki's inauguration dinner showed considerably more use of indigenous ingredients and recipes than that served up five years previously. Kalahari truffles, *mogodu*, *morogo* and *umngqusho* all made appearances. Whether the amarula mousse-filled chocolate *potjiekos* pots garnished with chocolate porcupine quills was a culinary and cultural step forward or backward is debatable.

Having relinquished the presidency of the ANC the previous year, Madiba was, for the first time since leaving prison nine years before, a private individual without any official responsibilities of state or party. He celebrated his first day of retirement with a day-long visit to Walter and Albertina Sisulu's house, after which he announced his intention to withdraw from public life, saying that he wanted to spend more time with his grandchildren. But hopes of retirement and sufficient solitude to concentrate on the second volume of his memoirs were not to be. As his friend Fatima Meer said: 'South Africa

has two precious commodities. The one is gold and the other is Nelson Mandela. Everyone fights to get access to them, and once they have access no one wants to give it up.'[319]

A WALK NOT ENDED

After June 1999, Madiba continued to be intensely involved with the issues which had interested him most during his Presidency and indeed which he had been committed to throughout his life. He worked tirelessly on fund-raising and awareness campaigns for the Nelson Mandela Children's Fund (which he had established five years earlier), the Mandela-Rhodes Foundation, the Nelson Mandela Foundation, the 46664 HIV/AIDS campaign, and peace-brokering on the African continent.

In his choice of causes and the approach he took to them, Madiba brought to bear his unparalleled global standing as a figure of moral authority. He had a flair for channelling the respect and affection he commands

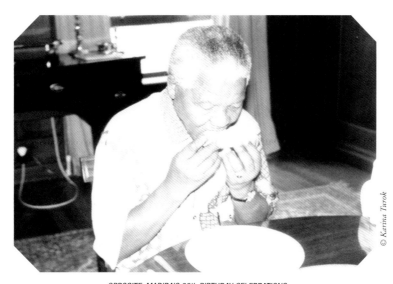

© Karina Turok

OPPOSITE: MADIBA'S 88th BIRTHDAY CELEBRATIONS
© Nelson Mandela Centre of Memory and Dialogue, Nelson Mandela Foundation
ABOVE: MADIBA ENJOYING A MEALIE FOR LUNCH

Morogo with Potato

2 BUNCHES *MOROGO* WILD SPINACH
1 ONION, FINELY CHOPPED
3 TABLESPOONS BUTTER
5 POTATOES, PEELED AND DICED
WATER
SALT AND PEPPER TO TASTE

Rinse the morogo *and chop finely.*
Sautée the onion in 1 tablespoon of the butter then
add the potatoes, morogo, *salt and water to cover.*
Let the mixture come to the boil, and
then simmer until the potatoes are soft, about
30 minutes. Add the remaining butter and
season to taste.

worldwide into such causes. In 1999, he was asked by leaders in the Great Lakes region to facilitate peace in Burundi and his approach broke with the pattern of fruitless talks, with a brutally frank confrontation of the leaders of the warring parties in a manner that facilitated their acting decisively to reach a settlement. Borrowing heavily from the South African experience, Madiba drove forward the peace process by insiting on inclusivity and staring down the delaying tactics of the various factions. His approach paid off with the signing of the Arusha Accord by all the parties one year later.

His considerable work load indicated that, to quote the final sentence of his autobiography: 'I have walked that long road to freedom. I have tried not to falter; I have made missteps along the way. But I have discovered the secret that after climbing a great hill, one only finds that there are many more hills to climb. I have taken a moment here to rest, to steal a view of the glorious vista that surrounds me, to look back on the distance I have come. But I can rest only for a moment, for with freedom comes responsibilities, and I dare not linger, for my long walk is not yet ended.'[320]

RETIRING FROM RETIREMENT

On 10 May 2004 Madiba addressed the South African Parliament on the occasion of the tenth anniversary of his accession to power. He started his speech by telling the Speaker that he was aware that an exception had to be made to the standing rules so as 'to allow a retired old pensioner, who is neither a Member of Parliament nor the serving head of state of any country, to address you'. This description was probably more wishful thinking than a matter of disengenuity, given his significant impact on both domestic and global politics in his post-presidential period. In June 2004 he announced that he was 'retiring from retirement'. This time he was resolute.

Any discussion of the second part of Madiba's post-presidential years needs to be respectful of the rights to privacy of a man who had explicitly removed himself from the public arena. His third wife, Graça Machel, has said of Madiba: 'The world needs symbols, probably nowadays more than before. He is a symbol and he is good at projecting what he represents, his values. But at the same time you have to look at him as a human being who has strengths and weaknesses. He is a symbol, that's correct but he's not a saint. Whatever happens to him, it is a mark of the liberation of the African people, particularly the South African people. He makes the point that he should be treated with dignity because he's absolutely aware of what he represents.'[321]

In the light of his wife's wise words, this chapter intends to maintain such dignity while providing a respectful window onto the dotage of a man who deserved a happy ending and got one.

LATE BREAKFASTS

The first thing to go was the prison-style breakfasting hours. Prior to his third marriage Madiba was in the habit of rising at 4 am, exercising and then breakfasting by 5 am. In 1998 Graça Machel remarked: 'When you love someone you really have to give up certain things. I'm not an early riser but I'm getting used to it.' By 2007, however, Xoliswa Ndoyiya commented: 'He used to be an early bird – we used to give him breakfast at five. But no more. Breakfast is now very late. He can come down at nine-thirty to ten. They will come down. At first it was earlier, but then Mama Machel said, "We aren't going to work. Why must we be down so early?" and so now breakfast is late.'[322]

And it was not just the timing of meals that changed. Their content also became far less austere. For most of Madiba's life he stuck to the disciplined dietary programme that he adopted in his youthful boxing days. But with age he was increasingly willing to believe that a little bit of what you fancy does you good. In his newfound, relaxed attitude to food he appeared to be using his grandchildren and great-grandchildren as his menu planners. Xoliswa Ndoyiya was surprised to find that he rejected her offer of porridge [which had hitherto been his standard morning meal] in favour of the Frosties breakfast cereal consumed by the children of the house. When she expressed concern at this change in his breakfasting habits, he remarked: 'I have honoured my mother enough. Now I will eat anything.'

This approach to matters dietary was not confined to the breakfast table. According to Thoko Mavuso, Madiba's communications co-ordinator: 'During the '90s when we started with him, he was a very strict person in terms of diet – in terms of the fact that he likes to eat fruit and no fat and plenty of greens – but now that he's ageing he's somebody that's craving for custard. Custard and ice-cream. Double toffee ice-cream. But in those days he used to say dried fruit and even discouraging the kids not to eat too much sweets. Now is the time of craving for ice-cream. Not every day, but sometimes he has such a craving.'[323]

His daughter Zindzi Mandela mused: 'In the past he was always concerned about too much fat. He had this thing about how cheese is bad for you … but now he's not very fussy about what he eats. I remember the kids were once with him overnight and I came to join them for lunch the next day and I had taken the children out to the Grillhouse [in Rosebank] the night before, so they had come back with doggy bags. I remember one of them had come back with spare ribs and so we are sitting down to lunch and I am asking, "Tata, what can

I dish for you?" and he looked around at all the nutritious things on the table and he said, "No, man, darling, what's that over there?" and he was pointing to the doggy bag of leftovers and I said, "I don't think you'll like it," but he insisted on having them and so he ate those ribs.'[324]

Even red wine was granted a place at the post-retirement Madiba table. Ahmed Kathrada recollected: 'One day I was going to Jo'burg and someone asked me to carry a case of wine for him to his house and I said, "No because he doesn't drink." I knew him all these years and so I refused to carry this wine. But then I told him about it and he said that the doctor had prescribed it – and he's a fanatic: if a doctor tells him to do it then he does – so now he drinks red wine. Doctor ordered red wine. Two weeks ago I had lunch with him and they gave him a little bit with his meal and he had some sips but you can see he doesn't like it. Even on doctor's orders he left most of it.'[325]

YOU CAN TAKE MADIBA OUT OF QUNU BUT YOU CAN'T TAKE QUNU OUT OF MADIBA

But even in the midst of eating 'anything', Madiba is more often than not honouring his mother. Wherever he is in the world, Madiba takes the tastes of Thembuland with him. His executive personal assistant and spokesperson Zelda la Grange said: 'Xoliswa always packs the Iwisa so that we can prepare Madiba's porridge for his breakfast in the morning. Wherever we are in the world the chefs in the kitchens have to prepare it. The problem is that I can't even boil water without burning it so I always have to ask the security guards to help me to show the chefs at the hotels around the world how to prepare the stiff porridge

THE GRILLHOUSE

Spare Ribs

{recipe supplied by owner Saul Mervis}

SERVES 6 TO 8 PEOPLE
6kg WHOLE CAGE PORK RIBS
(ABOUT 4 TO 5 RACKS)
400ml SOYA SAUCE
200ml WORCESTERSHIRE SAUCE
100ml BROWN VINEGAR
100ml LEMON JUICE
4 TEASPOONS OF TABASCO SAUCE
200ml ORANGE JUICE
200ml COCA-COLA
400ml TOMATO SAUCE
4 TABLESPOONS BBQ SAUCE
4 TABLESPOONS MILD MUSTARD
4 TABLESPOONS PICCALILLI
400g BROWN SUGAR
400ml RED WINE

Boil the ribs in a large pot of water for about 45 minutes. Test if they are ready by pushing the meat off the bone. If it separates relatively easily from the bone, it is ready to be grilled. For best results allow the ribs to cool before grilling. Combine the soya sauce, Worcestershire sauce, vinegar, lemon juice, Tabasco sauce, orange juice and Coke. Bring the mixture to the boil. Once it is boiling, add the tomato sauce, BBQ sauce, mild mustard, piccalilli, brown sugar and red wine. Whisk the mixture constantly and allow it to reduce to a thick sauce. Remove from the heat and cool completely. Grill the ribs on an open flame, turning regularly so as to ensure that the flesh becomes crispy on the outside but not burnt. Dip the ribs in the sauce 3 to 4 times during the grilling process. Remove and eat – with your hands.

XOLISWA NDOYIYA'S

Umphokoqo

2 CUPS WATER
1 TEASPOON SALT
2 CUPS MEALIE MEAL
1*l* AMASI

*Bring the salted water to a boil. Add the
mealie meal, stirring constantly. Lower the heat
and, stirring throughout, cook until the
porridge is soft, approximately 25 minutes.
After 25 minutes, stop stirring. Reduce
the heat to an absolute minimum and cover the
pot with a lid for 15 minutes or until the
texture is totally soft (if there are still granules,
the mixture is not yet cooked). Remove from
the heat, turn the contents of the pot into a
large bowl and allow it to cool completely.
Serve with soured milk on the sides so that
each diner can determine how sour they
would like their* umphokoqo *to be. The soured
milk is then stirred into the porridge.*

Madiba prefers for breakfast.'[326] Similarly, Vimla Naidoo, personal assistant to Nelson Mandela and Graça Machel, recalled a trip to London that she made with the former President. 'Zelda sent me an email from London before I could travel saying, "You're not going to believe this and you are actually going to laugh but

MADIBA WITH HIS GREAT GRANDSON, ZWELAMI MANDELA, AT ZENANI MANDELA'S BIRTHDAY, 2008

Kevin Joseph © Mandela family collection

laughing, but she was amazing – she packaged it so it looked like a birthday gift. They put it in a Tupperware and then wrapped it in gift wrap and put it in a box, and then I had this beautiful gift bag so it looked like I was taking someone a lovely birthday present. And

Madiba is tired of having food at the hotel." He had been away for a long time and I think he was missing Xoliswa. And what he was asking for was *umphokoqo*. That's what he wanted. He was in the finest of international hotels but that's what he felt like eating. So I had to call Thoko and Xoliswa at the house in Houghton and say, "I don't know how we are going to do this but this is what he wants." Initially when I spoke to Xoliswa she was

that's what I flew with. And Zelda called me before I left and she said, "Have you got Madiba's food? Because Madiba says if anything goes wrong you must call him immediately – because you are not allowed to come to the Dorchester without his food." Zelda said (and I'm sure she was joking) that, "If anybody stops you at customs, you are to call immediately, and if necessary an approach will be made to Tony Blair."'[327]

Sources and interviews

Bibliography

Published sources
Books
Ahmed Kathrada, *Memoirs*, Cape Town, Zebra, 2004
Allister Sparks, *The Mind of South Africa*, London, Heinemann, 1990
Anne Marie du Preez Bezdrob, *The Nelson Mandela Story*, Cape Town, Samoja, 2006
Anthony Sampson, *Mandela: The Authorized Biography*, London, HarperCollins, 2000
Charlene Smith, *Mandela: In Celebration of a Great Life*, Cape Town, Struik, 2003
Debora Patta, *One Step Behind Mandela: The Story of Rory Steyn, Nelson Mandela's Chief Bodyguard*, Johannesburg, Zebra, 2000
Eddie Daniels, *There and Back*, Bellville, Mayibuye Books, 1998
Elinor Sisulu, *In Our Lifetime*, Cape Town, David Philip, 2002
Fatima Meer, *Higher than Hope*, Johannesburg, Skotaville, 1988
Frieda Matthews, *Remembrances*, Cape Town, Mayibuye Centre, 1995
George Bizos, *Odyssey to Freedom*, Johannesburg, Random House, 2007
Helen Joseph, *Side by Side*, London, William Morrow & Co., 1987
Indres Naidoo, *Island in Chains*, London, Penguin, 1982
Institute of Race Relations, *1970 Survey of the South African Institute of the Race Relations*
Ismail Meer, *A Fortunate Man*, Cape Town, Zebra Press, 2005
Jeff B Peires, *The House of Phalo*, Braamfontein, Ravan Press, 1987
Joel Carlson, *No Neutral Ground*, New York, Crowell Collier Press, 1973
Luli Callinicos, *The World That Made Mandela*, Johannesburg, STE, 2006
Mike Nicol et al, *Mandela: The Authorized Portrait*, Wild Dog Press, Johannesburg, 2006
Mark Gevisser, *Thabo Mbeki: The Dream Deferred*, Johannesburg, Jonathan Ball, 2007
Mary Benson, *Nelson Mandela, the Man and the Movement*, Harmondsworth, Penguin, 1994. Updated from 1986 edition
Michael Dingake, *My Fight Against Apartheid*, Kliptown Books, London, 1987
Nelson Mandela, *Long Walk to Freedom*, London, Abacus, 1994

Nelson Mandela: *I am prepared to die*, International Defence and Aid Fund for Southern Africa, 1984
Rusty Bernstein, *Memory Against Forgetting*, London, Viking, 1999
Thomas Karis and GM Carter (eds) *From Protest to Challenge*, volumes 1-5. Stanford, Hoover Insititution Press, 1977–1997
Tom Lodge, *Black Politics in South Africa since 1945*, London, Longman, 1983
Truth and Reconciliation Commission of South Africa Report, volumes 1–5, 1998
Winnie Mandela, *Part of My Soul Went With Him*, London, Penguin, 1978

Newspapers, periodicals, websites and public lectures
Alan Fine, *Business Day,* 15 June 1999
Arthur Maimane, *The Golden City Post,* 25 May 1958
Bill Keller, *New York Times,* 19 November 1993
Franz Kemp, *You* magazine, 20 July 1989
http://www.sahistory.org.za
http://www.anc.org.za

PBS Frontline, 2003, url http://www.pbs.wgbh/pages/frontline/shows/mandela/interviews.html
R.L. Doty, *Handbook of Olfaction and Gustation*, Marcel Dekker, 1995
Verne Harris, *Cultural Value of Oral History*, University of Glasgow public lecture, 24 July 2007

Unpublished sources
African diary of Nelson Mandela, 1961; Percy Yutar Papers, Brenthurst Collection
Court Records of the Case of the State vs. Nelson Mandela and others
Nelson Mandela Private Papers, Nelson Mandela Centre of Memory and Dialogue, Nelson Mandela Foundation

Oral interviews not conducted by the author
Barbara Masekela, quoted in Anthony Sampson, *Mandela: The Authorized Biography*
Jack Swart, interview with PBS Frontline, 2003, url http://www.pbs.wgbh/pages/frontline/shows/mandela/interviews.html
Mabel Mandela, quoted in *Mandela*, a film by Menell and Gibson, 1994
Nelson Mandela, interview with Associated Press Television, 1995

Niël Barnard quoted in Anthony Sampson's *Mandela: The Authorized Biography*

Rica Hodgson, interview with PBS Frontline, 2003. url http://www.pbs.wgbh/pages/frontline/shows/mandela/interviews.html

Oral interviews conducted by the author

Ahmed Kathrada, Johannesburg, 8 October 2007
Amelia Grobelaar, telephonic, 11 December 2007
Amina Cachalia, Johannesburg, 5 October 2007
Anthony Xaba, telephonic, 9 February 2008
Barbara Harmel, Johannesburg, 22 September 2007
Barbara Waite, Johannesburg, 15 January 2008
Christo Brand, Cape Town, 16 October 2007
Ella Govender, telephonic, 15 January 2008
Esmenia Gemo, Maputo, on behalf of the author by Denise Vedor, 8 February 2008
Estelle Brand, Cape Town, 16 October 2007
Farida Omar, Cape Town, 18 October 2007
Fatima Meer, telephonic, 7 January 2008
Fiona Reed, Johannesburg, November 2007
François Ferreira, Stellenbosch, 16 October 2007
George Bizos, Johannesburg, 10 December 2007
Gladys Xhoma, Alexandra, 26 November 2007
Ilse Wilson, Johannesburg, 25 September 2007
Jack Swart, telephonic, 1 December 2007
Jacques Human, telephonic, 15 January 2008
Joe Matthews, Johannesburg, 26 October 2007
John Reinders, telephonic, 12 January 2008
Laloo Chiba, Lenasia, 21 November 2007
Lavinia Crawford-Browne, telephonic, 28 September 2007
Lillian Ngoboza, Cape Town, 17 October 2007
Madanjit Ranchod, conversation, July 2005
Makaziwe Mandela, Johannesburg, 10 October 2007
Mandlenkosi Ngcebetshana, Qunu, 15 November 2007
Marcia Kriek, telephonic, 20 November 2007
Michael Dingake, email, November 2007
Monde Ngcebetshana, Mvezo, 14 November 2007
Naga Naidoo, telephonic, 10 January 2008
Nat Bregman, Johannesburg, 27 November 2007
Nelson Mandela, conversation, Johannesburg, 4 December 2007
Nkosi Zwelivelile (Mandlesizwe Mandela), Mvezo, 15 November 2007
Nkosi Zwelivelile (Mandlesizwe Mandela), Qunu, 16 November 2007
Nthato Motlana, telephonic, 15 January 2008
Philemoen Tefu, telephonic, 9 February 2008
Sally Rowney, Pretoria, 9 November 2007
Shanthie Naidoo, Johannesburg, 29 November 2007
Sigrid Langebrekke, Nobel Foundation, email, 16 January 2007
Sitsheketshe Morrison Mandela, Qunu, 17 November 2007
Sonia Cabano, telephonic, 21 December 2007
Thanga Kolopan, Pretoria, 4 December 2007

Thoko Mavuso, Johannesburg, 11 September 2007
Tokyo Sexwale, telephonic, 29 November 2007
Vasugee Moodley, née Pillay, Pretoria, 4 December 2007
Vimla Naidoo, Johannesburg, 20 November 2007
Winnie Madikizela-Mandela, Johannesburg, 6 December 2007
Winnie Toni, Harding, 12 November 2007
Xoliswa Ndoyiya, Johannesburg, 20 September 2007
Xoliswa Ndoyiya, Johannesburg, 8 October 2007
Zelda la Grange, email, 1 February 2008
Zindzi Mandela, Johannesburg 5 December 2007

Photographic Credits

Photographers

Photographs by Richard Goode except where credited

Alet van Huyssteen
Alf Kumalo
Benny Gool
Eli Weinberg
Graeme Williams
Henner Frankenfeld
Jurgen Schadeberg
Karina Turok
Kevin Joseph
Louise Gubb
Mark Skinner
Morris Zwi
Rashid Lombard
Vanessa Grobelar

Family collections

Bregman personal collection
Charles van Onselen personal collection
Mandela family collection
Naidoo family collection
Pahad family collection
Pillay family collection
Reed family collection
Sisulu family collection

Institutional collections and agencies

Avusa Media
Baileys African History Archive
Images 24
MuseuMAfrica
Nelson Mandela Foundation, Centre of Memory Archive
Reuters
Robben Island Mayibuye Archives, University of the Western Cape
The Bigger Picture
University of the Witwatersrand historical papers collection

Culinary and political glossary

abakhwetha – Xhosa term for young men undergoing the ceremonial initiation period.

Afrikaners – ethnic settler group with predominantly European origins associated with southern Africa and the Afrikaans language.

alikreukel – Afrikaans term for a giant periwinkle.

amadombolo – Zulu word meaning steamed dumplings.

amasi – Xhosa term for soured milk.

African National Congress (ANC) – the most widely supported South African liberation movement, founded in 1912, banned in 1960, and legalised in February 1990.

Aromat – monosodium glutamate-based flavour enhancer.

besan gram – Indian term for chickpea flour.

biltong – traditional Afrikaner dried beef or game meat flavoured with coriander seed.

biryani – spicy rice, lentil and potato mélange which commonly but not always has a meat addition.

Black Consciousness Movement (BCM) – grassroots anti-apartheid organisation which emerged in South Africa in the late 1960s and argued that political liberation required a combination of fighting for structural political changes and also transforming the minds of black South Africans to replace mental inferiority. The organisation was opposed to co-operation with whites. In 1977 all BCM groupings were banned and its national leader, Steve Biko, was murdered while in the custody of the South African security police.

boerewors – beef and pork coriander-laden South African sausage.

Broederbond – Afrikaans secret society formed in 1918 and dedicated to the advancement of Afrikaner interests.

calabash – hard-shelled gourd (sometimes referred to as a bottle gourd) which has been hollowed out and dried and is used as a storage vessel.

Congress of Democrats – organisation founded in 1952 in which white people opposed to apartheid co-operated with the African National Congress (ANC), the South African Communist Party (SACP) and the South African Indian Congress (SAIC) within the broad Congress Alliance. Banned in September 1962.

Defiance Campaign – non-violent resistance campaign in 1952 under the leadership of the ANC and the SAIC during which volunteers defied apartheid laws and provoked arrest.

dermpies – the diminutive of innards.

dhal – Indian term for legumes that have been split and the cooked dishes made with them. In South Africa the term is commonly used to denote a spiced lentil soup served as an accompaniment to curries.

dhania – Indian term for coriander.

Diwali – Hindu religious festival also known as the Festival of Light which celebrates the victory of good over evil and brightness over darkness.

Eid ul-Fitr – Muslim festival of the breaking of the fast that occurs immediately after the month of Ramadan fasting.

frikkadel – traditional Afrikaner dish of meatballs prepared with onion, bread, eggs and spices.

fufu – West and Central African staple food made by boiling starchy root vegetables (usually but not always either yams or cassavas) in water and pounding into a thick paste.

ghee – clarified butter used in Indian cooking.

Government of National Unity (GNU) – first democratically elected government in which the National Party and Inkatha had cabinet positions alongside the ANC between 1994 and 1996.

Groote Schuur – official residence of the President in Cape Town.

IEC – Independent Electoral Commission.

imifino – Xhosa term that means green vegetables in general but is often used to denote a mealie meal and wild spinach mélange.

inconco – Xhosa term for a fermented mealie meal and sorghum sour porridge.

Inkatha – cultural organisation founded in the 1920s and revived in 1975; in July 1990 it was launched as a non-racial political party. Its membership is predominantly Zulu and based in KwaZulu-Natal.

inkobe – Xhosa term for a porridge-like dish made from husked, dried mealies.

isonka sombhako – Xhosa term used to describe a fire-baked pot bread.

Jehovah's Witnesses – Christian religious sect. Jehovah's Witnesses are politically neutral and argue that they owe allegiance to God's Kingdom rather than secular governments or political parties. They believe that participating in politics would be tantamount to worshipping an idol.

katkop – Afrikaans term (literally, cat's head) which is used in prison parlance to denote a chunk of bread and a lump of margarine.

kitke – also known as challah; a plaited egg-enriched yeast-leavened bread traditionally eaten by Ashkenazi Jews on the Sabbath, holidays and other ceremonial occasions.

koeksisters – deep-fried, twisted and syrup-laden doughnut common in Afrikaans and Cape Malay confectionery traditions.

koringbier – traditional Afrikaans-style fermented wheat beer.

kramat – tomb of a Muslim saint.

ladoo – Indian-style sweetmeat made from chickpea flour, almonds and icing sugar.

liquid glucose – sometimes referred to as glucose syrup, this thick, clear syrup controls the formation of sugar crystals when sugar is heated and is commonly used in confectionery.

makatane – Xhosa term to describe a melon-like vegetable, traditionally called *kafferwaatlemoen* in Afrikaans.

malva pudding – traditional Afrikaans baked vinegar pudding which contains apricot jam and is soaked in a cream-laden custard.

marhewu – Xhosa term for a mildly fermented mealie meal beverage.

masala – (also known as *massala*) a term used in Indian cuisine to describe a mixture of many spices.

mealie – maize on the cob.

melugueta **pepper** – small, tapered green chilli pepper used in Mozambican poultry and seafood dishes.

milk tart – traditional Afrikaner custard tart.

MK – Umkhonto weSizwe, the armed wing of the ANC.

mogudu – Xhosa term for tripe; also used to mean a spicy tripe stew traditional to the Eastern Cape.

morogo – Tswana term for vegetables, used in common South African parlance to mean a range of wild spinach-like vegetables.

Nesquik – flavoured powdered milk concentrate.

Orania – small settlement in the Northern Cape administered as a racially and culturally exclusive Afrikaner enclave.

Pan Africanist Congress of Azania (PAC) – South African liberation movement founded in 1959 as a breakaway from the ANC because of objections to the latter's non-racial policies.

pap – Afrikaans term for mealie meal porridge.

pellagra – nutritional deficiency disease caused by a lack of vitamin B.

perlemoen – Afrikaans term for a shelled, mollusc-like sea creature with a muscular foot which clings to rocky surfaces. Commonly known as abalone outside South Africa.

phuzamandla – Xhosa term (literally, drink of strength) commonly used to denote a powdered drink made from a mixture of iron-fortified sorghum and maize served by prison authorities in South Africa to prisoners.

potjie – heavy, black iron pot with three legs used for cooking over an open fire. A range of traditional Afrikaner stews are cooked in a *potjie* and are commonly referred to as *potjiekos*.

rhwabe – Xhosa term for green leafy vegetable indigenous to the Eastern Cape region of South Africa. Often used in *imifino*.

roti – thin, rolled, unleavened Indian bread, also known as *chapati*.

rusk – hard, dry biscuit or dried bread dough, often but not always twice-baked.

samoosa – small triangular savoury pastry with a spiced filling.

samp – roughly broken dried mealie.

shmaltz – rendered chicken fat that is used instead of butter in kosher cooking.

South African Indian Congress (SAIC) – formed in 1924 to oppose legislation to segregate the Indians. In the late 1940s, it spearheaded a passive resistance campaign in which over 2 000 people went to prison in protest against a new law restricting Indian land-ownership. The ANC and SAIC jointly launched the Defiance Campaign of 1952 and shortly thereafter both became members of the Congress Alliance.

terroir – term commonly used in the French viticultural environment to refer to the combination of soil, topography, climate, culture and history of a region and the impact of those on the wine.

Third Force – paramilitary force that attacked anti-apartheid organisations and individuals; covertly supported by the apartheid government.

Truth and Reconciliation Commission (TRC) – court-like body constituted after the end of apartheid so that victims of apartheid crimes could come forward and recount their stories and perpetrators of such crimes could also give testimony and apply for amnesty from prosecution.

umbozo – green leafy vegetable indigenous to the Eastern Cape region of South Africa. Often used in *imifino*.

umngqusho – Xhosa term used to describe a dish consisting of samp (roughly broken, dried corn kernels) and beans.

umphokoqo – Xhosa term to describe a dish consisting of mealie meal porridge and sour milk.

United Democratic Front – coalition of community, labour, religious, youth and other organisations sympathetic to the ANC. It was formed in 1983 to fight apartheid.

Endnotes

1 Nelson Mandela, *Long Walk to Freedom*, London, Abacus, 1994, p. 750.
2 No one is more aware and appreciative of his humanity than Madiba himself. In notes in the margin of an early draft of *Long Walk to Freedom*, he wrote: 'The issue that deeply worried me in prison was the false image that was unwittingly projected to the outside world of my being regarded as a saint. I was never one, even on the basis of an earthly definition of a saint as a sinner who keeps on trying.'
3 Dr Alan Hirsch of the Taste Treatment and Research Foundation in Chicago, quoted in MX, Melbourne, Australia, 28 January 2003.
4 R.L. Doty, *Handbook of Olfaction and Gustation*, Marcel Dekker, 1995.
5 Verne Harris, 'Cultural Value of Oral History', University of Glasgow public lecture, 24 July 2007.
6 Letter dated 31 August 1970, Nelson Mandela Centre of Memory and Dialogue.
7 Tokyo Sexwale, telephonic conversation with author, 29 November 2007.
8 Nelson Mandela, *Long Walk to Freedom*, p. 9.
9 Sitsheketshe Morrison Mandela, interview with the author, Qunu, 17 November 2007.
10 Nelson Mandela, *Long Walk to Freedom*, p. 10.
11 Nelson Mandela, interview with Associated Press Television, 1995.
12 Nkosi Zwelivelile, interview with the author, Qunu, 16 November 2007.
13 Nkosi Zwelivelile, interview with the author, Qunu, 16 November 2007.
14 Nkosi Zwelivelile, interview with the author, Qunu, 16 November 2007.
15 Mabel Mandela, interview for the film Mandela, by Menell and Gibson, 1994.
16 Anthony Sampson, *Mandela*, London, Harper Collins, 2000, p. 46.
17 Letter dated 1 April 1971, Nelson Mandela Centre of Memory and Dialogue.
18 Nelson Mandela, *Long Walk to Freedom*, p. 11.
19 Mandlenkosi Ngcebetshana, interview with the author, Qunu, 15 November 2007.
20 Letter dated 1 August 1970, Nelson Mandela Centre of Memory and Dialogue.
21 Mandlenkosi Ngcebetshana, interview with the author, Qunu, 15 November 2007.
22 Nelson Mandela, conversation with the author, 4 December 2007.
23 Winnie Toni, interview with the author, Harding, 12 November 2007.
24 Anthony Sampson, *Mandela*, p. 17 (interview with Mrs Knipe 2 February 1998 conducted by Anthony Sampson).
25 Nkosi Zwelivelile, interview with the author, Qunu, 16 November 2007.
26 Nelson Mandela, interview with Associated Press Television, 1995.
27 Nelson Mandela, *Long Walk to Freedom*, p. 31.
28 Nelson Mandela, *Long Walk to Freedom*, p. 35.
29 The Freedom Charter, Congress of the People, Kliptown, 26 June 1955.
30 Nelson Mandela, interview with Associated Press Television, 1995.
31 Joe Matthews, interview with the author, Johannesburg, 26 October 2007.
32 Peter Reinhart, *The Bread Baker's Apprentice*, Berkeley, Ten Speed Press, 2001.
33 Nelson Mandela, *Long Walk to Freedom*, p. 57.
34 Luli Callinicos, *The World That Made Mandela*, Johannesburg, STE, 2006.
35 Joe Matthews, interview with the author, Johannesburg, 26 October 2007.
36 Tom Lodge, *Black Politics in South Africa since 1945*, London, Longman, 1983, p. 12.
37 Gladys Xhoma, interview with the author, Alexandra, 26 November 2007.
38 Gladys Xhoma, interview with the author, Alexandra, 26 November 2007.
39 Nelson Mandela, *Long Walk to Freedom*, p. 91.
40 Nat Bregman, interview with the author, Johannesburg, 27 November 2007.
41 Nelson Mandela, *Long Walk to Freedom*, p. 85.
42 Nat Bregman, interview with the author, Johannesburg, 27 November 2007.
43 Nelson Mandela, *Long Walk to Freedom*, p. 85.
44 Nat Bregman, interview with the author, Johannesburg, 27 November 2007.
45 Elinor Sisulu, *In Our Lifetime*, Cape Town, David Philip, 2002, p. 68.
46 Joe Matthews, interview with the author, Johannesburg, 26 October 2007.
47 Elinor Sisulu, *In Our Lifetime*, p. 65.
48 Nelson Mandela, *Long Walk to Freedom*, p. 56.
49 Elinor Sisulu, *In Our Lifetime* interview with Nelson Mandela, 11 August 1993.
50 Letter dated 31 August 1970, Nelson Mandela Centre of Memory and Dialogue.
51 Dr Makaziwe Mandela, interview with the author, Johannesburg, 10 October 2007.
52 Anthony Sampson, *Mandela*, p. 36.
53 Dr Makaziwe Mandela, interview with the author, Johannesburg, 10 October 2007.
54 Sitsheketshe Mandela, interview with the author, Qunu, 16 November 2007.
55 Nelson Mandela, *Long Walk to Freedom*, p. 121.
56 Dr Makaziwe Mandela, interview with the author, Johannesburg, 10 October 2007.
57 Nelson Mandela, *Long Walk to Freedom*, p. 125.
58 Joe Matthews, interview with the author, Johannesburg, 26 October 2007.
59 Amina Cachalia, interview with the author, Johannesburg, 5 October 2007.
60 Nelson Mandela, *Long Walk to Freedom*, p. 121.
61 Joe Matthews, interview with the author, Johannesburg, 26 October 2007.
62 Letter dated 31 August 1970, Nelson Mandela Centre of Memory and Dialogue.
63 Monde Ngcebetshana, interview with the author, Mvezo, 14 November 2007.
64 Xoliswa Ndoyiya, interview with the author, Johannesburg, 8 October 2007.
65 Joe Matthews, interview with the author, Johannesburg, 26 October 2007.
66 Ella Govender, telephonic interview with the author, 15 January 2008.
67 Rica Hodgson, interview with PBS Frontline, 2003, url http://www.pbs.wgbh/pages/frontline/shows/mandela/interviews.html
68 Winnie Madikizela-Mandela, interview with the author, Johannesburg, 6 December 2007.
69 Barbara Harmel, interview with the author, Johannesburg, 22 September 2007.
70 Barbara Harmel, interview with the author, Johannesburg, 22 September 2007.
71 Winnie Madikizela-Mandela, interview with the author, 6 December 2007.
72 Barbara Harmel, interview with the author, Johannesburg, 22 September 2007.
73 Amina Cachalia, interview with author, Johannesburg, 5 November 2007.
74 Barbara Harmel, interview with the author, Johannesburg, 22 September 2007.
75 Ahmed Kathrada, interview with author, Johannesburg, 8 October 2007.
76 Barbara Harmel, interview with the author, Johannesburg, 22 September 2007.
77 Winnie Madikizela-Mandela, interview with the author, Johannesburg, 6 December 2007.
78 Winnie Madikizela-Mandela, interview with the author, Johannesburg, 6 December 2007.
79 Zindzi Mandela, interview with the author, Johannesburg, 5 December 2007.
80 Franz Kemp, *You* magazine, 20 July 1989, p. 8.
81 Letter dated 31 August 1970, Nelson Mandela Centre of Memory and Dialogue.
82 Anthony Sampson, *Mandela*, p. 113.
83 Winnie Madikizela-Mandela, interview with the author, 6 December 2007.
84 Zindzi Mandela, interview with the author, Johannesburg, 6 December 2007.
85 Winnie Madikizela-Mandela, interview with the author, 6 December 2007.
86 Letter dated 2 June 1986, Nelson Mandela Centre of Memory and Dialogue.
87 Winnie Madikizela-Mandela, interview with the author, 6 December 2007.
88 Zindzi Mandela, interview with the author, Johannesburg 5 December 2007.
89 Letter dated 20 June 1970, Nelson Mandela Centre of Memory and Dialogue.
90 Charlene Smith, *Mandela: In Celebration of a Great Life*, Cape Town, Struik 2003 p. 46.
91 Nelson Mandela, *Long Walk to Freedom* p. 106.
92 Ahmed Kathrada, interview with author, Johannesburg, 8 October 2007.
93 Ismail Meer, *A Fortunate Man*, Cape Town, Zebra Press, 2005, p. 101.
94 Letter dated 1 October 1970, Nelson Mandela Centre of Memory and Dialogue.
95 Shanthie Naidoo, interview with the author, Johannesburg, 29 November 2007.
96 Joe Matthews, interview with the author, Johannesburg, 26 October 2007.
97 Barbara Harmel, interview with the author, Johannesburg, 22 October 2007.
98 Ahmed Kathrada, interview with the author, Johannesburg, 8 October 2007.
99 Joe Matthews, interview with the author, Johannesburg, 26 October 2007.
100 Nelson Mandela, *Long Walk to Freedom*, p. 98.
101 George Bizos, interview with the author, Johannesburg, 10 December 2007.
102 Nelson Mandela, *Long Walk to Freedom*, p. 462.
103 Ilse Wilson, interview with the author, Johannesburg, 25 September 2007.
104 George Bizos, interview with the author, Johannesburg, 10 December 2007.
105 Ahmed Kathrada, interview with the author, Johannesburg, 8 October 2007.
106 Amina Cachalia, interview with the author, Johannesburg, 5 November 2007.
107 Sitsheketshe Mandela, interview with the author, Qunu, 15 November 2007.
108 Ilse Wilson, interview with the author, Johannesburg, 25 September 2007.
109 Joe Matthews, interview with the author, Johannesburg, 26 October 2007.
110 Ahmed Kathrada, interview with author, Johannesburg, 8 October 2007.
111 George Bizos, interview with the author, Johannesburg, 10 December 2007.
112 Ruth Mompati, quoted in *Mandela: The Authorized Portrait*, Wild Dog Press, Johannesburg, 2006, p. 56.
113 Barbara Harmel, interview with the author, Johannesburg, 22 October 2007.
114 Ahmed Kathrada, interview with the author, Johannesburg, 8 October 2007.
115 Letter from Nelson Mandela to Sanna Teyise dated 22 December 1970, Nelson Mandela Centre of Memory and Dialogue.
116 George Bizos, interview with the author, Johannesburg, 10 December 2007.
117 Madanjit Ranchod, conversation with the author, July 2005.
118 Professor Z.K. Matthews, letter to his wife dated 12 December 1956, in Frieda Matthews, *Remembrances*, Cape Town, Mayibuye Centre 1995, p. 111.
119 Ahmed Kathrada, interview with the author, Johannesburg, 8 October 2007.
120 Ismail Meer, *A Fortunate Man*, Cape Town, Zebra Press, 2005, p. 184.
121 George Bizos, interview with the author, Johannesburg, 10 December 2007.
122 Gillian Slovo, email interview with the author, 22 September 2007.
123 Joe Matthews, interview with the author, Johannesburg, 26 October 2007.
124 George Bizos, interview with the author, Johannesburg, 10 December 2007.
125 Helen Joseph, *Side by Side*, London, William Morrow & Co., 1987, p. 233.
126 Ahmed Kathrada, interview with the author, Johannesburg, 8 October 2007.
127 Mary Benson, *Nelson Mandela, the Man and the Movement*, Harmondsworth: Penguin, 1994. Updated from 1986 edition, p. 87.
128 Helen Joseph, *Side by Side*, London, William Morrow & Co., 1987, p. 240.
129 Thanga Kolopan, interview with the author, 4 December 2007. She is the mother of Jody Kollapen, Chairperson of SA Human Rights Commission – her surname was incorrectly recorded by apartheid-era functionaries.
130 Shanthie Naidoo, interview with the author, Johannesburg, 29 November 2007.
131 Ilse Wilson, interview with the author, Johannesburg, 25 September 2007.
132 Shanthie Naidoo, interview with the author, Johannesburg, 29 November 2007.
133 Vasugee Moodley, née Pillay, interview with the author, Pretoria, 4 December 2007.
134 Sinda Naidoo, interview with author, Johannesburg, 29 November 2007.
135 Vasugee Moodley, née Pillay, interview with the author, Pretoria, 4 December 2007.
136 Amina Cachalia, interview with the author, Johannesburg, 5 October 2007.
137 Ahmed Kathrada, interview with the author, Johannesburg, 8 October 2007.
138 Nelson Mandela, *Long Walk to Freedom*, p. 329.
139 Ahmed Kathrada, interview with the author, Johannesburg, 8 October 2007.
140 Winnie Madikizela-Mandela, interview with the author, Johannesburg, 6 December 2007.
141 Joe Matthews, interview with the author, Johannesburg, 26 October 2007.
142 Percy Yutar Papers, Brenthurst Collection, Johannesburg.
143 Joe Matthews, interview with the author, Johannesburg, 26 October 2007.
144 Naga Naidoo, telephonic interview with the author, 10 January 2008.
145 Nelson Mandela, *Long Walk to Freedom*, p. 374.
146 Fatima Meer, telephonic interview with the author, 7 January 2008.
147 Joe Matthews, interview with the author, Johannesburg, October 26 2007.
148 Zindzi Mandela, interview with the author, Johannesburg, 5 December 2007.
149 Winnie Madikizela-Mandela, interview with the author, Johannesburg, 5 December 2007.
150 Philemoen Tefu, telephonic interview with the author, 9 February 2008.
151 Michael Dingake, *My Fight Against Apartheid*, Kliptown Books, London, 1987, p. 140.
152 Anthony Sampson, *Mandela*, p. 191.
153 Mike Nicol et al, *Mandela, the Authorized Portrait*, Wild Dog Press, Johannesburg, 2006.
154 George Bizos, interview with the author, Johannesburg, 10 December 2007.
155 Nelson Mandela, *Long Walk to Freedom*, p. 433.
156 Elinor Sisulu, *In Our Lifetime*, p. 168.
157 Anthony Sampson, *Mandela*, p. 195.

158 George Bizos, interview with the author, Johannesburg, 10 December 2007.
159 George Bizos, interview with the author, Johannesburg, 10 December 2007.
160 Marcia Kriek, telephone interview with the author, 20 November 2007.
161 Michael Dingake, interview with the author by email, November 2007.
162 Indres Naidoo, *Island in Chains*, London, Penguin, 1982, p. 71.
163 Nelson Mandela, *Long Walk to Freedom*, p. 466.
164 Ahmed Kathrada, interview with the author, Johannesburg, 8 October 2007.
165 Michael Dingake, *My Fight against Apartheid*, p. 140.
166 *1970 Survey of the South African Institute of Race Relations.*
167 Nelson Mandela, *Long Walk to Freedom*, p. 455.
168 Nelson Mandela, *Long Walk to Freedom*, p. 599.
169 Laloo Chiba, interview with the author, Lenasia, 21 November 2007.
170 Fatima Meer, interview with Anthony Sampson, Durban, 27 July 1996.
171 Laloo Chiba, interview with the author, Lenasia, 21 November 2007.
172 Nelson Mandela, *Long Walk to Freedom*, p. 515.
173 Nelson Mandela, *Long Walk to Freedom*, p. 494.
174 Laloo Chiba, interview with the author, Lenasia, 21 November 2007.
175 Ahmed Kathrada, interview with the author, Johannesburg, 8 October 2007.
176 Nelson Mandela, *Long Walk to Freedom*, p. 482.
177 Mike Nicol et al, *Mandela, the Authorized Portrait*, p. 140.
178 Michael Dingake, email correspondence with the author, November 2007.
179 Laloo Chiba, interview with the author, Lenasia, 21 November 2007.
180 Laloo Chiba, interview with the author, Lenasia, 21 November 2007.
181 Anthony Xaba, telephonic interview, 9 February 2008.
182 Ahmed Kathrada, interview with the author, Johannesburg, 8 October 2007.
183 Anthony Xaba, telephonic interview, 9 February 2008.
184 Michael Dingake, *My Struggle Against Apartheid*, p. 110.
185 Laloo Chiba, interview with the author, Lenasia, 21 November 2007.
186 Laloo Chiba, interview with the author, Lenasia, 21 November 2007.
187 Farida Omar, interview with the author, Cape Town, 18 October 2007.
188 Mike Nicol et al, *Mandela, the Authorized Portrait*, p. 178.
189 Laloo Chiba, interview with the author, Lenasia, 21 November 2007.
190 Anthony Sampson, *Mandela*, p. 236.
191 Christo Brand, interview with the author, Cape Town, 16 October 2007.
192 Laloo Chiba, interview with the author, Lenasia, 21 November 2007.
193 Ahmed Kathrada, interview with the author, Johannesburg, 8 October 2007.
194 Laloo Chiba, interview with the author, Lenasia, 21 November 2007.
195 Philemon Tefu, telephonic interview, 8 February 2008.
196 Nelson Mandela, *Long Walk to Freedom*, p. 554.
197 Ahmed Kathrada, interview with the author, Johannesburg, 8 October 2007.
198 Laloo Chiba, interview with the author, Lenasia, 21 November 2007.
199 Wilton Mkwayi, interview with the archivist, Robben Island, Mayibuye Archives, University of the Western Cape.
200 Mike Nicol et al, *Mandela, the Authorized Portrait*, p. 148.
201 Laloo Chiba, interview with the author, Lenasia, 21 November 2007.
202 Sinda Naidoo, interview with author, Johannesburg, 29 November 2007.
203 Shanthie Naidoo, interview with the author, Johannesburg, 29 November 2007.
204 Sinda Naidoo, interview with author, Johannesburg, 29 November 2007.
205 Nelson Mandela, Speech by President Nelson Mandela at an Intercultural Eid Celebration, Johannesburg, 30 January 1998, Office of the President.
206 Mike Nicol et al, *Mandela, the Authorized Portrait*, p. 165.
207 Laloo Chiba, interview with the author, Lenasia, 21 November 2007.
208 Letter dated 31 August 1970, Nelson Mandela Centre of Memory and Dialogue.
209 Mike Nicol et al, *Mandela, the Authorized Portrait*, p. 140.
210 Tokyo Sexwale, telephonic conversation with the author, 29 November 2007.
211 Dr Makaziwe Mandela, interview with the author, Johannesburg, 10 October 2007.
212 Letter dated 1 April 1971, Nelson Mandela Centre of Memory and Dialogue.
213 Nkosi Zwelivelile, interview with the author, Qunu, 16 November 2007.
214 Anthony Sampson, *Mandela*, p. 253.
215 Dr Nthato Motlana, telephonic interview with the author, 15 January 2008.
216 Winnie Madikizela-Mandela, interview with the author, 6 December 2007.
217 Anthony Sampson, *Mandela*, p. 250.
218 Winnie Madikizela-Mandela, interview with the author, 6 December 2007.
219 Joel Carlson, *No Neutral Ground*, New York, Crowell Collier Press, 1973, p. 291.
220 Winnie Madikizela-Mandela, interview with the author, 6 December 2007.
221 Dr Nthato Motlana, telephonic interview with the author, 15 January 2008.
222 Letter dated 1 December 1974, Nelson Mandela Centre of Memory and Dialogue.
223 Letter dated 1 December 1970, Nelson Mandela Centre of Memory and Dialogue.
224 Zindzi Mandela, interview with the author, Johannesburg, 5 December 2007.
225 Shanthie Naidoo, interview with the author, Johannesburg, 29 November 2007.
226 Zindzi Mandela, interview with the author, Johannesburg, 5 December 2007.
227 Fatima Meer, *Higher than Hope*, Johannesburg, Skotaville, 1988, p. 377.
228 Ilse Wilson, interview with the author, Johannesburg, 26 September 2007.
229 Zindzi Mandela, interview with the author, Johannesburg, 5 December 2007.
230 Helen Joseph, *Side by Side*, p. 247.
231 Zindzi Mandela, interview with the author, Johannesburg, 5 December 2007.
232 Ilse Wilson, interview with the author, Johannesburg, 26 September 2007.
233 Zindzi Mandela, interview with the author, Johannesburg, 6 December 2007.
234 Winnie Madikizela-Mandela, interview with the author, Johannesburg, 6 December 2007.
235 Dr Nthatho Motlana, telephonic interview with the author, 15 January 2008.
236 Winnie Madikizela-Mandela, interview with the author, Johannesburg, 6 December 2007.
237 Zindzi Mandela, interview with the author, Johannesburg, 6 December 2007.
238 Mary Benson, *Nelson Mandela, the Man and the Movement*, Harmondsworth, Penguin, 1994, p. 170.
239 Barbara Waite, interview with the author, Johannesburg, 15 January 2008.
240 Zindzi Mandela, interview with the author, Johannesburg, 6 December 2007.
241 Winnie Madikizela-Mandela, interview with the author, Johannesburg, 6 December 2007.
242 Sonia Cabano, telephonic interview with the author, 21 December 2007.
243 Meyer de Waal, email interview, 21 December 2007.
244 Winnie Madikizela-Mandela, interview with the author, Johannesburg, 6 December 2007.
245 Zindzi Mandela, interview with the author, Johannesburg, 6 December 2007.
246 Nelson Mandela, *Long Walk to Freedom*, p. 718.
247 François Ferreira, interview with the author, Stellenbosch, 16 October 2007.
248 Letter dated 12 April 1986, quoted in Anthony Sampson, *Mandela*, p. 344.
249 Letter to Ismail Meer dated 22 January 1985, Nelson Mandela Centre of Memory and Dialogue.
250 Desk diary, 2 October 1982, Nelson Mandela Centre of Memory and Dialogue.
251 Ahmed Kathrada, interview with the author, Johannesburg, 8 October 2007.
252 Christo Brand, interview with the author, Cape Town, 16 October 2007.
253 Ahmed Kathrada, interview with the author, Johannesburg, 8 October 2007.
254 Estelle Brand, interview with the author, Cape Town, 16 October 2007.
255 Christo Brand, interview with the author, Cape Town, 16 October 2007.
256 Nkosi Zwelivelile, interview with the author, Qunu, 16 November 2007.
257 Farida Omar, interview with the author, Cape Town, 11 October 2007.
258 Ahmed Kathrada, interview with the author, Johannesburg, 8 October 2007.
259 Christo Brand, interview with the author, Cape Town, 16 October 2007.
260 Zindzi Mandela, interview with the author, Johannesburg, 6 December 2007.
261 Truth and Reconcilliation Commission Day 1: 26 November 1996.
262 Christo Brand, interview with the author, Cape Town, 16 October 2007.
263 Elinor Sisulu, *In Our Lifetime*, p. 335.
264 Jack Swart, telephonic interview with the author, 1 December 2007.
265 Niël Barnard, quoted in Anthony Sampson's *Mandela, the Authorized Biography*, p. 366.
266 Mark Gevisser, *The Dream Deferred*, Johannesburg, Jonathan Ball, 2007, p. 503.
267 Ahmed Kathrada, *Memoirs*, Cape Town, Zebra, 2004 letter to Shehnaaz Meer, 2 January 1988, p. 326.
268 Fiona Reed (née Duncan), interview with the author, Johannesburg, November 2007.
269 Jack Swart, telephonic interview with the author, 1 December 2007.
270 Letter from Walter Sisulu to Connie Njongwe, quoted in Elinor Sisulu, *In Our Lifetime*, p. 364.
271 Zindzi Mandela, interview with the author, 6 December 2007.
272 George Bizos, interview with the author, Johannesburg, 10 December 2007.
273 Zindzi Mandela, interview with the author, 6 December 2007.
274 Tokyo Sexwale, telephonic interview with the author, 26 November 2007.
275 Amelia Grobelaar, telephonic interview with the author, 11 December 2007.
276 Jack Swart, interview with PBS Frontline, 2003, url http://www.pbs.wgbh/pages/frontline/shows/mandela/interviews.html
277 Farida Omar, interview with the author, Cape Town, 11 October 2007.
278 Jack Swart, interview with PBS Frontline, 2003, url http://www.pbs.wgbh/pages/frontline/shows/mandela/interviews.html
279 Nelson Mandela, *Long Walk to Freedom*, p. 673.
280 Lavinia Crawford-Browne, telephonic interview with the author, 28 September 2007.
281 Lillian Ngoboza, interview with the author, Cape Town, 17 October 2007.
282 Sally Rowney, interview with the author, Pretoria, 9 November 2007.
283 Nelson Mandela, *Long Walk to Freedom*, p. 682.
284 Zindzi Mandela, interview with the author, Johannesburg, 6 December 2007.
285 Anthony Sampson, *Mandela*, p. 252.
286 Nelson Mandela, *Long Walk to Freedom*, p. 683.
287 George Bizos, *Odyssey to Freedom*, Johannesburg, Random House, 2007, p. 341.
288 Nelson Mandela, *Long Walk to Freedom*, p. 719.
289 Nat Bregman interview with the author, Johannesburg, November 2007.
290 Nelson Mandela, *Long Walk to Freedom*, p. 696.
291 Allister Sparks, *The Mind of South Africa*, London, Heinemann, 1990, p. 368.
292 François Ferreira, interview with the author, Stellenbosch, 15 October 2007.
293 François Ferreira, interview with the author, Stellenbosch, 15 October 2007.
294 Sigrid Langebrekke, Nobel Foundation, email interview with the author, 16 January 2007.
295 Anthony Sampson, *Mandela*, p. 474.
296 Barbara Masekela, interview in Anthony Sampson, *Mandela*, p. 453.
297 Zindzi Mandela, interview with the author, Johannesburg, December 2007.
298 Xoliswa Ndoyiya, interview with the author, Johannesburg, 20 September 2007.
299 Mandlesizwe Mandela, interview with the author, Qunu, 15 November 2007.
300 Xoliswa Ndoyiya, interview with the author, Johannesburg, 20 September 2007.
301 Bill Keller, *New York Times*, 19 November 1993.
302 Kevin Gibbs, telephonic interview with the author, 15 January 2008.
303 Anthony Sampson, *Mandela*, p. 491.
304 Joe Matthews, interview with the author, Johannesburg, October 2007.
305 Alan Fine, 'Insights into Mandela's Reign', *Business Day*, 15 June 1999.
306 Ella Govender, telephonic interview with the author, 15 January 2008.
307 John Reinders, telephonic interview with the author, 12 January 2008.
308 Anthony Sampson, *Mandela*, p. 523.
309 Amina Cachalia, interview with PBS Frontline, 2003, url http://www.pbs.wgbh/pages/frontline/shows/mandela/interviews.html
310 Jacques Human, telephonic interview with the author, 15 January 2008.
311 Amina Cachalia, interview with PBS Frontline, 2003, url http://www.pbs.wgbh/pages/frontline/shows/mandela/interviews.html
312 Zelda la Grange, quoted in Debora Patta, *One Step Behind Mandela*, Johannesburg, Zebra Press, 2000, p. 194.
313 Rory Steyn, quoted in *One Step Behind Mandela*, p. 177.
314 Esmenia Gemo, interview with the author, Maputo (translation by Denise Vedor), 8 February 2008.
315 Mandlesizwe Mandela, interview with the author, 15 November 2007.
316 Xoliswa Ndoyiya, interview with the author, Johannesburg, September 2007.
317 Rory Steyn, *One Step Behind Mandela*, p. 180.
318 Anthony Sampson, *Mandela*, p. 448.
319 Fatima Meer, telephonic interview with the author, 7 January 2008.
320 Nelson Mandela, *Long Walk to Freedom*, p. 617.
321 Anthony Sampson, *Mandela*, p. 533.
322 Xoliswa Ndoyiya, interview with the author, 11 September 2007.
323 Thoko Mavuso, interview with the author, Johannesburg, 11 September 2007.
324 Zindzi Mandela, interview with the author, Johannesburg, 6 December 2007.
325 Ahmed Kathrada, interview with the author, Johannesburg, October 2007.
326 Zelda la Grange, interview by email, 1 February 2008.
327 Vimla Naidoo, interview with the author, Johannesburg, 20 November 2007.

Index

African National Congress 8, 24, 26,
    27, 32, 45, 52, 57, 61, 76, 78, 83–85,
    95, 103, 107, 134, 137, 145, 147,
    149, 160, 161, 165, 168, 173, 175,
    176, 178, 180, 182, 185, 187, 190,
    201
    members 27, 30, 66
    National Conference 60
    Shell House (head office) 64
African Mineworkers' Union 24
Alexandra Bus Boycott 24, 25
Alexandra township 21, 22, 24
alikreukel 96, 97
amasi xv, 2, 10, 34, 35, 83, 84
ANC Youth League (ANCYL) 27, 32,
    49, 52

Barnard, Niël 149, 150
biryani 51, 54, 110, 191, 193, 194
Bizos, Alexi 71, 74, 75, 170
Bizos, George xv, 54, 56, 63, 68, 69, 71,
    73, 75, 91–93, 96, 126, 159, 160
Black Consciousness Movement
    (BCM) 95, 112, 185
Boipatong Massacre 176, 178
Bopape, David 27, 49
Botha, P.W. 137, 145, 147, 149, 160, 161,
    189, 190
    Elize 138, 190, 191
Botha, Pik 187, 189
Brand, Christo 107, 139–142, 147, 148
Brand, Estelle 140, 142, 143
Bregman, Nat xiv, 22, 25, 26, 171, 173
Buthelezi, Mangosuthu 176, 185

Cabano, Sonia (née De Waal) 132–134
Cachalia
    Amina 33, 42, 56, 57, 78, 79, 156,
        190, 191
    Yusuf 56, 57, 156, 160
Chiba, Laloo 99, 101, 104–109,
    110–112
Coetsee, Kobie 132, 141, 144, 145, 147,
    149, 150, 156
Communist Party 24, 26, 39, 83, 84, 85
    149, 161, 185
Congress of Democrats 73, 76
Congress of the People 60, 61, 69, 185
Convention for a Democratic South

Africa (Codesa) 176, 187
Crayfish 96, 107

Dalibhunga *see* Mandela, Nelson
De Klerk
    F.W. 160, 161, 175, 178, 182, 189, 190
    Marike 175, 178
Defiance Campaign 57, 58, 63, 68, 192
Department of Native Affairs 2
De Waal 132
    Piet 132, 134, 144
    Adele 132–134
dhal 54, 87
Dingake, Michael 91, 96, 98, 101, 104

Ethiopia 85–88

Ferreira, François 137, 139, 175, 176,
    178, 179
Fischer
    Bram 54, 55, 91
    Molly 54, 55, 124
Fort Hare 18, 27
Freedom Charter 14, 58, 60, 61, 69
frikkadels 124, 160

Govender, Ella 36, 189, 191, 193–195
Government of National Unity
    (GNU) 176, 185, 190
Gregory, James 148, 149, 152, 155, 160

Harmel 43
    Barbara 39–41, 43, 52
    Michael 39–41
    Ray xv, 39–41
hunger strikes xi, 91, 95, 101, 103, 104,
    142

imifino 2, 6
inconco 101, 102
Inkatha Freedom Party 176, 185
inkobe xv, 68

Joseph, Adelaide 45, 58
Joseph, Helen 73, 122, 124, 129, 131

Kapitan's 38, 51, 66, 68, 171
Kathrada, Ahmed 43, 49, 52, 56, 57,
    60, 66, 68, 69, 73, 84, 85, 98, 99, 101,
    103, 107, 108, 139, 141, 142, 144, 149,
    156, 161, 183, 187, 190, 204
katkop 96, 101
Kliptown 60, 122
Kolopan (Kollapen), Thanga 73, 81
koringbier 156
koeksisters 190
Kriek, Marcia 96, 97

La Grange, Zelda 26, 194, 204, 207
Liberal Party 73, 185
Long Walk to Freedom xi, 7, 30, 31, 38,
    54, 89, 107
Luthuli, Chief Albert 84, 87

Machel, Graça 184, 194, 196–200, 202,
    207
Madiba *see* Mandela, Nelson
Madiba clan 1
Madikizela-Mandela, Winnie (née
    Nomzamo Winnie Madikizela)
    xii, xv, 36, 38–43, 56, 82, 85, 89,
    90, 93, 117, 119–122, 126, 127, 129,
    131, 132, 134, 139, 144, 164, 165,
    168–170, 198
    daughters 115
    Madiba's letters to xi, 27, 35, 46, 112
    sisters 117, 120, 121
Magubane, Peter 120, 121
Maharaj, Mac 101, 107, 110
    Robben Island veteran 287
Makoena, Joe 19
Mandela and Tambo Attorneys 63, 64,
    68, 78
Mandela, Dr Makaziwe 30–32, 115
Mandela, Evelyn (née Evelyn Mase)
    xv, 28–32, 38, 58, 114, 115
Mandela, Makgatho 30, 115
Mandela, Mandlesizwe (Nkosi
    Zwelivelile) x, 5, 7, 13, 116, 117, 142,
    144, 154, 180, 196
Mandela, Mandla *see* Mandela,
    Mandlesizwe
Mandela, Nelson (Madiba) xi, xv,
    15, 19, 28–30, 32, 33, 35, 49, 52,
    55–58, 66, 117, 119–121, 198

ANC leadership 32
arrests and detention of 58, 88, 90
Constantiaberg Medi-Clinic 150,
    152, 155
courtship of and marriage to Evelyn
    Mase 30
courtship of and marriage to Graça
    Machel 94, 96, 98
courtship of and marriage to
    Winnie Madikizela 38, 39, 41–46,
    49, 134
early 1990s 174, 175, 178, 180, 182,
    183
early years xiv, 1, 2, 7, 8, 10–22, 49
eighty-eighth birthday 200, 201
father of see Mphakanyiswa, Nkosi
first wife of see Mandela, Evelyn
food and 34, 36, 51, 54, 56, 88, 124
grandchildren of x, 5, 7, 114, 115,
    142, 144, 168, 174, 180, 194, 196,
    201, 204, 207
lawyer 24–27, 62–64, 68, 69, 71
mother of see Mandela, Nosekeni
Nobel Prize for Peace 178
Pollsmoor Prison 137, 139, 140, 142,
    144, 145, 147–149
President 182–191
release from prison 164–166, 168,
    170, 171, 173
retirement 201, 203, 204, 207
Rivonia Trial 91–93,
Robben Island xii, xv, 45, 67, 90, 91,
    95–112, 116
second wife of see Madikizela-
    Mandela, Winnie
sisters of 7, 8, 35
third wife of see Machel, Graça
Treason Trial 41, 73, 77, 78, 83
underground operative (as David
    Motsamayi) 83–87
Victor Verster Prison 148, 155, 156,
    159–161
Mandela, Nkosi Mphakanyiswa Gadla
    see Mphakanyiswa, Nkosi
Mandela, Nosekeni (Ma Mandela) 2,
    33, 35, 116, 117
Mandela, Nosisa 3, 37
Mandela, Sitsheketshe Morrison 2, 3,
    30, 37, 58
Mandela, Thembekile 30, 115, 116
Mandela, Zenani (Zeni) 85, 89, 120–
    122, 124
Mandela, Zindzi 39, 44, 46, 89, 120–
    124, 126, 129, 131, 134, 136, 142,
    147, 159, 170, 171, 180, 204

Madiba's letter to 121
Manse, Alice 26, 27, 52
Manuel, Trevor 165
    UDF activist 187
marhewu 2, 12
Mase, Evelyn 28–30
Matanzima, Kaiser (K.D.) 36, 38, 39
Matthews, Joe 17–20, 27, 32, 35, 51, 54,
    58, 86–89, 187
Matthews, Z.K. 17, 58, 68
Matyolo, Winnie see Toni, Winnie
Mbashe River xvi, 1
Mbeki, Govan 17, 84
Mbeki
    Thabo 39, 149, 182, 189, 201
    Zanele 185
Meer
    Fatima 87, 89, 99, 124, 201
    Ismail 8, 49, 51, 69, 87, 123, 124, 139
Meligqili, Nkosi 14, 15
Meyer, Roelf 176, 182
MK see Umkhonto weSizwe
Mkwayi, Milton 107, 108, 110
Moodley, Vasugee (née Pillay) 76, 171
Moretsele, Elias 65, 66
morogo 65, 201, 202
Motlana, Dr (Harrison) Nthato 117,
    120, 122, 126, 160
Mphakanyiswa, Nkosi 2, 5, 7, 10, 15
Mqhekezweni 11, 12
Mvezo 1, 2, 5, 7, 8

Naidoo
    Manomoni (Amma) 50–52, 121, 122
    Naranswamy (Roy) 51
    Shanthie 51, 73, 76, 110, 122, 172
Naidoo, Naga 87, 90
Naidoo, Sinda (née Pillay) 50, 76, 110
Natal Indian Congress 84
National Party 145, 147–149, 160, 161,
    176, 178, 187, 190
Ndoyiya, Xoliswa xiv, 34, 35, 180, 181,
    198, 203, 204, 207
Nelson Mandela Centre of Memory
    and Dialogue see Nelson Mandela
    Foundation
Nelson Mandela Foundation xiv
Ngoboza, Lillian Nosipho xv, 166, 167
Nokwe, Duma 27, 30, 42, 63
    mother of 191
nongwe 10

OAU (Organisation of African
    Unity) 87
Omar 141
    Dullah 105, 141, 144, 165
    Farida 105, 141, 144–146, 165

Pap 32, 90, 137, 185
Passive Resistance Campaign 54, 73
phutu 42
phuzamandla 96, 98, 99, 111, 112, 137
Pahad
    Amina xv, 52–54, 68
    Goolam 54
    Meg 53, 54
Pan African Congress (PAC) 76, 95,
    161, 185
perlemoen 96, 97, 108
Pillay, Thayanayagee xv, 73, 76, 81,
    110, 171, 172
Pollsmoor 136, 137, 139, 142, 144

Qhobozela 10
Qunu 1, 8, 10–12, 14, 15, 34, 35, 116,
    117, 173, 194, 196, 198

Radebe, Gaur xiv, 24
Ramaphosa, Cyril 168, 171, 176, 182
Ranchod, Madanjit 68, 171
Reconstruction and Development
    Programme 185
Reed, Fiona (née Duncan) 150, 152,
    153
Resha, Robert 56, 73
Rhodes University 20
rhwabe 6
rice water 98, 99
Rivonia Trial 54, 92, 93, 115, 139, 190
    lawyers 91
    comrades 90, 104, 109, 112, 160, 175
    trialists 90, 91, 140
Robben Island xii, xiv, xv, 8, 10, 12,
    94–113, 116, 117, 120, 124, 137, 139,
    140–142, 148, 155, 160, 171, 187
roer bread 156
Rolihlahla see Mandela, Nelson
roti 38, 58, 141, 144
Rowney, Sally 168–170

Samoosa xi, 105, 110, 141, 144
samp 32, 36
Sexwale, Tokyo xv, 112, 126, 160
Sharpeville Massacre 29
Sidelsky, Lazar 22, 160, 171
Sisulu 26, 27
    Albertina 82, 93, 201

Ma Sisulu (Alice Manse) 26, 27, 52
    Walter 22, 24, 26–28, 30, 49, 51, 76,
        78, 84, 93, 101, 103, 107, 109, 137,
        140, 156, 161, 190, 201
Slovo 43
    Gillian 69, 72
    Joe 49, 63, 69, 71, 72, 84
South African Indian Congress 52
Soweto 26, 32, 35, 39, 42, 44, 64, 121,
    129, 131, 134, 142, 147, 168, 170, 180
Soweto Uprising 112, 126
Suppression of Communism Act 29,
    58
Swart, Jack 148, 155, 156, 159, 160,
    161, 165
sweet chicken xiv, 178, 180, 181

Tambo
    Adelaide 38, 87, 191,192
    Oliver 19, 27, 30, 38, 63, 64, 68, 78,
        160, 173, 194
        godfather to Mandela children 196

Tefu, Philemon 90, 103, 107
Thembu 7, 8, 12, 14, 15, 17, 73
Thembuland 1, 2, 7, 15, 204
Toni, Winnie (née Matyolo) 9, 11, 12
Transkei 5, 36
Transvaal Indian Congress (TIC) 8,
    51, 57, 58, 73
Treason Trial 41, 45, 60, 61, 66, 68, 69,
    73, 76, 78, 83, 171
    trialists 66, 67, 71, 80, 89
Truth and Reconciliation Commission
    147, 185
Tutu, Archbishop Desmond 117, 166,
    168

Umbhako xii, 130, 131
Umkhonto weSizwe 84, 85, 87, 91
umleqwa 9
umngqusho xiii, xiv, 8, 32, 36, 37, 156,
    182, 201
umphokoqo xi, 8, 180, 207
umqeqe 19

Uncle Ish see Meer, Ismail
United Democratic Front (UDF) 137,
    147, 149, 160, 165, 170, 176, 185
    comrades 165

Victor Verster Prison 152, 154–161

Waite, Barbara xiv, 128, 129, 131
Wilson, Ilse (née Fischer) 54, 58, 73,
    124, 125
Witkin, Sidelsky & Eidelman 22, 24,
    25

Xaba, Anthony 103
Xhoma, Gladys 21–23

Zwelivelile, Nkosi see Mandela,
    Mandlesizwe

The Recipes

Adele de Waal's Herb-roasted
    Chicken 133
Amina Cachalia's Mutton Curry 79
Amina Pahad's Dry Chicken Curry 53

Barbara Waite's Milk Tart 128
Beef Stew 65
Besan Ladoos 70
Brandfort-style Biltong 135

Constantiaberg Chocolate Mousse
    151

Elize Botha's Malva Pudding 138
Ella Govender's
    Biryani 193
    Crayfish Curry 195
Estelle Brand's Christmas Cake 143
Evelyn Mandela's Jelly with a Twist 31

Farida Omar's Chicken Curry 146
Fort Hare Rye Bread 18
François Ferreira's Chicken Broth 179
Fufu 88

George Bizos's Lemon and Oregano
    Lamb 75
Gloria Ngcebetshana's Imfino 6
Graça Machel's
    Caranguejo com Camarão (Crab
        and Prawn Curry) 199
    Caranguejo Recheado (Stuffed
        Crab) 197

Harriet Xhoma's Pig's Head with
    Gravy 23

Ilse Wilson and Molly Fischer's
    Frikkadels 125
Inconco 102
Ismail Meer's Fried Eggs 123
Isonka Sombhako 130

Jack Swart's
    Koringbier (wheat beer) 158
    Wholewheat Bread 157
Joe Slovo's Salad Dressing 72

Kitfo 88
Koeksisters 188

Laloo Chiba's Christmas Cake 111
Lillian Nosipho Ngoboza's Chicken
    Curry 167

Madiba's Birthday Treat 113
Manomoni Naidoo's Crab Curry 50
Marcia Kriek's
    Perlemoen 97
    Sautéed Alikreukel 97
Molly Fischer's Rusks 55
Moretsele-style Phutu Pap 65
Morogo with Potato 202
Mrs Naga Naidoo's Lamb Kebabs 90
Mrs Pillay's
    Chicken Curry 81
    Green Mango and Fish Curry 172
Mrs Xhoma's Gravy 23

Nosisa Mandela's
    Marhewu 3
    Umngqusho 37

Phutu Pap 65
Phuzamandla 100

Ray Harmel's Chopped Liver 40
Rice Water 100

Sally Rowney's Mushrooms 169
Sugar Cages 177

The Grillhouse Spare Ribs 205

Umhluzi Wetamatisi ne Anyanisi
    (Tomato and Onion Relish) 65

Winnie Madikizela-Mandela's
    Chicken Dumplings 127
    Preserved Peaches 118
    Spaghetti and Mince 47
Winnie Matyolo's Chicken 9

Xoliswa Ndoyiya's
    Qunu Amasi Recipe 34
    Sweet Chicken 181
    Umphokoqo 206